Philippine Duchesne

A Woman with the Poor

Painting of Mother Philippine Duchesne

The artist and the exact date of this painting are unknown. It was most probably commissioned by the Ursuline nuns of New Orleans about 1870, eighteen years after Mother Philippine's death. No photographs or paintings of the saint have come down to us from her lifetime, but it is believed that the model, probably an older Ursuline, was chosen because she resembled Philippine in looks. One argument for its attempt to be a true likeness is that it is not a flattering painting, and we know that Philippine was not attractive.

PHILIPPINE DUCHESNE:

A Woman with the Poor

by
Catherine M. Mooney, R.S.C.J.

PAULIST PRESS
New York/Mahwah, N.J.

Cover art is based on present-day artist William Schickel's original painting of Philippine Duchesne.

The publisher gratefully acknowledges the use of selected excerpts from: *Constitutions: Society of the Sacred Heart of Jesus*. Permission granted from Tipografia Poliglotta della Pontificia Universita Gregoriana, Rome, n.d., *Philippine Duchesne: Frontier Missionary of the Sacred Heart 1799–1852* by Louise Callan. Copyright © 1957 by the Newman Press, Westminster, Maryland. Permission granted by Paulist Press.

Maps by Sheri Marcus.

Library of Congress Cataloging-in-Publication Data

Mooney, Catherine M.
   Philippine Duchesne : a woman with the poor / by Catherine M. Mooney.
     p. cm.
   Includes bibliographical references.
   ISBN 0-8091-3116-1
   1. Duchesne, Philippine, Saint, 1769–1852. 2. Christian saints—United States—Biography. I. Title.
BX4700.D8M66 1989
282'.092—dc20
  [B]
                                             89-38117
                                              CIP

Published by Paulist Press
997 Macarthur Boulevard
Mahwah, New Jersey 07430

Printed and bound in the
United States of America

CONTENTS

v

Maps

DEDICATION

To my parents,
Joseph W. Mooney and Margaret McCarthy Mooney,
with love and gratitude

FOREWORD

The canonization of Philippine Duchesne on July 3, 1988, has awakened considerable interest in the life of this French missionary to the American frontier. This book is an attempt to respond to that need. It is both a simple retelling of her life and a personal reflection on what she might have to say to us today.

The writing of saints' lives is a tradition tracing back to the earliest years of the Christian Church's existence. For all the differences there are in the thousands of saints' lives written over the last two thousand years, almost all of them include two types of writing. On the one hand, the author includes facts of the saint's life, what we today would call "historical writing." On the other hand, the writer includes personal reflections on the meaning of the saint's life. These are intended to inspire those reading about the saint. Such reflections have more in common with preaching and theological speculation.

Until recently, most writers of saints' lives did not bother to make the distinction between these two types of writing. Since the point of most written saints' lives was to edify and impress the reader with the miracles *God* worked through the individual, it did not matter much how the facts of the *human life* of the saint were recounted, stretched or even invented. If the story served to inflame fervor in the hearts of the faithful, then the real cause of Truth, God, was being served. Even fairly recent biographies of canonized saints sometimes tend to gloss over their human failings and to overdraw their virtues.

My own training as an historian has led me to keep these two types of writing clearly distinguished in this book. There is nothing edifying today about over-rating virtues or underplaying peccadillos. There is, I think, a profound reason for this. When we read the lives of the saints, we expect to learn something about holiness. But the only real holiness there is in life is that which we find enfleshed in our own, very human lives. Our lives are tapestries woven not only of our gifts and stunning successes, but also of our flaws and bitter failures. It is through the medium of all these earthy, mundane realities that we grow into holiness, into human wholeness. Indeed, the life of this graced woman, Philippine Duchesne, easily touches our own precisely because it is so very human.

Philippine was, above all, a woman dedicated to the poor. In recent years, the Church, theologians and many other people of good will have called attention to the needs of the poor. Yet studies show that the poor continue to grow poorer while the rich grow richer. This growing disparity not only widens the breach separating wealthy nations from poor nations; it also increases the distance between the wealthy and the poor within individual countries, regardless of the country's general economic condition. In keeping with Philippine's own spirit, I have devoted special attention in this book to the poor and marginalized groups of her own time: the materially poor of France and America, blacks, native Americans and orphans. The situation of eighteenth- and nineteenth-century women, another marginalized though not minority group, is one I have frequent opportunity to touch upon. My hope is that reflection on the poor and marginalized groups of Philippine's time will, by analogy, enrich our reflection on the situation of poor and marginalized peoples today.

This book could never have been written without the work of many people before me, especially Louise Callan. Her biography of Philippine included the first publication of much of Philippine's correspondence in addition to extensive excerpts from many other primary source documents. Although my interpretation of Philippine Duchesne differs from Callan's in significant ways, the present book could never have been written without her invaluable assistance. Thanks to the dedicated work of Srs. Jeanne de Charry, Claire Dykmans and many others, we now have the complete edition of the correspondence between Philippine Duchesne and Madeleine Sophie Barat and easy access to many other archival materials.

There are many other people to whom I am indebted for their generous advice and support during the writing of this book. It was Cornelia Dinnean who gave me the idea and then prodded me to write this book. I am grateful to the Sisters of the Visitation, Francis Marie O'Connor and Mary Grace McCormack, for reading the parts of the manuscript on the Visitation order. Many members of the Society of the Sacred Heart of Jesus also shared their insights with me: I want to thank particularly Maureen Aggeler, Jean Ford, Regina Griffin, Anne O'Neil, Mary Quinlan and Ellen Snee. Barbara Rogers proved a valued companion and critic throughout the writing process. I am profoundly grateful to both Dr. Francine J. Cardman and to Teresa Jorgen for their advice and constant friendship. Finally, my most heartfelt thanks go to Sue Costa. Her honest and always astute criticisms improved the book immeasurably. And her wit and friendship made the re-writing a pleasure.

This book is dedicated to my parents, Joseph W. Mooney and Margaret McCarthy Mooney. They were the first to teach me that authentic sanctity is not some other-worldly phenomenon. It only happens here.

CHRONOLOGY

1769   August 29, Philippine Duchesne is born in Grenoble, France.

1781   Philippine and her cousin Josephine are sent to the Visitation monastery of Saint Marie to prepare for their first communion.

1783   Philippine is withdrawn from Saint Marie and returns home.

1788   Philippine enters the Visitation monastery of Saint Marie.

1792   The monastery of Saint Marie is forcibly closed and the nuns are dispersed by the revolutionary French government.

1793–1801   Philippine undertakes charitable work in Grenoble. For brief periods she also lives with her family in the country, with her grandmother, and with a group of nuns in the monastery of St.-Marcellin.

1800   Foundation of the Society of the Sacred Heart of Jesus by Madeleine Sophie Barat and Joseph Varin in Paris.

1801   Philippine reacquires the monastery of Saint Marie.

1802   Most of the Visitation nuns who had returned to Saint Marie abandon Philippine and the monastery. Philippine decides to associate Saint Marie with a different order.

1804   Frs. Joseph Varin and Pierre Roger visit Saint Marie in July to judge its suitability for association with the Ladies of the Faith [later "Society of the Sacred Heart of Jesus"]. Madeleine Sophie Barat, superior of the Ladies of the Faith, arrives in December and remains for a year.

1805–15   Philippine is occupied with multiple duties at Saint Marie: secretary to the superior, head of the boarding school, teacher, infirmarian and overseer of the material necessities of the school and convent.

1815   Philippine travels to Paris for the Second General Council of the Society of the Sacred Heart. She remains there afterwards as Sophie Barat's secretary.

1818   Philippine departs for America with four other religious. They stop in New Orleans and St. Louis before making their first foundation in St. Charles, Missouri.

1819   The religious leave St. Charles and make a new foundation in Florissant, Missouri.

1821   Foundation of Opelousas [Grand Coteau] in Lower Louisiana. Eugénie Audé is sent as superior.

1825   A school for Indian girls is opened by Philippine. It does not flourish and is closed by 1831.

1825   Foundation of St. Michael's, near New Orleans, with Eugénie Audé as superior. Xavier Murphy becomes superior of Opelousas.

1827   Foundation of the City House in St. Louis. Philippine leaves Florissant to become superior there and remains until 1834.

1828   Foundation of La Fourche. Hélène Dutour is sent as superior. The convent and school are closed in 1832.

1828   The St. Charles foundation is re-opened, with Lucille Mathevon as superior.

1829   Meeting in St. Michael's, Louisiana, of Philippine with the three southern superiors, Audé, Murphy and Dutour. Unity among them is not achieved.

1831   Sophie Barat withdraws Philippine as superior of the St. Louis house, but is then persuaded by Bishop Rosati to reverse her decision.

1833   Sophie Barat names Eugénie Audé Assistant General for the United States, requests that Audé visit the five American foundations and then report to France.

1834   Sophie Barat withdraws Philippine as superior of the St. Louis house. Philippine returns to Florissant as superior, where she remains until 1840.

1836	Word is sent from France that Eugénie Audé will not be returning to America.
1840	Arrival of Elizabeth Galitzin as Provincial and Visitatrix for the houses of Missouri and the southern United States. Philippine is finally relieved as superior. She moves to the St. Louis house as a simple member of the community.
1841	Foundation of the Sugar Creek mission among the Potawatomi tribe in present-day Kansas. Lucille Mathevon is superior and travels there with Philippine and two other religious. Philippine is sent away after a year due to her failing health.
1842	Philippine joins the community of St. Charles where she remains for the last ten years of her life.
1843–47	Philippine receives no letters from Sophie Barat. Finally, Sophie Barat sends word to her friend through Philippine's niece, Amélie Jouve. Correspondence between Philippine and Sophie resumes, but remains sporadic.
1852	November 18, Philippine Duchesne dies in St. Charles, Missouri.

I.

Sainthood

Sainthood is an elusive concept for many of us, and this is no surprise given the word's broad use. The meaning of sainthood varies dramatically from century to century and from place to place, not only because the ecclesiastical rules defining sainthood have not been uniform, but also because cultural notions of what constitutes sanctity have continued to change. For example, Simeon the Stylite, the Syrian saint who spent the last forty years of his life living on pillar-like rock formations up to thirty-five feet high, probably inspires fewer of us today than he did in the fifth century. In thirteenth-century England, a Jew named Koppin was falsely charged with torturing, scourging, crowning with thorns and then crucifying nine-year-old Hugh of Lincoln. After Koppin was brutally murdered along with numerous other Jews, a saint's cult grew up around Hugh. Yet this story tells us little about Hugh or sainthood. Rather, it reveals the virulence of Christian hatred of Jews at this time. Christina the Astonishing's fondness for lofty places frequently inspired her to climb trees or fly into church rafters. On one such occasion, she soared to the roof of a church and came down only when ordered to by the priest saying mass (he must have been distracted). Her contemporaries saw these events as signs of her holiness. To us they are simply exotic and bizarre. Catherine of Bologna, canonized formally in the eighteenth century, was admired for repeating a thousand Hail Marys on Christmas night. Yet it is the temptation she resisted which probably attracts most of us: an overpowering desire to sleep.

Saints, in short, whether popularly acclaimed so or formally canonized by the papacy after exhaustive expert investigations, often tell us much more about the societies in which they were considered holy than they do about the saints themselves. Their selection for canonization by bishops and popes also offers us insight into the types of sanctity which the hierarchical Church wishes to foster among the faithful in each age.

The canonization of Philippine Duchesne is significant not only because of her extraordinary life, but also because it is a window into some of our own religious values and assumptions. For this reason, I will devote the remainder of this chapter to the larger religious issues surrounding sainthood and her canonization in particular. Readers interested only in Philippine's life may wish to turn directly to chapter two where her biography begins.

The first issue regarding sainthood concerns the history of the canonization process itself: in short, who chooses the saints? While all Christians are called to be saints, only a very small minority of the Christian saints are ever officially given the title "saint." But who makes this choice? In the first centuries of the Church, the saints were chosen by all the faithful of the Christian community. Little by little during the early Middle Ages, it became the prerogative of bishops. Finally, for the last few centuries, it has been in the hands of the Roman, or Papal Curia, which submits its recommendations to the pope himself for ratification. Philippine's canonization, therefore, is the outcome of a process managed by an office of the Papal Curia and then finalized by the pope.

Second, I will discuss what "types" of people have been considered apt candidates for sainthood. It may surprise some people to know that there are very definite patterns to sainthood and that certain groups have tended to dominate among the saints. For example, relatively few middle and lower class people have been chosen for canonization. The majority of saints, moreover, have come from certain areas of Western Europe, even today when Christianity has truly become a "world" religion and has millions of followers in places such as Latin America, Asia and Africa. The vast majority of saints are also men. While a relatively greater number of women are being canonized in the twentieth century, they represent a very specific idea of what female holiness should be. Lay people are only a tiny minority of the saints being named in any period, including the twentieth century. These patterns and their significance will be elaborated in this second section.

Third and finally, I will share my own thoughts about why saints' lives often seem so removed from our own. Many of us find them impressive, but irrelevant to our daily living. My assumption in writing this book about Philippine is that if a saint is really to touch our lives, as impressive as she may be, she must be presented as a real human being, gifts and limitations together. I hope that these three discussions of sainthood will lead us to deepen our awareness that authentic holiness is not something that belongs in heaven. It happens here.

1. THE HISTORY OF SAINTHOOD AND CANONIZATION[1]

Thus far, I have been using the terms "sainthood" and "sanctity" to refer to a broad range of people, from those popularly held to be holy, for whom the title "saint" has less juridical value, to those who have succeeded through the most recent and arduous papal processes of canonization. "Canonization," a term in use since the eleventh century,[2] refers to the Church's official recognition of an individual's sanctity. But the process of determining sainthood has evolved over the past two thousand years. In different historical periods it has been primarily in the hands of the Christian faithful, of bishops, or of the pope and his appointees. Today the process is managed by the Congregation for the Causes of Saints, an office of the Papal Curia which is under the jurisdiction of the pope. But this is the outcome of a long historical process in which the notion of sainthood and, more particularly, the process of choosing the saints, has evolved considerably.

---

[1] I have drawn principally on the following studies concerning sainthood and canonization: John F. Broderick, "A Census of the Saints (993–1955)," *The American Ecclesiastical Review* 135 (1956): 87–115; Pierre Delooz, *Sociologie et canonisations* (Liège: Faculté de Droit, 1969); and for a very abbreviated English version, see Delooz, "Towards a sociological study of canonized sainthood in the Catholic Church," pp. 189–216, in *Saints and their Cults: Studies in Religious Sociology, Folklore and History*, ed. Stephen Wilson (Cambridge, England: Cambridge University Press, 1983); Mariano Foralosso, *Indagine sociografica sulle cause dei santi* (Rome: Pontificia Studiorum Universitas a S. Thoma Aq. in Urbe, 1987); Katherine and Charles H. George, "Roman Catholic Sainthood and Social Status: A Statistical and Analytical Study," *Journal of Religion* 35 (1955): 85–98; Michael Goodich, *Vita perfecta: The Ideal of Sainthood in the Thirteenth Century*, Monographien zur Geschichte des Mittelalters, Band 25 (Stuttgart: Anton Hiersemann, 1982), pp. 21–47; Ludwig Hertling, "Canonisation," *Dictionnaire de Spiritualité*, 1953– ed.; Paul Molinari, "Canonization of Saints (History and Procedure)," *New Catholic Encyclopedia*, 1967 ed.; Pitirim A. Sorokin, *Altruistic Love: A Study of American "Good Neighbors" and Christian Saints* (Boston: The Beacon Press, 1950); André Vauchez, *La sainteté en occident aux derniers siècles du Moyen Âge: D'après les procès de canonisation et les documents hagiographiques*, Bibliothèque des Ecoles Françaises d'Athènes et de Rome 241 (Rome: École française de Rome, 1981); and Donald Weinstein and Rudolph M. Bell, *Saints and Society: The Two Worlds of Western Christendom, 1000–1700* (Chicago: University of Chicago Press, 1982).

[2] Goodich, *Vita perfecta*, p. 21, n. 1; and Vauchez, *La sainteté en occident*, p. 25.

How have people been chosen to be saints in the past? We assume that they have been chosen for their sanctity. But who has been involved in making this choice? Who were the final arbiters in conferring "sainthood" upon an individual?

The Early Christian Community: The early Christians were fervent believers in the afterlife, so much so that they formed "cults of the dead" to honor their deceased friends and relatives. When the period of Roman persecutions and martyrdom began, these cults of the dead were transformed quite naturally into the cult of "saints." Christians invoked these heroic and saintly martyrs to intercede in heaven for them.

The first Christian saints were, therefore, all martyrs. They were chosen by the *vox populi*, the voice of the people. The sociologist Pierre Delooz points out that the first Christian saints were chosen by a "spontaneous social selection," not by tribunals or formal inquests as they are today. The cult of saints was originally a simple fact of history rather than the logical outcome of any doctrinal teaching.[3]

300 to 1000 A.D.: The Origins of Episcopal Canonization:[4] The persecution of Christians ended in the fourth century, putting an end to the possibility of physical martyrdom, but sainthood and martyrdom remained powerful ideals among Christians. In fact, this is one of the reasons thousands of Christians, both men and women, fled to the deserts of Syria and Egypt to live ascetic lives of fasting, prayer and sacrifice, a "living martyrdom" as some called it. By the fifth century, not only these austere desert dwellers, but bishops, abbots, missionaries and even civil rulers such as kings and queens had joined the ranks of the holy. A virtuous Christian *life* was beginning to supplant death through martyrdom as the main road to sainthood.

Gradually, and somewhat haphazardly, bishops became involved in the selection of the saints. The rapid spread of Christianity created a need for their leadership in discerning who, indeed, was holy. The bishop presided at liturgical celebrations commemorating the saint's feast or honoring the saint's relics. Bishops also helped to control the rapid multiplication of saints' cults in the early Middle Ages. A well-known and popular saint's cult attracted pilgrims to visit the saint's tomb and this in turn meant money and prestige for the town. Some

---

[3]Delooz, *Sociologie et canonisations*, p. 23; see also Vauchez, *La sainteté en occident*, pp. 15–16.

[4]Delooz, *Sociologie et canonisations*, pp. 23–27; and Vauchez, *La sainteté en occident*, pp. 16–24.

towns dug up the relics of a little known person and fabricated a saint or, at best, stretched the truth considerably in order to lay claim to a powerfully miraculous saint—not to mention a lucrative tourist attraction. A good bishop could control such abuses.

His intervention was not always disinterested, however. An ambitious bishop was not immune to confirming the "authenticity" of questionable relics or touching up the written life of a saint associated with his diocese if such acts would enhance his prestige or, arguing from a higher plane, edify his faithful.

Bishops in the early Middle Ages were well aware of the strength saints could lend to their episcopal authority. In the first few centuries of the Church, for example, influential and wealthy Christians often controlled saints' cults since they owned the relics which Christians longed to visit. These individuals clearly posed a threat to the bishop's authority. Astute bishops forbade the private possession of relics and demanded that these be brought into the public domain of the Church, that is, their churches. They thereby managed simultaneously to diffuse their rivals' power and to enhance their own prestige through the special relation established between the bishop's "home," his church, and the presence of a powerful intercessor.[5]

But throughout this entire period, the *initiative* for proclaiming someone a "saint" still remained in the hands of the community at large. The bishop's intervention was always subsequent to the community's recognition of a person's sanctity. There was no special commission to investigate the person's life, no team of experts to test the veracity of the miracles recounted in the saint's biography and no questioning of witnesses, if indeed, there were any, who might have known the saint. Most of these cults are still recognized as legitimate today and some of them have even received explicit papal approval through "equivalent canonization." In equivalent canonizations there is no formal inquest to prove the saint's historical existence, heroic virtue or miracles. They must simply be believable, a slippery criterion at best when it comes to judging miracles.

1000 to 1600 A.D.: The Origins of Papal Canonization: Popes did not become involved in the canonization process until the tenth century, when the bishop of Augsburg proposed a saint for canonization to the Lateran Council of 993.[6] No doubt he recognized the enhanced prestige

---

[5] Peter Brown, *The Cult of the Saints: Its Rise and Function in Latin Christianity,* Haskell Lectures on History of Religions, n.s. 2 (Chicago: University of Chicago Press, 1981).

[6] Delooz, *Sociologie et canonisations,* p. 28; Goodich, *Vita perfecta,* p. 22; but also see Eric

of a canonization confirmed not only by him, but by an assembly of five bishops, nine cardinals and the pope. Soon it was common for bishops to seek the pope's approval of the canonizations in their dioceses.

The popes of this time were also powerful political, social and economic leaders. By the thirteenth century, the pope's court, or "Papal Curia," had become an elaborate and effective bureaucracy influencing legal, political and religious affairs throughout Western Europe. The power of the popes had to be reckoned with in practically all domains of life. The process for selecting the saints was no exception. Popes of this time ruled that only they had the right to canonize and they made this decision part of canon, that is, Church law. The lives and miracles of proposed candidates were examined during a canonization trial, which followed specific procedures developed by the papacy. The popes were quick to realize how they could use the powerful tool of canonization to define papal policy, to fight heresy and to reward religious orders or political dynasties who were friendly to papal policies and causes.[7]

By the fourteenth century, papal decisions regarding a person's sanctity rested primarily in the hands of a commission of three appointed cardinals who reported to the pope. Experts such as priests and physicians, in addition to theologians, were soon employed to evaluate the life and miracles of people proposed for canonization. The fact that the Dominicans were the theologians appointed by the papacy to examine canonization documents in the thirteenth century explains in part the large numbers of mendicants such as Dominicans and Franciscans who were canonized during this period.[8] By the fifteenth and sixteenth centuries, so many documents were necessary for canonization—biographies, records of miracles, interrogations of witnesses, expert testimonies—that even more officials were employed to manage the process. Finally, in 1588, Pope Sixtus V formed an entire institution within the Vatican, the Sacred Congregation of Rites and Ceremonies. Its two main functions were to manage the many steps leading toward canonization and to regulate the Latin liturgy.

The juridical and bureaucratic procedures for canonization in the

---

Waldram Kemp, *Canonization and Authority in the Western Church*, (Oxford: Oxford University Press, 1948), pp. 56–58; and Giuseppe Löw, "La canonizzazione papale o universale," *Enciclopedia Cattolica*, 1949–1954 ed. The earlier cases cited by Kemp and Löw, as Kemp points out, are based on questionable sources. A thorough discussion of the origins and growth of papal canonization can be found in Vauchez, *La sainteté en occident*, pp. 25–120.

[7]Goodich, *Vita perfecta*, pp. 29–30, 38–47.

[8]Goodich, *Vita perfecta*, p. 30.

papal court became so complicated and costly that few groups promoting a canonization could persist through the entire procedure. Canonizations were no longer the prerogative of the Christian community at large, but of powerful individuals and groups who had the money and influence necessary to push the canonizations through. As Pierre Delooz notes, the sixteenth-century Pope Julius II could still echo his twelfth-century predecessor Celestine III in claiming that canonization was a divine rather than a human judgement about a person's sanctity. But, the human verdict regarding the judgement of God had assumed an ever increasing importance![9]

Papal Canonization: 1600 to the Present: Few significant changes have taken place over the last four centuries in the Congregation of Rites' process for evaluating candidates submitted for canonization. Beatification was added as a step leading toward canonization in 1662. In the eighteenth century, Benedict XIV set down in writing the detailed procedures and norms necessary for papal canonization. In 1914, Pius X divided the Congregation of Rites into two sections, one for liturgy and the other for beatifications and canonizations. Pius XI added an historical section in 1930, and in 1948 Pius XII added a college of medical experts. These experts of "secular knowledge" help the Congregation evaluate the lives and miracles of the individuals proposed for canonization. In more recent times, both Paul VI[10] and John Paul II[11] have made efforts to streamline the administration of this complicated office. Pope Paul VI abolished the Congregation of Rites in order to divide its work among two separate Congregations, one to deal with sacraments and divine worship, and the other, the Congregation for the Causes of Saints, to deal solely with beatifications, canonizations and the preservation of relics.

In spite of these changes, canonization is still a long, arduous and very expensive process. The investigations carried on by the Congregation for the Causes of Saints are as thorough as possible. The Congregation undertakes a lengthy examination of documents, testimonies and other evidence. Beatification is conferred upon martyred Christians, that is, those who have died defending the faith, without evidence of miracles. Beatification for a non-martyr, on the other hand, first requires incontrovertible evidence of the individual's "heroic virtue" in

---

[9]Delooz, *Sociologie et canonisations*, p. 37.

[10]See his apostolic constitutions, *Sacra Rituum Congregatio* (1969), and *Constans Nobis* (1975).

[11]See his apostolic constitution, *Divinus Perfectionis Magister* (1983).

life. At this point, the person is considered "venerable." It literally takes a miracle then, two in fact, for a non-martyred individual to be beatified. The miracles, which the Church understands as having been performed by God after the faithful have turned in prayer to the individual in question, are taken as God's confirmation of the person's holiness. Beatification permits the faithful of a specified territory or religious order to render public cult to the one proclaimed "blessed."

Canonization requires yet another investigation of the blessed's life, writings and miracles. Evidence of at least one more miracle is the last requirement for the final step of canonization, for martyrs and non-martyrs alike.[12] Canonization is an irrevocable pronouncement by the Church that the person is among the saints of God. Public veneration of the saint is mandated throughout the universal church and the saint receives his or her own liturgical feastday. Each of the miracles, by the way, is submitted to rigorous expert examination by physicians or other competent authorities. In short, it is tougher to join the circle of saints than it is any club on earth.

It is also more expensive. The Congregation for the Causes of Saints charges the costs of its investigations to the group, usually a religious order, promoting the canonization. This group also pays for the costs of the canonization ceremony itself in St. Peter's Basilica in Vatican City. It is quite common for holy cards, commemorative medals and relics of the new saint to be distributed as gifts on that day. If the relics are first class, they must be sent to the Congregation for the Causes of Saints and then be placed in reliquaries by nuns who specialize in this work. These expenses alone and other festivities usually sponsored by a religious congregation on the days surrounding a canonization easily amount to tens of thousands of dollars.

But there are numerous other hidden expenses which are harder to calculate. For example, most religious congregations and other groups sponsoring an individual for canonization have to work for decades in the promotion of the individual's cause. This frequently involves the disposition of personnel, the publication of pamphlets or booklets making the cause of their individual known, and so forth. Some religious congregations commission members of their orders to undertake in-depth historical research on the individual's life. This research is then handed over to the Congregation for the Causes of Saints as evidence to

---

[12]For a thorough discussion of the requirement of miracles for beatification and canonization, see Paul Molinari, "I miracoli nelle cause di beatificazione e canonizzazione," *La Civiltà Cattolica* n. 3079 (1978): 21–33.

be used in the investigatory process. In addition, one must add in the previous costs of the beatification, since this is a necessary step leading toward canonization. If all the hidden expenses are taken into account, a conservative estimate of the cost of a canonization is in the neighborhood of a few hundred thousand dollars. Some canonizations have been known to cost religious congregations several million dollars.

Of course, cases vary considerably. Some individuals must wait centuries to be canonized, while others are canonized within a few decades or even years after their death. An overwhelmingly popular figure whose virtuous life is beyond doubt, or someone who is especially attractive to the individuals who work in the Congregation for the Causes of Saints, will pass through the process with greater ease. It is no coincidence that Maximilian Kolbe was the second saint named by John Paul II. His canonization makes him one of just five Poles to be canonized by the papacy in four hundred years and, coming a mere eleven years after his beatification, it was an astonishingly quick canonization by Vatican time.

This brief overview of the last two thousand years chronicles a steady shift away from the Christian community's role in choosing models for sanctity. Technically, the suggestion of someone for canonization should still come from the faithful, but the pivotal role belongs to the Congregation for the Causes of Saints within the Papal Curia. The Congregation currently has a backlog of about fifteen hundred individuals awaiting final examination for canonization.[13] It involves many years, indeed, centuries sometimes for an individual to proceed through the three steps of veneration, beatification and canonization. One of the unfortunate aspects of such an arduous verification process is that canonization has typically become the preserve of groups with the time, money and influence to see the process through to its successful conclusion. Religious orders, which sometimes have reserves of personnel and money, have not surprisingly dominated this process.

The Canonization of Philippine Duchesne: The canonization of Philippine Duchesne adds a new line to the history of sainthood. The process for her beatification was initiated in St. Louis in 1895. By 1909 her cause had been officially introduced in Rome, which meant that the title "Venerable" could be attached to Philippine's name. Her own congregation, the Society of the Sacred Heart, was principally respon-

---

[13]See Congregatio pro Causis Sanctorum, *Index ac Status Causarum* (Vatican City: Guerra, 1988).

sible for the promotion of her cause. Those seeking her canonization were encouraged when on May 12, 1940, Pope Pius XII beatified her.

Since that time, many people have continued their devotion to Philippine, especially members of her own religious order and students and alumnae of Sacred Heart schools around the world. Her religious congregation initially hoped that her cause would move beyond the step of beatification to canonization itself. In the 1960s, however, the religious of the Society of the Sacred Heart decided not to promote her cause beyond beatification. It was not, of course, that they doubted her holiness. Rather, their decision was a response to the new calls of the Church since the Second Vatican Council. Every religious order was called to return to the initial vision of its foundress or founder and to reassess its service in the world. Rediscovering their initial spirit of simplicity and hearing the Church's new call to service of the poor, the Society of the Sacred Heart felt that the personnel, time and expense involved in pursuing the canonization were not justified. Nor did it seem in keeping with the spirit of Philippine Duchesne herself.

It is highly unusual for a religious to be canonized when the cause has not been actively promoted by the members of his or her own order. Since the Congregation for the Causes of Saints does not make many aspects of its deliberations public, it is not easy to assess the significance of this canonization. It is most likely that the Congregation for the Causes of Saints itself re-opened the case for Philippine Duchesne's canonization. Many of us who know of her life can be glad that her brave pioneer spirit and dedication to the poor and marginalized will be made known to millions of Christians. Her canonization is additionally relevant, however, because it represents another shift in the process for determining sanctity away from the Christian faithful and toward an office of the Papal Curia. It is ironic that the canonization of Philippine Duchesne and so many other simple men and women dedicated to serving the poor is the outcome of such a complex and costly process.

2. SAINTLY SOCIETY

Now that we have examined the evolution of the process for selecting the saints, let us consider the people themselves who have been chosen as exemplars of the Christian ideal. The composition of saintly society, in fact, has varied a great deal over the last two thousand years. Social status, geographical distribution, sex and state of life—all of these are revelatory not only of which groups have shown their holiness in each age, but also of what ideals of sanctity have governed the choices of those with the power to canonize.

Social Status:[14] Throughout most of Christian history, people from the privileged classes have dominated within saintly society. A study of almost 2500 persons identified as "saint" or "blessed," a third for whom social class can be determined, indicates that seventy-eight percent of these holy persons have come from the upper class (aristocracy, landed nobility and the economically wealthy), seventeen percent were members of the middle class (merchants, industrialists, professionals and free farmers), and five percent belonged to the lower class (all others, slave or free, who have depended on manual labor for their livelihood). It is relevant to recall that the proportion of upper, middle and lower classes has been approximately the reverse of these figures. That is, the five percent of holy people from the lower class come from the class which accounted for roughly seventy-eight percent of the entire Christian population, while the seventy-eight percent of upper class holy people have been selected from a class representing only about five percent of the population. Even admitting a certain bias on the part of the authors of this study, and their considerable margin of error given the large number of holy people for whom no social class can be determined, their findings are telling.[15]

The over-representation of the upper class in saintly society has many explanations. First, the upper class, through its wealth and power, has always drawn more attention to itself, so such holy people naturally stand out more among their contemporaries. Second, written biographies, miracle tales, etc. have been key elements in virtually all canonizations and beatifications. Throughout most of Christian history, such documents exist almost only for the literate, that is, the wealthy and powerful. Third, as we have seen above, the increasingly complex and costly nature of obtaining a canonization restricted this privilege even more to the upper class. Fourth, in significant periods of Christian history, the high social status of Christian leaders and holy people was important to attract converts. For example, the conversion of entire barbarian peoples often came about not through any great

---

[14]George and George, "Roman Catholic Sainthood and Social Status," *Journal of Religion* 35 (1955): 85–98. See also Broderick, "A Census of the Saints (993–1955)," *The American Ecclesiastical Review* 135 (1956): 112–13; Sorokin, "Class Origins," *Altruistic Love*, pp. 122–35; Weinstein and Bell, "Class," *Saints and Society*, pp. 194–219; and Vauchez, *La sainteté en occident*, pp. 324–28.

[15]For a critique of the George and George study, see Broderick, "A Census of the Saints (993–1955)," *The American Ecclesiastical Review* 135 (1956): 112–13, n. 17.

preaching or teaching of the masses, but through the single conversion of the barbarian king. As he believed, so believed his nation. Effective evangelization of the masses meant making known to them that society's leaders were accepting Christianity. An easy way to do this was to raise some of these leaders to the status of saint.

But the prevalence of the powerful among the saints has not been consistent during Christian history. Less than half of all first-century holy people came from the upper class, forty-one percent came from the middle class and twelve percent from the lower class. Such figures reflect in part the humble origins of Christianity. The modern period has varied even more, with the upper class losing ground consistently beginning in the eighteenth century. It is not coincidental that the middle and lower classes began to make progress "religiously" at the same time they were gaining ground economically, politically and educationally. In the eighteenth century, thirty-nine percent of the canonized and beatified came from the upper class, forty-eight percent from the middle class and thirteen percent from the lower class. In the nineteenth century, twenty-nine percent came from the upper class, fifty-three percent from the middle class and eighteen percent from the lower class. Twentieth-century figures indicate that the lower and middle classes continue their upward rise in saintly status.

In some respects, Philippine Duchesne represents the majority of Christian saints. Her family was wealthy and influential. We will see in later chapters how her social status affected both her and her family's attitudes toward the French Revolution, education of the poor and charitable works. She speaks, however, to both the poor and the rich among us. Philippine chose to use her wealth on behalf of those less fortunate and, throughout her life, she threw herself on the side of the poor and marginalized. Philippine's contact throughout her life with both the rich and the poor, her own wealthy background and her personal choice of a life of poverty are an important testimony to us today.

Geography:[16] Three Western European cultures have dominated

---

[16]See Delooz, *Sociologie et canonisations*, pp. 171–77, 183–87, and 193–94 for statistics covering the years 1000 to 1967. Information covering the years 1968 through 1987 is based on my own study, Catherine M. Mooney, "Statistical Study of Canonized Saints (1968–1987)," unpublished manuscript. These statistics are drawn from the *Acta Apostolicae Sedis: Commentarium Officiale*, vols. 60–79 (1968 to 1987). Large martyr groups, a relatively recent phenomenon in canonizations, can easily skew statistics. They have been excluded from this discussion except where relevant. The groups include the twenty-two Martyrs of Uganda (subtracted from Delooz' statistics) and four groups in my own study: the four martyrs of the Order of Friars Minor, canonized in 1970; the Forty English and Welsh

the ranks of canonized saints and, despite a widening of the circle in recent years, this continues to be true today. An examination of the 371 saints who have died between the years 1000 and 1987 and whose canonizations have received formal approbation by the papacy offers some startling statistics. One third come from the area of modern-day Italy. Together with saints from the territory of modern-day France, they account for over half of all canonizations. When saints from modern-day Spain are added to them, these three areas account for over sixty-five percent of *all* papally canonized saints.[17]

Even factoring in the larger Catholic populations in these areas, there is little significant correlation between the numbers of Catholics in each territory and the percentage of persons canonized.[18] For example, despite Ireland's overwhelming Catholicity, only one Irish[19] person has been canonized since the Congregation of Rites began to manage papal canonization proceedings in the late sixteenth century.[20] Cardinal Suenens of Belgium forthrightly complained of this imbalance during the Second Vatican Council and called for changes in the canonization selection process.[21]

Nevertheless, the last twenty years indicate no shift away from this bias. Between the years 1968 and 1987, twenty-eight saints were

---

martyrs, canonized in 1970; the 103 Korean martyrs, canonized in 1984; and Lorenzo Ruiz and Fifteen Companion Martyrs, canonized in 1987. See also Broderick, "A Census of the Saints (993–1955)," *The American Ecclesiastical Review* 135 (1956): 113–14; Sorokin, *Altruistic Love*, pp. 108–21; Vauchez, *La sainteté en occident*, pp. 318–24; and L.E. Whatmore, "The Statistics of Haloes: A Breakdown of Eleven Hundred Causes," *The Tablet* 28 (1964): 1222–23, 1270.

[17]Delooz, *Sociologie et canonisations*, pp. 193–94; and Mooney, "Statistical Study of Canonized Saints (1968–1987)." See also Broderick, "A Census of the Saints (993–1955)," *The American Ecclesiastical Review* 135 (1956): 113–14; Sorokin, *Altruistic Love*, p. 109; and Whatmore, "The Statistics of Haloes: A Breakdown of Eleven Hundred Causes," *The Tablet* 28 (1964): 1222–23, 1270.

[18]Delooz, *Sociologie et canonisations*, pp. 186–87.

[19]The terms "Irish," "Italian," "French," etc. are used throughout this section to refer to the geographical areas of the saints, rather than their nationality *per se*. "Nationality" is a notion tied to the existence of nation-states. Since these did not exist during the earliest period under discussion, it would be anachronistic to speak of the "nationality" of some of these saints. Similarly, the term "country" refers to a general territory within boundaries which have varied during the last one thousand years. Delooz employs the political boundaries in effect in 1960 in assigning the country of each saint in his study.

[20]The seventeenth-century archbishop and martyr of Armagh, Oliver Plunkett, canonized in 1977, by Pope Paul VI.

[21]*Acta Synodalia Sacrosancti Concilii Oecumenici Vaticani II*, vol. III, part I (Rome: Typis Polyglottis Vaticanis, 1973), pp. 430–32.

individually canonized. Nineteen, that is, about seventy percent, came from Italy (7), Spain (7) and France (5) combined. Are we to conclude that the Italians, French and Spanish are simply holier than the people of the other twenty-eight countries who account for the remaining thirty percent of canonized saints?[22] Hardly.

One possibility, but still inadequate as an explanation, is the birth-places of the popes themselves in this same time period. They are overwhelmingly Italian, with France running a distant second.[23] There are some cases in which political or other "worldly" considerations have influenced their choices. For example, Pope Boniface VIII can-onized King Louis IX, the "Good King" of France devoted to the Church and papacy, as an example to the French king, Philip the Fair, who was resisting papal authority regarding matters he considered to be French business.[24] But such cases are atypical. Popes, moreover, do not initiate canonization proceedings and they have a close hand in overseeing very few.

The key lies elsewhere: an examination of all other saints in the last one thousand years, that is, the 1190 who have not been *formally* recognized by the papacy, but who have been honored locally by bishops, monastic groups and the laity, indicates the same overwhelm-ing preponderance of Italian and French saints, who together account for over half of all the saints. Twenty-seven other countries split the remainder.[25] The message is that the groups who promote a saint's cult, either through the papacy *or* at the local level, have been determin-ing factors in who becomes identified as "saint." The Italians and French have been particularly successful in understanding the can-onization process, gathering the necessary documentation, and promot-ing their saints' causes before the proper authorities.[26] In fact, even the large groups of martyred Asians who have been beatified or canonized in recent years are causes which were promoted especially by Western Europeans who were interested in the causes because their own mis-

---

[22]Delooz, *Sociologie et canonisations*, pp. 193–94, lists twenty-three other countries. To these must be added Lebanon, the Philippines, Scotland, the United States and Yugoslavia [Bohemia], for saints canonized between 1968 and 1987.

[23]Delooz, *Sociologie et canonisations*, p. 196.

[24]Delooz, *Sociologie et canonisations*, p. 174.

[25]Delooz, *Sociologie et canonisations*, p. 178, based on his study of the years 1000 through 1967.

[26]A more nuanced and detailed explanation of the geographical distribution of saints can be found in Delooz, "Les données géographiques," *Sociologie et canonisations*, pp. 169–225.

sionaries were included in the group.[27] The success of the Italians, French and Spanish in promoting canonizations derives especially from their "social proximity" to the papacy, that is, their historically friendly relations with the papacy, their relatively numerous contacts with members of the Curia and their presence within the Curia itself.[28]

Again, Philippine Duchesne represents the majority of canonized saints geographically. As a woman from a Latin-speaking country, she joins the majority of the saints, fully sixty-five percent, who come from countries speaking one of the romance languages, Italian, French, Spanish or Portuguese. Until about 1960, her cause was being promoted by her own French-born religious congregation. On the other hand, Philippine herself was a pioneer. She abandoned the comfort of her own language and culture and set out for the New World. There she dedicated herself to the education of young women who were Creole, native American, or one of the many other cultures present in nineteenth-century North America. She took upon herself the gospel injunction to "go and teach all nations," reminding us that the call to holiness is universal and favors the boundaries of no nation, political system, culture or race.

Sex and State of Life:[29] Many people believe that women are more religious than men. But were we to judge by any of the statistical studies of saints, whether they focus on early Christian or modern times, formally canonized or popularly acclaimed saints, clergy, religious orders or the laity, we would conclude that men are far holier than women. Between the years 1000 and 1987, for example, 371 saints have been formally approved by the papacy. Only seventy-five were women, that is, about one in five.[30] Significantly, over half of

[27]Delooz, *Sociologie et canonisations*, pp. 189–91.

[28]Vauchez, *La sainteté en occident*, p. 319.

[29]Delooz, "Y-a-t-il plus de saints que de saintes?" and "Y-a-t-il des saints laïcs?," *Sociologie et canonisations*, pp. 255–76 and 323–74; see also, Pierre Delooz, "Béatifications et canonisations à venir," *La Revue Nouvelle* 40 (1964): 595–600; Weinstein and Bell, "Men and Women," *Saints and Society*, pp. 220–38; and Vauchez, *La sainteté en occident*, pp. 310–14.

[30]Delooz, *Sociologie et canonisations*, p. 270–71, for statistics through 1967; and Mooney, "Statistical Study of Canonized Saints (1968–1987)." A scholarly study of the seventy-one causes opened by the papacy between 1198 and 1431 reveals that about eighteen percent were women. Fifteen percent of those finally approved were women; see Vauchez, *La sainteté en occident*, pp. 316–17. A less rigorous study, but using a much larger data base including all the saints and blesseds of Butler's *Lives of the Saints* in addition to several other sources is Pitirim Sorokin, *Altruistic Love*. This study of 3090 saints from early Christian history until about 1925 indicates that eighty-two percent of all saints and blesseds have been men. If the recently canonized martyr groups are added to persons individually canonized, women account for 127 out of 556, still about one out of five.

these women have been canonized in the twentieth century. This is owing in part to the growing numbers of women religious relative to men religious and clerics in the past few centuries.[31] But the shift is also a sign of the growing consciousness about the inequality women have suffered throughout history. The change is stunning. Yet even today men's canonizations continue to dominate the canonization process. For example, thirty percent more men than women have been canonized among saints canonized as individuals this century. If martyr groups are also considered, then men are being canonized at double the rate of women.[32]

What sense can we make of these figures? The first and most obvious factor is the predominance of men in positions of power and leadership throughout Christian history, and indeed, Western history itself. Women have been excluded by definition from virtually all of the evangelizing roles—pope, bishop, priest, confessor and preacher—which put one in positions traditionally identified as saintly. Even in missionary efforts which included both women and men, the women quite often assumed a secondary role as helper to the men. There is some evidence of this in Philippine's own life.

Second, a long tradition in Christian theology, one which has been very slow to die, has considered women to be the moral and spiritual inferiors of men. Virtually all of the Church Fathers portrayed women as seducers of men. Many argued that Eve's responsibility for the Fall had tainted all women after her. Tertullian (160–230 A.D.) contended that women's subjection to men and the pain they endured during childbirth were simply God's just judgement upon the particularly sinful condition of their sex. He wrote concerning women in general:

You are the devil's gateway . . . you are the first deserter of the divine law; you are she who persuaded him whom the devil was not valiant enough to attack. You destroyed so easily God's image, man. On account of your desert—that is, death—even the Son of Man has to die.[33]

---

[31]Foralosso, *Indagine sociografica sulle cause dei santi*, pp. 111–13.

[32]Delooz, *Sociologie et canonisations*, pp. 270–71; see also Delooz, "Béatifications et canonisations à venir," *La Revue Nouvelle* 40 (1964): 596–97.

[33]Tertullian, "On the Apparel of Women"; quoted in Katherine M. Rogers, "The Troublesome Helpmate: A History of Misogyny in Literature," in *Women: From the Greeks to the French Revolution*, ed. Susan G. Bell (Belmont, California: Wadsworth Publishing Company, 1973), p. 84.

St. John Chrysostom (c.347–407 A.D.), less extremely inclined than Tertullian, wrote:

> How often do we, from beholding a woman, suffer a thousand evils; returning home, and entertaining an inordinate desire, and experiencing anguish for many days. . . . The beauty of woman is the greatest snare.[34]

The misogyny of the early Christian Church profoundly affected subsequent Christian theology. Every major Christian writer through the sixth century, in fact, considered women to be the mental and moral inferiors of men.

This bias softened slightly in the late Middle Ages,[35] a period in which holy women and feminine imagery became especially attractive to religious men. As Caroline Bynum has persuasively demonstrated, these men were attracted to the "female" because the conception of gender constructed by male writers "stressed male as power, judgment, discipline, and reason" as opposed to female, which represented "weakness, mercy, lust and unreason."[36] Female imagery was particularly attractive to male religious writers because it helped them renounce authority, power and wealth, realities peculiarly associated with these men and in sharp contrast to the extreme world-denial demanded by late medieval Christianity. As Bynum points out:

> The male writer who saw his soul as a bride of God or his religious role as womanly submission and humility was conscious of using an image of reversal. He sought reversal because reversal and renunciation were at the heart of a religion whose dominant symbol is the cross—life achieved through death. . . . Because women were women, they could not embrace the female as a symbol of renunciation. Because society

---

[34]John Chrysostom, "An Exhortation to Theodore After His Fall"; quoted in Rogers, "The Troublesome Helpmate," in *Women: From the Greeks to the French Revolution*, ed. Bell, p. 86.

[35]Vauchez, *La sainteté en occident*, pp. 428–31.

[36]See her sophisticated discussions of these points in " ' . . . And Woman His Humanity': Female Imagery in the Religious Writing of the Later Middle Ages," in *Gender and Religion: On the Complexity of Symbols*, ed. Caroline Walker Bynum, Stevan Harrell and Paula Richman (Boston: Beacon Press, 1986), pp. 257–88, especially 277–80; and in *Holy Feast and Holy Fast: The Religious Significance of Food to Medieval Women* (Berkeley, California: University of California Press, 1986), pp. 282–88.

was male-dominated, they could not embrace the male as a symbol of renunciation. To become male was elevation, not renunciation. . . .[37]

But the late medieval exaltation of attributes genderized as female—weakness, mercy, tenderness, nurturing—and the enhanced importance of holy women, particularly for men, still betrayed a fundamentally misogynist perspective, a perspective which has continued to typify most theologians until the modern era.

It is significant that these theologians were all celibate clerics. To focus exclusively on their feelings—and sometimes fears—about women is to lose the larger context. Their opinions about women were often only a secondary consequence of their rejection, even revulsion, concerning the body, sexual desire and marriage. But their extreme ascetical ideals kept very few men and women from marrying, and the radical misogyny evident in their writings was not fully reflected in the everyday life of Christians in the Middle Ages. Nevertheless, their theories reinforced the conventional idea of woman as the devil's instrument.[38] The Christian theological position became just one more justification for the subjection of women to men, a subjection, it should be recalled, which predated the advent of Christianity.

In fact, "virtue," a word in use long before the Christian era, derives from the Latin word *vir*, meaning "man." Thus, it is true in a sense to say that "to be virtuous, one must be manly." Most women, until quite recently, have internalized this judgement about themselves. Thus we find that even female religious leaders, including Philippine Duchesne and the foundress of her religious order Madeleine Sophie Barat, counseled other women to be "manly" in their religious life and to avoid "womanly" weakness.[39] In light of these deeply-rooted

---

[37]Bynum, " ' . . . And Woman His Humanity'," in *Gender and Religion*, ed. Bynum, Harrell and Richman, p.273; see also Caroline Walker Bynum, "Jesus as Mother and Abbot as Mother: Some Themes in Twelfth-Century Cistercian Writing," in *Jesus as Mother: Studies in the Spirituality of the High Middle Ages* (Berkeley: University of California Press, 1982), pp. 135–69.

[38]See Eileen Power, "The Position of Women," in *The Legacy of the Middle Ages*, ed. C.G. Crump and E.F. Jacob (New York: Oxford University Press, 1926), pp. 403–33, for examples of independent women who depart from the stereotype of early Christian theologians.

[39]See, for example, Philippine's 1824 letter to Gonzague (Adeline) Boilvin, quoted in Louise Callan, *Philippine Duchesne: Frontier Missionary of the Sacred Heart, 1769–1852* (Westminster, Maryland: The Newman Press, 1957), pp. 480–81. Sophie Barat uses such language rather infrequently, but a good example is found in her unpublished letter to Eugénie Audé, March 18, 1837 (Religious of the Sacred Heart Archives, Rome, Italy).

historical presuppositions, it is not surprising that far fewer women than men have been considered saints in Christian history.

Third, it is probable that "sainthood" is less likely to be conferred upon women since it is ultimately decided by an almost all male bureaucracy. Sociologists tell us that social perceptions inevitably reflect the social structure of the perceiving group. It stands to reason, therefore, that the perceptions of holiness formed (and fostered) by the hierarchical church should reflect the all-male composition of its social structure.[40]

Numbers, however, can mean many things. Even today as women are being canonized in ever greater numbers, it is important to look at the specific women being canonized, Philippine among them. Do they share any common traits? Is there a message to be deciphered in examining the types of women who have been canonized? Do these women speak to our contemporary world, about its problems, about the role of women in the Church and in the world? To what extent might the models of female holiness being chosen today by the Papal Curia subtly skew or constrict our notions of what constitutes women's holiness? Let us first examine common themes among women saints in general, and then see how the female saints of this century either fit or break from these earlier patterns.

One study of saints formally canonized between 993 and 1955,[41] provides a fascinating starting point for a reflection on women's sanctity. This study counts fifty-six women in a group of 283, less than one in four. A close examination of these fifty-six women reveals that their sanctity is quite often associated with two factors: 1) the nurturing aid they lend to others, often men, and 2) their virginity or choice of celibate chastity. Even the more atypical cases of women whose lives diverge significantly from traits common to most female saints show this to be true. For example, although of the sixty-nine saints listed as martyrs in this study, only two are women, their lives too reflect the characteristics of nurturing service, and virginity or celibate chastity. Let us look briefly at each.

The first is Wiborada, a woman born in a Swiss canton of the tenth century. The details her biographer chooses to include as evidence of her virtue clearly reflect cultural assumptions about women's proper role. For example, when her brother became a priest, she made

---

[40]Delooz, "Béatifications et canonisations à venir," *La Revue Nouvelle* 40 (1964): 595–96.

[41]Broderick, "A Census of the Saints (993–1955)," *The American Ecclesiastical Review* 135 (1956): 87–115.

his clothes for him. She worked in the monastery where he studied, and cared for the books in the library. Her brother also brought her sick people whom he asked her to tend, which she did. In her later life, she withdrew as a recluse, and led a life of extraordinary mortification. During this period, she foresaw an attack by invading Hungarians. She immediately warned the male clergy and monks of her region and thereby saved them all. She, however, remained in her cell and was murdered by the Hungarian warriors. Wiborada was helper and nurturer, virgin, and a self-sacrificing penitent. These attributes have been long admired by Christians and are common in many saints' lives, both male and female. For reasons which will be discussed below, they have played an especially prominent role in the lives of women saints.

The other female martyr is Maria Goretti. She was born in 1890 in Italy and lost her father at age nine. Evidence proffered for her holiness, even at this age, is that she helped to care for her younger siblings and was devoted to helping with the household tasks, such as cleaning, sewing, cooking and buying the groceries. In a spirit of reparation, she also did good deeds and undertook various religious practices to intercede for the soul of her deceased father. When Maria was eleven years old, an eighteen-year-old neighbor tried to convince her to have sex with him. She naturally refused. In a third and brutal encounter, he himself quoted her as saying, "No, no, God does not want this. Whoever does this goes to hell." In a violent scene, the young man stabbed the resisting girl repeatedly. She lived until the next day, sufficient time in which to forgive him, and then she died, a virgin. Like Wiborada, Maria's sanctity, the sanctity imputed to her by her contemporaries, is intimately tied to nurturing service and virginity.[42]

Nurturing and service of others are, of course, characteristics the popular imagination today associates with all saints, not just women. As exemplars of the Christian life, we expect saints to be models in fulfilling the central gospel injunction of loving thy neighbor. Charity and nurturing do indeed characterize many saints' lives, both male and female, but it is a theme particularly prevalent in women's lives. The reasons for this are primarily cultural. Males have always had open to them all the traditional roads to sainthood: priesthood, preaching, martyrdom, evangelizing, in addition to roles and practices open to women, such as penance, supernatural power and charitable service.

---

[42]See, for example, C.E. Maguire, *Saint Maria Goretti: Martyr of Purity, 1890–1902* (New York: Catholic Book Publishing Co., 1950).

Male saints are found in all of these categories, but proportionately their saintly reputations depend more on their roles of authority and leadership. They are apt to be admired for both spiritual *and* temporal leadership: as preachers and peacemakers, as reformers and rulers, as evangelizers and educators.

Women saints, however, have by definition been excluded from the evangelizing roles of priest and preacher. They were unlikely to be in roles of religious leadership, and rarely held temporal authority. Women were seldom martyred and, as missionaries, they usually followed the male missionary founders and then assumed helping roles. Most women were denied the education, not to mention the possibility, of becoming theologians at the service of the Christian community. Service of others, that is, nurturing, clearly falls in their domain. For example, studies show that holy women have helped the sick, aided the poor, and assisted widows and children, in greater proportions than their male counterparts.[43]

Not surprisingly, their sanctity often follows the models open to women in general, but raised to a spiritual sphere. Even as virgins, they are often called the spiritual mothers of the nuns or lay followers who surround them. They are wives to their husband, Christ, and daughters of God the Father. They even continue to care for others in the womanly task of nurturing and feeding their "families."[44] Women saints, for example, are much more likely than men to perform miracles in which food is multiplied and made available to the hungry.[45]

Nor is it coincidental that women, much more than men, have been devoted to the eucharist, which is after all, food.[46] Women were first to promote the feast of Corpus Christi and their devotion to the eucharist, a meal which accentuates the leadership role of ordained men to the exclusion of laymen and all women, is markedly stronger than men's throughout Christian history. Their eucharistic devotion became particularly pronounced in the thirteenth century, precisely

---

[43]See, for example, Weinstein and Bell, *Saints and Society*, p. 232.

[44]On the continuity of women's symbols and sense of self with their social and biological roles, see Bynum, *Holy Feast and Holy Fast*, pp. 288–94; and Caroline Walker Bynum, "Women's Stories, Women's Symbols: A Critique of Victor Turner's Theory of Liminality," in *Anthropology and the Study of Religion*, ed. Frank Reynolds and Robert Moore (Chicago: Center for the Scientific Study of Religion, 1984), pp. 105–25.

[45]See, for example, Bynum, *Holy Feast and Holy Fast*, pp. 76 and 192–94.

[46]For excellent discussions of the next two paragraphs, see Bynum, *Holy Feast and Holy Fast;* and Caroline Walker Bynum, "Women Mystics and Eucharistic Devotion in the Thirteenth Century," *Women's Studies* 11 (1984): 179–214.

the period in which clericalism had hardened within the Church. The role of the ordained minister and his control of the sacraments was accentuated, laypeople were prohibited from receiving the chalice at communion and women, specifically, were kept from any contact with the altar vessels.[47]

Food is curiously associated with women's secondary status, both in the temporal and spiritual domains. In the temporal sphere of the home, women have traditionally been the food-preparers, a task until recently considered more menial than most men's employments. In the spiritual sphere, on the other hand, laymen and all women receive food, the eucharist, prepared by ordained men. In this instance, the task of food preparation is curiously accorded an exalted status. Moreover, devotion to the eucharist, a devotion especially strong among women, has traditionally focused on a cult rendered to a male God, not just in the person of Christ, but also by association with God the Father and, to a lesser extent, his Holy Spirit.

Many theologians in previous centuries assumed that the shared equality among the three persons of the Godhead was best described in human terms by reference to three masculine, and therefore "equal," persons. In recent years, this skewed emphasis on the masculine in the Godhead has been critiqued. Pope John Paul I pointed out that God, the Creator, is both Mother and Father.[48] The equality and relational aspects of the Trinity are more adequately described today by employing either the complementarity of the masculine and feminine principles, or even by reference to three androgynous persons, the Creator, Redeemer and Spirit.

Virginity and celibate chastity, a second theme central to female saints' lives, have also been emphasized consistently as saintly virtues for *both* men and women throughout most of Christian history. Curiously, virginity and celibate chastity are also key to the sanctity of most canonized laypersons. I remind the reader that the term "laity" as used here excludes all religious.[49] So before discussing virginity as a charac-

---

[47]Bynum, *Holy Feast and Holy Fast*, pp. 55, 76–83, 93, 123, 227–33 and *passim*.

[48]John Paul I, "Angelus Message, September 10, 1978" in *Il tempo d'un sorriso: i discorsi del breve pontificato di Giovanni Paolo I*, ed. Tullio Visconti (Rome: Edizioni Logos, 1978), p. 92, and see also pp. 74 and 97; and *The Message of John Paul I*, ed. Daughters of St. Paul (Boston, Massachusetts: St. Paul Editions, 1978), p. 100, and see also pp. 82 and 106.

[49]According to canon law, the term "laity" technically includes all non-ordained persons, including religious women and men. It is used here in its more colloquial sense to denote all persons who are not clergy or religious.

teristic of canonized women, let us consider it first with regard to the canonized laity.

Laypersons, married or not, have always comprised a minority of the saints, even though they account for the overwhelming preponderance of the faithful. Of the 393 saints recognized by the papacy from the year 1000 through 1987, seventy-six, or a little less than twenty percent are laypeople.[50]

The state of life can be known for sixty-three of these laypeople. Significantly, over half never married, while another eight percent were widows. Only about forty-one percent of the laypeople canonized died in the married state, and many of these were martyred either as individuals or in a group. Since signs of "heroic virtue" in *life* are necessary only for the canonization of non-martyrs, it is clear that these martyred laypeople are not generally being offered to the faithful as models of holy *living*. In fact, we know very little indeed about most of their lives. And significantly, a much greater percentage of laypeople than clergy or religious achieve sainthood through martyrdom. Of all the saints canonized between 1588 and 1967, for example, fully seventy-five percent of the laypeople were martyred contrasted with just twenty-three percent of ecclesiastics.[51] And rather than diminishing, this breach has been growing even wider since the Second Vatican Council. It is telling that the sanctity of laypeople tends to be associated more with the way they died than with the way they lived.

Twenty laywomen have been canonized from the year 1000 through 1987. Just as with canonized religious women, virginity and celibate chastity have played more pronounced roles in laywomen's lives than in the lives of their male counterparts. Ten never married, six were widows, and of the four who died in the married state, one was celibate and at least one of the others lived the semi-religious life of a tertiary. Married women, even more than married men, are rarely canonized unless they are either virgins, widows, or renounce engaging in sexual relations with their husbands.

Although it would be natural to expect an increase in the numbers of laypeople, married and single, in the last twenty years, that is not the case. A study as late as 1975 shows that of the over thirteen

---

[50]Delooz, *Sociologie et canonisations*, pp. 330, 351–52; and Mooney, "A Statistical Study of Canonized Saints (1968–1987)." It is impossible to use Delooz' statistics on the laity without including the Ugandan martyr-group of twenty-two men, most of whom were laymen. Were they subtracted, lay saints would be even fewer.

[51]Delooz, *Sociologie et canonisations*, p. 356.

hundred causes then introduced for canonization, not including martyrs for whom state of life is often difficult to determine, 11.3 percent were laypeople, with just 4.5 percent having ever married. If widows and widowers, founders and foundresses of religious institutes were subtracted from this latter group, then only 3.1 percent of all the cases before the Congregation for the Causes of Saints in 1975 would represent models of holiness for married Christians.[52]

In fact, of the twenty-eight persons who have been canonized as individuals from 1968 through 1987, only one was a layperson, the Italian, Giuseppe Moscati, who died in 1927. He was canonized in 1987, the "Year of the Laity." But it is worth noting that Moscati took a vow of perpetual chastity at age seventeen before dedicating himself to a life of medicine. Ironically, then, the only layperson meriting canonization in recent years for a life of heroic virtue is one who conspicuously resembles a religious.

There have of course been greater numbers of laypersons, married and single, in the large groups of martyrs canonized recently. Yet most of these saints receive little or no individual attention for their personal sanctity during life. Furthermore, the individuals singled out for attention in each martyr-group are usually the few clergy or religious who died with the group. Lorenzo Ruiz and his Fifteen Companions, all martyred in Japan, are an exception to this rule. Ruiz, the first Filipino ever canonized, was one of the few laypersons in his martyr group, but he is always singled out for attention. It is significant that he too was canonized during the "Year of the Laity." Yet it is seldom pointed out that when Ruiz set out for Japan, he abandoned his wife and children in the Philippines. Close examination of the saints shows that celibate chastity or virginity are the preferred routes to sainthood for all men and women, including laypeople. For women, it is a virtual necessity.

Important background for understanding the importance of virginity or celibate chastity in the lives of holy women is the fact that, until the modern era, women have generally been considered to be more concupiscent than men and less able to resist temptation.[53] Their sexual behavior, or lack thereof, has excited more attention in the saints' lives written about them. These biographies, almost always written by

---

[52]Foralosso, *Indagine sociografica sulle cause dei santi*, Table 1, p. 77; pp. 95–96; and Table 8, p. 97.

[53]See, for example, Thomas Aquinas, *Summa Theologica*, IIa, IIae, q. 149, art. 4; and IIa, IIae, q. 165, art. 2.

men, portray many women as beset by carnal struggles. St. Jerome, though a friend to many women, held that a woman could overcome her inherent weakness only by living celibately and becoming, therefore, like a man. An extensive study of almost nine hundred saints shows that one out of six women had to struggle to maintain her chastity in her quest for holiness, while only one out of thirteen men had to do so.[54] Moreover, the men who struggled with sexual temptation usually attributed it to outside sources, such as a woman-temptress or the devil. Women, on the other hand, perhaps because they had internalized cultural assumptions about themselves as carnally weak, tended to look for the source of their struggles within themselves.[55] It is particularly noteworthy that these women's feelings and actions have been handed on to us primarily through male writers. They no doubt project their own assumptions and fears about women onto their subjects. As the authors of this study say:

> While male saints often were gifted with a special form of clairvoyance that enabled them to sniff out the faintest odor of sin in their fellows, it was woman's part to root out the evil within herself rather than to act as champion of morality and censor of the hidden sins of others. In the world of the spirit as in the world of the flesh, men and women were different and unequal.[56]

A clear message ringing through all saints' lives, but particularly those of women, is that celibate chastity is better than married chastity, and virginity is the best of all.

Women Saints in the Twentieth Century: In today's world, the situation of women has been rapidly changing in many societies. It is therefore not surprising that their situation in the Church is also beginning to change, affecting even the numbers of women selected for canonization. Such a radical change in the present helps reverse the common assumption in earlier centuries of women's moral inferiority.

On the other hand, the themes that characterize female saints' lives, while modified to a certain degree, remain essentially the same. Nurturing and serving others are still more dominant themes in their

---

[54]Weinstein and Bell, *Saints and Society*, Table 3, pp. 129 and 220; see especially, "Chastity," pp. 73–99, and "Men and Women," pp. 220–38.

[55]Weinstein and Bell, *Saints and Society*, pp. 87, 235–36.

[56]Weinstein and Bell, *Saints and Society*, p. 236.

lives than in male saints' lives. One has only to think of the numerous women canonized in this century who were the foundresses of educational orders or orders dedicated to the care of the poor and sick. Many of these women were leaders who forthrightly addressed societal ills. For example, Elizabeth Bayley Seton, the first United States-born saint to be canonized, cared for the poor and sick from her early years. After bearing five children and becoming widowed, she continued her commitment to the welfare of the poor, founding the Sisters of Charity in the United States. Her authority, and the perception of holiness her contemporaries formed about her, clearly derived from her admirable commitment to the womanly task of nurturing. There is no doubt that such women provide important role models for both women *and* men today. Yet a question should be raised: are they perceived as models for *both* women and men, or is their selection for canonization intended as a special model for women? Most women canonized this century continue to reflect traditional and sometimes even antiquated assumptions about activities appropriate to women. Will women who exercise religious leadership outside the bounds of the traditional cultural restraints placed on them be admitted to canonized sainthood in the coming years?

Virginity and celibate chastity also continue to be central to almost all saints canonized in this century, and this is true especially of women. For example, of the forty-two women canonized from 1900 through 1987, thirty-eight were members or foundresses of religious orders. This is perhaps surprising given the Church's new attention to the role of the laity. The four laywomen who have been canonized in the twentieth century confirm the first characteristic, discussed above, of service to others. Significantly, they also confirm the second characteristic, virginity and celibate chastity. Although laywomen, their lives do not provide models of saintliness in the full context of women's sexuality. None of them were spouses, none mothers. All were virgins.

The lives of these four women also highlight a third characteristic, as yet to be discussed, particularly prevalent among women saints, penance and private religious practices. A brief examination of the lives of these laywomen well illustrates the centrality of this third characteristic of women's sanctity. A question to keep in mind regarding each of these women is their aptness as models of holiness for women in general in the twentieth century, and for laywomen in particular. The first laywoman is Maria Goretti, canonized in 1950, whose life has already been described.

The second laywoman is Joan of Arc, who was canonized in 1920. This well-known fifteenth-century saint was directed by supernatural voices to lead the French army to victory over the English. When she was captured after some significant victories, the man she had helped so much, King Charles, did nothing to rescue her. Joan was sold to the English, who tried her for heresy and witchcraft. The witchcraft charge was becoming more common in Western Europe at this time. Supernatural gifts, such as hearing voices, could be from the devil as well as from God, but it is notable that charges of sorcery were leveled almost exclusively at women.[57] The English questioned her about her voices, her faith and her loyalty to the Church. They were particularly vexed by her male attire and asked her pointedly if she had wanted to be a man. They contrived to find her guilty of heresy and then burned her alive at age nineteen.

Third is Gemma Galgani, who was born in 1878 in Italy and canonized in 1940. Since childhood, she meditated on Christ's passion. Suffering and recurring illnesses filled her short life. Gemma's meditations were accompanied by a personal experience of the passion: she received the stigmata (the wounds of Christ in her own body), experienced being scourged and crowned with thorns, and felt the sweat of blood experienced by Christ. Gemma died at age twenty-five.

Last is Mariana de Paredes, canonized in 1950. Together with Maria Goretti, Mariana is the most recent model of lay sanctity presented to women in this century. She was born in seventeenth-century Ecuador and was orphaned. Even as a child she was known for her extreme penance and fasting. Mariana lived in an austerely furnished room in her sister's house and used to dress in a black cassock like that of her Jesuit confessors. She cared for the poor and hungry and was both teacher and nurse to Ecuadoran Indians. She died at age twenty-six and was buried in her "Jesuit" clothing.

The lives of all forty-two women chosen for canonization in the twentieth century, religious and laywomen together, clearly continue to emphasize service to others, celibate chastity and virginity as central to their sanctity. The third characteristic suggested by their lives, penance and private religious practices, merits further examination.

Penance, personal mortification and other private religious practices are important expressions of piety for women because they are available to them in the privacy of their religious cloisters or own homes. In a study covering the period 1000 to 1700, in which women account for only 17.5 percent of approximately nine hundred saints, they nevertheless comprise over half of all the saints in whose lives

[57]Weinstein and Bell, *Saints and Society*, pp. 94, 227–28.

fortitude in illness was recognized as a major virtue. For what other activities do their lives show a disproportionate emphasis? long periods of reclusion, extreme humility, extreme dedication to poverty and self-flagellation.[58]

Two principles are operative here. First, with many religious roles closed to them, women *could* do all of these things. Like women in general, holy women have been expected to assume primarily domestic roles. Just as the home was the domain of so many married women, so religious women were confined to the cloister, even when, in the case of Clare of Assisi, for example, they expressed a desire to evangelize in "the world." This fact helps to explain the more private nature of women's spirituality. Fasting, personal poverty, all night vigils of prayer and other practices involving self-denial were some of the few aspects of women's lives in which they *were* in control and through which they could choose to express themselves. Their practices were personal and private expressions of their religious zeal. In earlier centuries women were more apt than their male counterparts to have visions and to prophesy. They were also more likely to be lifted into heaven, or at least to the church rafters. These private expressions of their religiosity, signs to others of their holiness, could take place in the cloister or at home and were not therefore dependent on their assuming roles open only to men—priest, preacher, evangelizer of other nations, author of religious doctrine, and so forth.

Second, private penance, as distasteful as some of its forms are to us today, also responded to the image of woman which society, until recently, had assigned to them. Self-mortification and self-abasement, ideals for all Christians, were especially suited to the sex which was seen as spiritually inferior and physically weaker. Furthermore, biblical exegesis, philosophical, theological and medical theories have tended to associate women with the flesh and men with the spirit or rational soul.[59] The thirteenth-century theologian Thomas Aquinas, for example, argued in his *Summa Theologica* that woman's subjection to

---

[58]Weinstein and Bell, *Saints and Society*, pp. 232–35.

[59]Vernon L. Bullough, "Medieval Medical and Scientific Views of Women," *Viator: Medieval and Renaissance Studies* 4 (1973): 485–501; Bynum, *Holy Feast and Holy Fast*, pp.261–69; Marie-Thérèse d'Alverny, "Comment les théologiens et les philosophes voient la femme," *Cahiers de civilisation médiévale* 20 (1977): 105–29; Joan M. Ferrante, "Biblical Exegesis," *Woman As Image in Medieval Literature from the Twelfth Century to Dante* (New York: Columbia University Press, 1975; reprint Durham, North Carolina: Labyrinth Press, 1985), pp. 17–35; Carolyn Osiek, "Inspired Texts: The Dilemma of the Feminist Believer," *Spirituality Today* 32 (1980): 140.

man was natural because "in man the discernment of reason is greater."[60] The association of women with flesh is one more factor predisposing women to express themselves religiously through the physical practices of mortification, although men too to a lesser extent have chosen this path to sanctity.

3. ARE SAINTS RELEVANT?

Saints have exercised the minds, hearts and imaginations of men and women since the earliest Christian times. How much great art would be lost if painters had not had the inspiration of the saints? Tens of thousands of Christians since early times have enjoyed the adventure of a pilgrimage to Rome or elsewhere owing to their devotion to places made holy by some saint. St. Francis of Assisi has inspired more men and women, Christian and non-Christian, than almost any other holy person in history. So much good religious fiction has been written about him, that it is hard to separate it from the equally vast corpus of historical documents relating to his life. He has even made it to the movies with "Brother Sun, Sister Moon." On a more serious note, people in all ages have felt protected, listened to and interceded for by one or another of the Christian saints. Some would even claim a miracle in their lives owing to the kindness of a saint.

Nevertheless, fewer Christians today pray to the saints or ask the saints to pray for them. Many people struggle to discover the relevance of saints' lives to their own. With scientific knowledge increasingly dominating our way of thinking, more people dismiss many saints' stories as relics of a bygone past, tainted by superstition. Some of the incidents recorded in biographies of the saints bear little relevance to the joys, disappointments, challenges and failures which face Christians in their everyday living. Such biographies, in fact, betray an infantile piety which leads people to treat the saints, in the words of the well-known Religious of the Sacred Heart Janet Erskine Stuart, "as inhabitants of a superior kind of doll's house."[61] Moreover, some of the saints who are being canonized in our own century seem to serve better the needs of Christians of another time.

In fact, it is the written saints' lives, the texts composed about them, more than the saints themselves that stand at the center of this

---

[60]Thomas Aquinas, *Summa Theologica*, Ia, q. 92, art. 1.
[61]*The Education of Catholic Girls* (London: Longmans, Green and Co., 1927), p. 10.

problem. In the early Church and in the Middle Ages, much as in other primitive societies today, people did not distinguish between miracle and human event the way many of us do today. What seems to us a miraculous element in a saint's life could have been an everyday occurrence for them. In other cases, the goal of the writer was precisely to astound the readers with stunning tales, or to scare them about the horrors of hell, or just to provide an entertaining evening of reading, much as we enjoy a good detective novel. Today, we do not write or read saints' lives for any of these reasons, yet the genre has not adapted itself. Many writers of saints' lives continue to emphasize the extremes of prayer, hardship, success, sacrifice, and so forth. Even when there is not exaggeration, the more human sides of the saints' lives sometimes receive short shrift. The peccadillos of the saint, the more mundane aspects of the life, the trying aspects of the saint's personality, plain old mistakes, so many of these are whisked away into the closet with the other skeletons. And *voilà*, we have swept this saint into a spiritual stratosphere which we mere humans can never hope to attain.

Yet saints are needed today as much as in any other period of history. People look to other people to show them the way, to set standards of good and just living, to inspire them when hope flags. In many societies, perhaps especially in the wealthier, industrialized nations, there are few or no heroes or heroines. There may be passing stars, people who rise to prominence for a brief period and then fall again from favor. They include politicians, entertainers, television preachers and business magnates. But there are few leaders of the moral stature or with the staying power of Gandhi, Martin Luther King, Dorothy Day or Bishop Oscar Romero. It is significant that all these models sustained harsh criticism during their lives. They did not dwell in a utopia; they each engaged in very human struggles; and their opponents seized every chance to make their failings known. In fact, their prayer, their charity, their joy in success and their acceptance of failure strike us as all the more holy precisely because these appear in the context of their humanity.

In Philippine Duchesne we find a woman who was fully human. Her failures, her weaknesses and her limits keep her within our reach, in touch with our reality. Her holiness was not some supernatural sanctity. She got it the old-fashioned way, as they say: she earned it, with bumps and bruises. Her human achievement speaks to us in many ways:

—She lived in a world that was complicated and unjust. It was difficult for her to discern at times the right thing to do in such a world. Her own struggles to reach beyond the boundaries and biases of her own culture and class can give courage to people today engaged in the works of charity and justice.

—She was a woman in a world and a Church run largely by men. Her life and choices reflect her reality as a nineteenth-century woman. They also give us food for thought as we seek to create a Church and a world in which the gifts of both men and women find full complementarity. As a woman on the frontier, she has something to say to women today who find themselves on frontiers of another sort.

—Philippine's life, like so many today, was frequently marked by a sense of loneliness and isolation. In a world marked increasingly by individualism and even alienation, we can learn from her attempts to give her life meaning through service of others.

—Although she felt a personal call to be with the poor, she spent much of her life in contact with the wealthy. The Church's call to be with the poor is much louder today, but many of us find ourselves in countries or situations of wealth. She is an example of someone who refused to live in just one world, ignoring the other. A woman of communion, she built bridges between worlds.

—Philippine's life was marked by failures. Living as we do in a world little tolerant of failure, her life has something to teach us all about what is really of value in life.

Dorothy Day, the Catholic socialist, pacifist and founder of the Catholic Worker movement, used to become irate at the suggestion of some people that she would someday be canonized. She said, "That's the way people try to dismiss you. If you're a saint, then you must be impractical and utopian, and nobody has to pay any attention to you. That kind of talk makes me sick."[62] I hope to paint a portrait of Philippine Duchesne as a woman who should not be dismissed—as a real saint. She is not an otherworldly spiritual being living in a utopian world, but rather a human being struggling and stumbling toward holiness as we all must. If we can learn to look at her and the other saints in all their *human* glory, we need not dismiss any of them.

---

[62]Quoted in William D. Miller, "Dorothy Day," in *Saints Are Now: Eight Portraits of Modern Sanctity*, ed. John J. Delaney (Garden City, New York: Image Books, 1983), p. 19.

II.

Family, the Feminine Arts, and Religious Vocation

1. FAMILY CONTEXT AND INTELLECTUAL CURRENTS

Philippine Duchesne was born on August 29, 1769 in Grenoble, France. It was a town of 25,000 people in the southeastern province of Dauphiny. She was baptized Rose-Philippine in honor of Rose of Lima, the first woman to be canonized in the Americas, but everyone called her Philippine. Her father, Pierre-François Duchesne, was a prominent lawyer and politician in Grenoble. Her mother, Rose-Euphrosine Périer, dedicated herself to managing the Duchesne home and raising their children. Philippine, though she was not the first-born, was left as the eldest child, with four younger sisters and a brother, when her older sister died. The family had already lost an infant girl.

In fact, there were really many more children than these in Philippine's childhood. Her cousins' the Périers' lived in an adjoining section of their enormous home and, between the two families, twenty children were born in a space of just twenty years. Significant ties bound the two families closely. The intimate friendship between Philippine's mother and her Aunt Périer provided Philippine with an important model of human affection. During these early years Philippine formed what would be the most abiding and supportive friendship of her life. Her cousin Josephine Périer was her confidant, benefactress and steadfast correspondent right through the last years of their lives. Josephine's loyalty never wavered even when for over thirty years they did not see each other.

The world of Philippine's childhood was a world of rapid change in the areas of economics, intellectual thought, and religion in France.

32

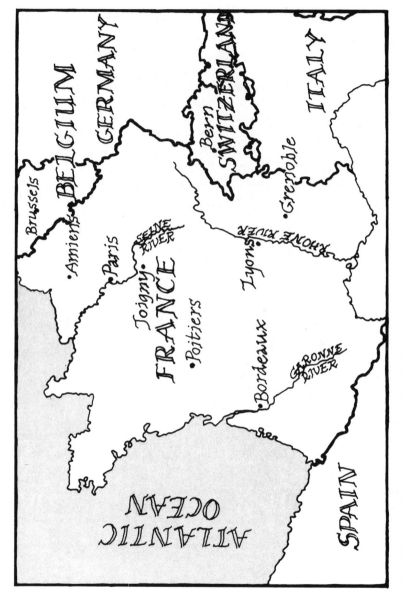

Map of France and its major cities in the life of Philippine Duchesne at the end of the 18th century.

Most Europeans were still impoverished, illiterate and working in agriculture. Commercial activity however was moving into a period of unprecedented growth. Both of Philippine's parents came from well-to-do families who had made their wealth riding the first waves of the industrial revolution. Her mother's dowry had been 100,000 francs or about twenty thousand dollars, a veritable fortune in those days. Philippine's Grandfather Périer had been so successful as a merchant that he could afford to lend large sums, sometimes charging excessive interest rates, to other aspiring businessmen in Dauphiny.[1] Her Uncle Claude Périer, who lived in the adjoining home and was a favorite of Philippine's, became one of the wealthiest men in Grenoble owing to his undertakings in textiles, banking, manufacturing and other capitalistic ventures both in France and overseas. Other relatives similarly acquired fortunes and fame in the businesses of banking, wine and overseas trade. The flip side of the unlimited individual wealth made possible by this new commercial activity was the wretched conditions it often caused for workers. These conditions, in fact, inspired the modern Church's forthright social teachings concerning production, workers' rights and the just distribution of wealth.[2]

Philippine, a member of the upper class, was raised in a world of ease. The family's enormous home, which still stands today, was prominently situated opposite the Palace of Justice on the Place Saint-André and was bordered on another side by Grenoble's principal street, the Grande Rue. The Duchesne children typically had more spending money than their neighbors. Yet Philippine was also raised with a sense of social responsibility toward those less fortunate. Like many other children of her social class, Philippine sometimes shared her "wealth" to make charitable gifts to the poor, a fact no doubt exaggerated in importance by Philippine's hagiographers. What is more significant is that her awareness that people come before material goods eventually led her as an adult to use all her wealth, material and personal, on behalf of those in need.

Philippine's family was successful and prominent not only in busi-

---

[1] François Hincker, *Expériences bancaires sous l'Ancien Régime* (Vendôme: Presses Universitaires de France, 1974), pp. 81–84.

[2] These documents are, significantly, seldom read by Catholics in many wealthy nations, who tend to focus instead on the Church's teachings regarding individual morality. The compelling nature of the social teachings make them at once less easy to dismiss and more challenging for Christians, a fact which perhaps explains their relative absence from Catholic preaching and teaching. A recent example of such teaching is the impressively nuanced encyclical of John Paul II, *The Social Concerns of the Church*.

ness, but also in the area of politics. Her father was a well-known lawyer in Grenoble, a member of the provincial Parliament and, on several occasions, the elected president of the local bar association. Duchesne helped to found and to organize a public library, serving as its director for a while. His active public service was not lost on his daughter. He was one of many successful and upwardly mobile businessmen who had been deeply influenced by ideas current in France during the period of the Enlightenment.

"The Enlightenment," as it has been called by historians, refers roughly to the years 1660 to 1789 and primarily concerns an intellectual movement in which new insights in the scientific field were popularized by writers such as Voltaire and Montesquieu. In brief, "enlightened" individuals assumed that the universe could be fully understood and that it was governed by natural, not supernatural, forces. They believed that all questions could be answered by dispassionately observing material evidence and that the human race could improve almost infinitely if only it were educated properly. These ideas had a dramatic impact on the intellectual, political and religious life of France. They also indirectly affected Philippine in at least three ways.

First, although few Enlightenment thinkers doubted the existence of God, their ideas were a critique of French Catholicism. Some thinkers criticized the Catholic Church because it upheld belief in miracles, the sacraments and other mysteries. Philippine's father was sympathetic to these Enlightenment ideas. He was one of many of Philippine's male relatives who rejected Catholicism; that is, until their deathbeds. The Church was also criticized because it was tremendously powerful, both politically and economically. When the French Revolution finally erupted in 1789, those who resented the Church encouraged the expulsion and death of some clergy, closed convents and churches, and prohibited the very practice of Catholicism. These events changed the course of Philippine's life. Expelled from the Visitation convent which she had entered, she had to devise her own sort of religious life "in the world," a fact particularly interesting for Christians choosing the lay life today. The virulence of the French Revolution's attacks on the Church also illuminates some aspects of her own spirituality. For example, the ills the Church suffered during this period inspired her to undertake some rather harsh penances to make amends for the hostile attacks directed against it.

Some enlightenment ideas were optimistic, however, and indirectly affected Philippine in a second way. Many people believed that God, much like a watchmaker, had created the world, provided it with perfect laws, and then abandoned it to run on its own. It was simply up to humans to understand these laws and act accordingly to improve their world. Her father's political activity, in Grenoble as a lawyer, as member of the municipal council, as a leader in the first stage of the French Revolution, and in various governmental posts thereafter, points to his belief that human activity could bring about change and establish an order of government superior to the eighteenth-century French monarchy. Although Philippine would hardly agree that God had abandoned the world and left everything up to human activity, her faith was clearly one which inspired action and favored a practical approach toward many religious issues. Her conscious choice to enter a religious order with an active apostolate of teaching instead of a contemplative order devoted primarily to prayer is one example of this.

Finally, although Philippine was "protected" from Enlightenment thinkers in her own formation, she was indirectly affected by them in a third way. They believed that the human race could improve almost infinitely with proper education. This confidence in the *possibility* of educating people is reflected in many changes in the educational sphere. The fact that Philippine would later belong to a religious order dedicated to educating young women is significant. The order she entered taught young women subjects traditionally considered suitable only to young men. She and her religious sisters are the first hint of a wave of educators who would believe that women were educable in areas other than the traditional "feminine" skills. They believed that educated women would have a dramatic impact on family and social life in France. Equally revolutionary was the fact that her order educated not only the wealthy, but also the poor. Until then, the poor had been considered uneducable by nature, a point which will be discussed more fully in chapter four.

2. EDUCATION FOR DOMESTICITY: LEARNING THE FEMININE ARTS

At home, Philippine was taught in the manner of other girls of her social class. She and Josephine were under the charge of a governess, while the boys had a tutor of their own. The education of girls at this time was less academic than that received by the boys. Their lighter academic load included reading, writing, and probably a smattering of history, arithmetic, and literature. The girls' education was completed by an introduction into the household duties that they were expected to assume as married women, as managers of the servants and children of their own families. Philippine's mother was responsible for these aspects of her child's education. She assigned Philippine the appropriate household chores and expected her, as the eldest girl, to care for her younger sisters and brother. Yet even at this early age, Philippine betrayed a certain stubborn streak and independence of mind which her mother found difficult to temper. Fortunately, her mother had little success. Philippine would need her determination, or "stubbornness," to get her through many tough times as an adult. Philippine also acquired religious fervor and learned the fundamentals of religion from her mother. Her disbelieving father, a forceful, even cantankerous type on occasion, chose not to interfere. Religious formation was women's work.

It is important to bear this in mind in considering the education Philippine received. Women, in the eighteenth- and early nineteenth-century middle class, were the religious and moral educators of the family. In Victorian England, a wife was even referred to as the "Angel in the House." Her duties were the management of the servants and children. A girl's education was important not in itself, but insofar as it was intended to serve the needs of her future husband and children. Her training in the "feminine arts" of music, singing, drawing and painting was to render her fit for entertaining in the parlor. In *Émile*, the "enlightened" French thinker, Jean-Jacques Rousseau (1712–1778) had this to say about the education of women:

> On the good constitution of mothers depends, in the first place, that of children; on the care of women depends the early education of men. . . . Thus the whole education of women ought to be relative to men. To please [men], to be useful to them, to make themselves loved and honored by them, to educate them when young, to care for them when grown, to counsel them, to console them, and to make life agreeable and sweet to them—these are the duties of women at all times, and what should be taught them from their infancy.

The education of many well-to-do women provided them with a smattering of geography, literature, history and arithmetic, but not so much as to provide them with a critical grasp of the events taking place outside their homes. Women were not expected to be the intellectual companions of their husbands. They were not expected to have opinions about the political events of the world. Rousseau goes on to say:

The search for abstract and speculative truths, principles,
and scientific axioms, whatever tends to generalize ideas,
does not fall within the compass of women; all their studies
ought to have reference to the practical; it is for them to make
the application of the principles which man has discovered,
and to make the observations which lead man to the establishment of principles. All the reflections of women which are
not immediately connected with their duties ought to be directed to the study of men and to that pleasure-giving knowledge which has only taste for its object; for as to works of
genius, they are out of their reach . . . [3]

Rousseau's views were not accepted in their entirety by everyone
in the eighteenth century. Indeed, just thirty years after he wrote this
passage he was severely criticized by Mary Wollstonecraft in her essay,
"A Vindication of the Rights of Woman." Her view, however, was that
of a minority. The educational ideas of Fénelon struck a middle ground
between Rousseau and Wollstonecraft. An ardent defender of the importance of women's education, he argued for broadening the curriculum in well-to-do girls' schools to include more arithmetic, reading,
writing, and the introduction of such subjects as the physical sciences,
law and pedagogy. Yet Fénelon, like Rousseau, argued that the value of
such learning for women attached to their role as the moral educators
of their families and help-mates to their husbands. [4]

It is difficult to assess the quality of Philippine's academic studies
either at home or those she undertook later at the Visitation boarding
school. But her education conformed generally to the bourgeois ideal.
The woman's place was in the home as religious and moral educator,
manager of the servants and children as well as charming entertainer
for her husband and his guests.

Philippine's tastes as a child give us other glimpses of her character. She did not like to play with dolls and never learned to cook
well. Those who lived with her years later attest to this failure! She
loved to go on long walks out of doors, to climb in the mountains
surrounding Grenoble or to pick flowers in a nearby meadow. Philip-

---

[3]This and the preceding quotation can be found in *Women: From the Greeks to the French
Revolution*, ed. Bell, p. 265.

[4]Léon Abensour, *La femme et le féminisme avant la révolution* (Paris: Editions Ernest
Leroux, 1923), pp. 34–51. See also Bonnie G. Smith, *Ladies of the Leisure Class: The Bourgeoisie
of Northern France in the Nineteenth Century* (Princeton, New Jersey: Princeton University
Press, 1981), pp. 165–86.

pine preferred nature to art, for which she had little talent. She already betrayed a certain reserve with regard to showing her feelings and a real capacity for solitude, which she would need more than she imagined later in life. When she was with the other children, both boys and girls, she was a leader, a fact not surprising as the eldest child. It is refreshing to find that she was not a "pious little girl." Her strong personality brought her trouble. She was often too domineering with the other children and had to be reprimanded at school. Her tastes in reading are also revelatory. She relished reading the lives of the saints, especially those of the martyrs. As children do in so many times and cultures, she dreamed of traveling to far-off lands. In her case, the destination was the missions. In later life she recalled one of her earliest influences in this regard:

My first enthusiasm for missionary life was roused by the tales of a good Jesuit Father who had been on the missions in Louisiana and who told us stories about the Indians. I was just eight or ten years old, but already I considered it a great privilege to be a missionary. I envied their labors without being frightened by the dangers to which they were exposed, for I was at this time reading stories of the martyrs, in which I was keenly interested. The same good Jesuit was extraordinary confessor at the convent in which I became a pupil. I went to confession to him several times, and I loved his simple, informal manner of speaking, a manner he had used with the savages.[5] From that time the words "Propagation of the Faith" and "Foreign Missions" and the names of priests destined for them and of religious in far-away lands made my heart thrill.[6]

---

[5] Philippine frequently used the word "savage" to refer to native Americans. It was a term current among Europeans at the time and had a less derogatory connotation than today. I employ the term "Indian" instead of the more correct term "native American" when the former term is more consistent with the sources and situations under discussion. Similarly, Louise Callan's translations, quoted below, often politely render the French word "sauvage" as "Indian."

[6] *Memoir of Philippine Duchesne to St. Madeleine Sophie* (Paris, 1818), Religious of the Sacred Heart Archives, St. Louis, Missouri. Translations from Philippine's letters and from other relevant primary source documents are, when not otherwise indicated, from Callan, *Philippine Duchesne*. I have made it a practice throughout the book to translate into English terms she has left in French and to adapt spelling and punctuation when that enhances uniformity or clarity.

On first consideration, this recollection of her early desire to be a missionary is remarkable, but it should be kept in its own historical context. Tales of the missions, especially those among "the savages" of America, were common fare among well-to-do Catholics of this period. The attraction of saving "the savages" was at once romantic, adventurous and altruistic. Wealthy Catholics felt that the greatest gift they could give to native Americans was the Catholic faith. Nor was a desire to go to the missions so different from the idealistic and adventurous dreams that children continue to dream today, to travel, to do something great, to change the world for the better. Nevertheless, the force of Philippine's early desire, and the vividness with which she recalls her encounters with so many missionaries, reveal just how determined she was to go to the foreign missions. It became one of the driving forces of her life.

3. CONVENT BOARDING SCHOOL

Philippine and her cousin Josephine were sent to a nearby boarding school in 1781. She was just entering adolescence, the age many girls of her class were sent off to the nuns to prepare for their first Holy Communion. The school chosen by her parents was St. Marie On High, a Visitation monastery built midway up the side of an Alpine mountain which overlooks Grenoble. From the top of the long staircase leading to the monastery, one can glimpse the fifth floor of the imposing Duchesne mansion, a building now divided into numerous apartments. As a pupil at St. Marie, Philippine studied academic subjects such as arithmetic, history and French literature. She also continued to develop "feminine" skills such as needlework. The education offered by the Visitation nuns was concerned above all with providing each girl with a strong grounding in her faith. The other subjects were just means toward her formation as a Christian woman who, in most cases as a wife and mother, would be responsible for making the home a place of Christian virtue for all.

While life at St. Marie might seem austere, to Philippine, a girl already given to self-sacrifice, this period recalls happy memories. Visitation spirituality is characterized by its emphasis on God's love, docility to the Spirit, humility, gentleness and patience. All of these spiritual virtues naturally affected the manner the nuns had with the children, no matter how strict the discipline. Years later, Philippine wrote to her cousin Josephine recalling that time. St. Marie, she said, was "the home of our childhood . . . the cradle of our faith and of the intimacy that has united us."[7] In fact, it was during these early adolescent years that she resolved to become a religious. One of her schoolmates recalls Philippine's efforts at prayer during this period:

She was continually praying before the blessed sacrament, and her fervor now led her to get up every day at the same hour as the nuns, in order to be in the choir and make her meditation when they did. Sometimes in mid-winter she would hurry down half dressed rather than omit the practice or shorten her hour of prayer. Her companions, who did not realize the strength of her will, used to laugh at this great zeal and prophesy that it would slacken soon, but nothing ever turned her from the practice; as long as she remained at school, she was faithful to it.[8]

This is our first glimpse of her strong attachment to the eucharist, an attachment for her to the incarnated reality of God within human life. Visitation also introduced her to devotion to the Sacred Heart, a vital current in French spirituality, especially in the Visitation order.

4. VISITATION MONASTIC LIFE

Philippine's parents learned through her schoolmates of her intention to be a nun. Like many parents then and today, they were not happy with the news. As Philippine wrote many years later, parents are often more open to allowing their sons to become priests than allowing their daughters to become nuns. The difference in the status accorded to each is the key factor here. A priest could still fulfill many of the roles expected of a successful man. He was a leadership figure; his words were influential; spiritually he could be a good father and provider. His priestly role changed his relationships, but left him deeply rooted within society. On the other hand, a woman who entered the cloister, a condition imposed on religious women of that time, distanced herself from society. She was abandoning the privileges and duties society expected of her. She would not have children, be a homemaker or be a devoted wife caring for her husband. Even her

---

[7]January 30, 1838.
[8]Madame de Coriolis, *Histoire de la Société du Sacré Coeur*. Religious of the Sacred Heart Archives, Rome, Italy.

spiritual role as "sister" to all, or even "mother" of schoolchildren, lacked the force attached to the paternal role of priests because women who became nuns, unlike priests, physically withdrew from society itself. Philippine's father wasted no time in removing his daughter from St. Marie's.

She returned to her home, which now belonged entirely to the Duchesne family. Her Uncle Claude Périer had just inherited two-thirds of the family fortune upon the death of his father and had purchased a six-story mansion elsewhere. Philippine dedicated her time to caring for the younger children. She also received some academic instruction from her cousins' and brother's tutor, the abbé Raillane. Raillane was a stern and severe person. The change for Philippine from her Visitation days must have been dramatic. She adjusted gracefully, however, aided no doubt by her own inclination to severity with herself. Penitential practices at this point were becoming a regular part of her life. She sought out the most unpleasant chores to be done around the house. Unbeknownst to her family, she also undertook more striking penances. For example, she used to heat a little silver cross and then press the hot metal to her bare flesh. Such practices are the first signs not only of Philippine's profound humility, but also of a sometimes exaggerated tendency toward self-abasement.

Philippine did not move in the slightest from her intention to be a nun during these five years at home. She went to parties and balls, but was not attracted by social life in Grenoble. Two of her younger sisters were married, although as the oldest, she should have been the first to marry. She was not beautiful and, in those days just as today, the physical appearance of the woman was of more importance than that of the man. Nevertheless, Philippine was eminently marriageable. At age eighteen, her father had found her a suitable marriage partner. She found her suitor quite agreeable, but absolutely refused to marry him.

The conflict with her parents then escalated. Rather than simply speak of her desire to be a nun, she began to live like a nun in the confines of the family home. She followed a routine of daily prayer. She refused to wear her beautiful clothing and was loath to go to dances or other social events. There was no giving in on these points. Her story echoes that of a surprising number of women saints from the Middle Ages on who have resisted parental insistence to marry and who have finally taken matters into their own hands. After a few months, Philippine persuaded her Aunt Périer, who was sympathetic to her desires, to accompany her to St. Marie to speak with the nuns. Much to her aunt's chagrin, once there, Philippine refused to leave.

Philippine's parents would remain skeptical of her choice for some time, but her will had worked its way.

Philippine received the novice's black habit and white veil on September 10, 1788, a few months after entering. It is interesting to note that the monastery document recording this event contains the signatures of both her Aunt and Uncle Périer as witnesses of the ceremony, but not those of her own parents.[9] Thirty years later, shortly before setting off for the New World, Philippine recalled this time in her memoir to Sophie Barat and provided some of the details of her religious formation:

> When I entered religious life at the age of eighteen and a half years, a desire to share in the apostolate made me choose the Visitation, where children were educated, in preference to Carmel [a contemplative order], which I loved very much. My community was animated by the spirit of the Jesuits, from whose Constitutions they boasted their own had been drawn. The library was enriched with nearly all the works of Jesuit authors, because at the time of the suppression of the Society of Jesus three of its members found a refuge in our chaplain's house, and when they died they left their library to the convent. During two whole years of my novitiate I read only Rodríguez, without ever tiring of it; and when we assembled after Vespers, I used to relate to my Sisters the lives of nearly all the saints of the Company of Jesus [Jesuits]. That of St. Francis Xavier appealed most strongly to me. . . . I loved his touching appeals to the European schools to send him missionaries. How often have I not said to him since then, in my impatience, "great Saint, why do you not call me? I would respond at once." He is the saint of my heart.

Several important aspects of her spirituality come to the fore in this passage: her fascination with the missions, her esteem for the Jesuits, her active approach to life, and her attraction to a life of self-sacrifice.

The work she tirelessly studied for two years is the *Practice of Perfection and Christian Virtues*, written primarily for religious by the sixteenth-century Spanish Jesuit, Alphonsus Rodríguez. This hefty work contains twenty-four treatises and runs to almost two thousand pages. It was a classic in Philippine's time. Rodríguez' work is a trea-

---

[9] I am grateful to Sister Françoise Darbois for this information.

sure of detailed and practical advice on a multitude of religious topics, such as prayer, community living, examination of conscience, mortification, feelings of happiness and sadness, and so forth. Although cast in a now outdated religious vocabulary, it shows a psychological subtlety which would surprise many modern readers. It also might frighten them with its harsh counsels to be dead to the world, to suffer need and to be forgotten. But such passages were an inspiration to men and women of Philippine's time.

But typical of much sixteenth-century Catholic writing, especially Jesuit, the spirituality Rodríguez proposes is also extraordinarily active. When you are having trouble in prayer, you do not just accept it as a cross God has sent you, rather you *do* something about it. The same principle applies to growth in humility, discovering God in work, fighting off temptations and dealing with all other aspects of life. Dependence on God's grace was a theological principle especially dear to Protestants of this period. Catholic theology accepted it, but urged above all that Christians *actively engage* in collaborating with that grace. That Philippine continued to find spiritual help in Rodríguez' work even in later years is true to her character: active, aggressive, ready to take on the new and never resigned to complacency.

The "saint of her heart" whom she mentions, Francis Xavier, is also revealing. Xavier, a friend of Ignatius Loyola, was one of the first great Jesuit missionaries, known mostly for his missionary activity in India and Japan. Like Philippine's other Jesuit missionary hero, John Francis Regis, Xavier was a tireless preacher and evangelizer. These two Jesuits were not to be the only ones to have a great influence on her life. In fact, Philippine's life is marked by encounters with numerous other Jesuits. The personal sacrifices she would make for them later in the New World were one of many signs of her constant affection for their order.

The years Philippine remained at the Visitation monastery did not change her inclination toward self-mortification. Francis de Sales and Jane de Chantal, the founder and foundress of the Visitation order, envisioned a congregation which limited corporal austerities so that the nuns could undertake a more active apostolate while remaining cloistered, a condition the Church mandated for all religious women. Philippine says her attraction to the educational apostolate made her forgo her preference for the Carmelite order. Her attraction to Carmel was not just attraction to prayer, but to its more austere lifestyle. In fact, only the Visitation Rule and the prohibitions of her superiors limited Philippine's requests for extra prayer at night and modified her corporal austerities. Regarding obedience, Philippine was true to her determined and self-severe character:

> The day I entered St. Marie On High I took the resolution never to fail on a single point of rule, and indeed I do not recall ever infringing a single one.[10]

Philippine mentions one other person who was significant in her formation, Marie of the Incarnation, the French Ursuline known for her work among Canadian Indian tribes. She read the *Life of the Venerable Mother Marie of the Incarnation* repeatedly during her years in the monastery and desired to pattern her own life after Marie's. The virtues which this text emphasizes, and which impressed Philippine, include personal sacrifice—Marie left her only child when he was just eleven to enter the convent —and extreme physical austerities. Marie wore a penitential shirt with knots and thorns, beat herself, ate wormwood and burned her own skin by drawing near to fire. She also showed unstinting dedication to her work among the Indians. When Marie went to the missions in 1639, she was the first cloistered religious woman ever allowed to do so.[11] Perhaps here also Marie's life was Philippine's inspiration. Philippine began once again to dream of the missions in the New World, despite the apparent contradiction between this call and her own choice to be a cloistered Visitation nun.

In September, 1789, a year and a day after receiving the novice's veil, Philippine should have made her vows of religious profession. The revolution in France had already begun, however, and her father sensed the many difficulties which this social movement posed for the Church and its property, for clergy and for convents. He did not want to see his daughter become a nun in any case. In deference to his wishes, Philippine reluctantly agreed not to make her vows until she reached the age of twenty-five, that is, not for another five years.

But the revolution changed the course of her religious life. Church property was confiscated. By the spring of 1790, the ancient monastic orders such as the Benedictines and Cistercians were suppressed. Only those devoted to nursing or teaching were allowed to continue. For the sake of individual liberty, all religious vows were forbidden. Almost all

---

[10]*Memoir of Philippine Duchesne.*

[11]*Word from New France: The Selected Letters of Marie de l'Incarnation*, trans. and ed. Joyce Marshall (Toronto: Oxford University Press, 1967), pp. 5–9.

religious men immediately deserted their convents. Women's congregations proved much more resistant to the pressure of authority. But by August of 1792, all religious orders of women and men were outlawed, even those charged with schools and hospitals. So, four years after entering Visitation and two years before her final profession, Philippine was forced to leave the Visitation monastery she loved so dearly. The revolution in her country was about to work another in Philippine's own life. But let us first consider her country's revolution and its impact on her family and the Catholic Church.

III.

The Historical Context:
The French Revolution

Philippine passed her childhood and youth in an atmosphere of peaceful security. But outside her home and school, her country was heading toward one of the most tumultuous events in modern Western history, the French Revolution. Just at the time it was sweeping across France, Philippine entered the Visitation monastery of St. Marie. Yet even there the Revolution would touch her life and change it dramatically. Although it would be impossible in these few pages to treat such a complicated event in any depth, it is important to understand how the Revolution affected Philippine's family, the Church and Philippine herself.

1. BACKGROUND OF THE REVOLUTION

The sudden and violent outbreak of the Revolution in 1789 took most French citizens by surprise. But the social tensions which are the background of this outburst had been building for generations.

France's population was traditionally divided into three estates. The first consisted of the Roman Catholic clergy and was dominated by powerful bishops, archbishops and cardinals. The aristocracy made up the second estate. The third estate included everyone else, from a small group of well-to-do merchants down to the majority of the French population—artisans, shopkeepers and peasants, many of whom lived in extreme poverty. For years the third estate had been vying for a greater voice within France. They could officially voice their opinions only when the men chosen to represent each of the estates met together in assembly. Even then, the powerful minorities represented by the first and second estates, Church and aristocracy, usually joined together to outvote the men of the third estate.

These tensions had long been present among the estates of Philippine's province as well. In the seventeenth century, the few landholders among the third estate in Philippine's native Dauphiny pointed out that they paid much more than their share of property taxes compared to the wealthy aristocracy and Church. The king responded to their complaint by forbidding the estates of Dauphiny to meet and the estates of all other provinces in France as well. The national Estates General of France had not met since 1614, depriving men of the third estate of an important forum in which to air their complaints.

Paris and each province did have a Parliament, however. But only aristocrats—members of the second estate—belonged to them. These Parliaments were not legislative bodies such as parliaments and congresses of democratic countries today. Rather, they were courts of record which received and registered decrees made by the king. In a sense, the king wrote the rules for the country and the Parliaments made these rules "legal" by putting their aristocratic rubber stamp on them. Naturally, these aristocrats used their power to strengthen their own position in the country.

When Philippine was a small girl, these social tensions were reaching crisis proportions. Poor harvests, rising taxes and prices affected all classes in France and exhausted the patience of rich and poor alike. In Dauphiny insufficient land for agricultural workers and growing unemployment both in the country and city aggravated relations between the governing and working classes.[1] France faced an administrative and financial crisis beyond the meager abilities of King Louis XVI to manage. Fifty percent of the national budget went to pay for the debt alone. Louis needed to raise more taxes, but for this, he needed the support of the provincial Parliaments.

The aristocratic Parliaments were reluctant to support him. For years they had been reasserting their independence and insisting on their rights and liberties. One of these rights was their exemption from major national taxes. Like the wealthy in so many societies, they preferred that the brunt of taxes be borne by the classes below them, in this case the industrious, working sector of the third estate.

---

[1] Bernard Bonnin, "Le Dauphiné à la veille de la Révolution: formes de l'économie et structures sociales," in *Les débuts de la Révolution française en Dauphiné, 1788–1791*, ed. Vital Chomel (Grenoble: Presses universitaires de Grenoble, 1988), pp. 30–31.

2. THE REVOLUTION HER RELATIVES SOUGHT

But the prospering members of the third estate who were expected to pay these taxes were also increasingly conscious of their
rights and liberties. These merchants and industrialists, among them
Philippine's relatives, were garnering fortunes which put them on a
financial par with some members of the aristocracy. Some, like Philippine's uncle Claude Périer, even bought their way out of the third
estate by purchasing aristocratic titles.[2] Hard work and know-how in
exploiting new industries were qualities they valued. Government,
they thought, should not be managed arbitrarily by those born with
titles, but by men with ability, regardless of their estate. These merchants and industrialists joined with progressive members of the aristocracy to resist the king's authority and assert their own.

In May, 1788, tensions finally came to a head. The king tried to
suspend the provincial Parliaments around the country in order to
establish a court system friendlier to his own interests. The Parliament
of Dauphiny was the first to resist these edicts, but the king disregarded its opinion and had the edicts registered by force. He also
forbade the members of the Parliament of Grenoble to gather, a directive which they defied in order to protest his actions.

Royal prohibition of the Parliament roused the anger of people
throughout the city. Philippine's father called a meeting of all the
lawyers of Grenoble, men whose professions—and livelihoods—were
intimately tied to the work of Parliament. They and other groups
vigorously protested the edicts, but to no avail. On June 7, the members of Parliament were ordered by the lieutenant of Dauphiny,
Clermont-Tonnerre, to leave Grenoble. An angry mob gathered to
oppose their exile. Poor merchant women who saw their livelihoods
threatened by the loss of their parliamentarian clients incited hundreds
of others to take to the streets.[3] Over a hundred people were wounded
in the violent exchange which ensued. They pitched roof tiles at government troops on the now well-known "day of Tiles," and compelled
Clermont-Tonnere to reverse his order.[4]

[2]Robert Chagny, "Grenoble: Les structures sociales d'une ville de province," in *De pain et d'espérance: Grenoble et le Dauphiné à la veille de la Révolution* (Grenoble: Musée Dauphinois, 1988), p. 96.

[3]Gérard Viallet, "La journée des Tuiles, accident de l'histoire ou première manifestation politique populaire à la veille de 1789?" in *Les débuts de la Révolution française en Dauphiné*, ed. Chomel, pp. 73–74.

[4]Gérard Chianéa, "Institutions dauphinoises, pré-révolution et identité provincial," in *Les débuts de la Révolution française en Dauphiné*, ed. Chomel, pp. 33–36.

Influential men such as the Duchesnes and Périers could appreciate the turn in events wrought by the unruly crowd. These poor men
and women were, in effect, defending the rights of the aristocratic
Parliament and the other influential men of Grenoble. After all, it was
the well-heeled lawyers, notaries and other professional men, those
whose livelihoods depended on the court system and the Parliament,
who had the most to lose through the king's proposed judicial reforms.
Some scholars even argue that these men, men such as Philippine's
father, were the pivotal force behind the insurrection. And without the
capital of men like Claude Périer, the deluge of anti-royalist pamphlets
which appeared immediately after the riot could never have been published. But these men were were also alarmed by the force of the
uprising. Without grasping fully what such violence augured for the
future of France, they also recognized the popular revolt as a potential
threat to their own governing power.[5]

After the "day of Tiles," the Périers and Duchesnes supported
the revolutionary decision to call a meeting of the three estates of
Dauphiny. This act was in open defiance of the king since all the
Provincial Estates of France had been suppressed for over 150 years.
The Provincial Estates of Dauphiny were the first, moreover, to double the size of the third estate, so that its votes, representing the
majority of the French population, would at least equal the number of
votes of the first and second estates together. Little did they realize
that they were setting a dangerous precedent for the future. When
the Estates General of all France met in May, 1789, in Versailles,
King Louis XVI felt compelled to double the third estate there also.
He thereby opened the floodgate of the third estate's feelings of
disenfranchisement.

Philippine's family was actively engaged in Dauphiny's revolutionary movement. Her father was an elected member of the province's
third estate. Since these estates were prohibited from meeting in Grenoble, her wealthy uncle Claude Périer offered his magnificent chateau
in nearby Vizille as a meeting place. His active role in these pre-
revolutionary events has often been misconstrued as whole-hearted
support for radical revolution in France. However, the Assembly at
Vizille aimed both to continue the protest against the royal edicts *and*

---

[5]Viallet, "La journée des Tuiles," in *Les débuts de la Révolution française en Dauphiné*, ed.
Chomel, pp. 63–94, especially pp. 82–85.

to contain the burgeoning popular movement.[6] When the Revolution finally broke out nationally in 1789, Philippine's father, uncle and other male relatives enthusiastically supported it. But their support was short-lived.

Duchesne and other liberal, forward-thinking men like him could hardly foresee the radical turns the Revolution would take. The "rights and liberties" which the provincial Parliaments had been protecting before the Revolution were the rights and liberties of the aristocratic class and of the wealthy members of the third estate. In the first phase of the Revolution, some enlightened nobles along with a growing cadre of wealthy merchants and industrialists sought to extend these rights and broaden participation in the affairs of their country. "Broaden" meant the inclusion of the growing group of landed and wealthy men, but it by no means included most men, or any women.

The Revolution which Philippine's family supported was essentially a middle-class affair and remained so until 1792. The absolute monarchy of the king was replaced with a limited monarchy controlled by the wealthy. Civil rights were accorded to everyone, but the vote was given only to citizens paying a certain amount in taxes. That included about half the country's men. Economic policy favored the interests of the prospering upper middle-class. Guilds, which might have helped poorer people, were suppressed and associations of urban workers were outlawed. The new land taxes which should have been drawn from the prosperous leaders of the Revolution could not effectively be collected. The most vivid images conjured by the French Revolution in the popular imagination today stem from later, radical stages of the Revolution. By comparison, this first phase was altogether conservative.

The laws enacted by the first revolutionary government favored the wealthy men of Philippine's family and their business ventures. They eased the expansion of her father's and uncle Claude Périer's burgeoning textile industry, and her brother-in-law Jean-Joseph Jouve's mercantile interests. Her Uncle Augustin formed the third French Company of the Indies. Such overseas trading companies became notorious for their often ruthless conquests of markets opening in the New World. Few "revolutionary" laws restrained him and his brother Claude in their overseas exportation ventures. Claude, for example,

---

[6]Robert Chagny, "De Vizille à Romans," in *Les débuts de la Révolution française en Dauphiné*, ed. Chomel, pp. 99–141.

was one of numerous French men to own a vast plantation in the French colony of Saint-Domingue, present-day Haiti. At the time, the colony had a population of 24,000 free people of color, 32,000 white landowners and 450,000 slaves. Claude's sugar plantation, which counted 250 slaves in its "workshop," was free from virtually all control.[7] It is no surprise that men like Périer would withdraw their support from the Revolution at just the time it began to support the interests of a broader cross section of the French populace, ceasing to lend particular support to their concerns.

In the second phase of the Revolution, from August, 1792, until the ascent of Napoleon in November, 1799, the moderate middle-class leaders were first replaced by radical republicans, the Jacobins. The Jacobins claimed to represent the interests of the common people. The unrestrained free-enterprise economy of the Revolution, they said, benefitted only the few, while subjecting the poor majority to the unstable and increasing prices of bread and other basics. They pursued a policy favoring "universal" suffrage—which granted the vote to all men, but no women—and promoted state programs which would benefit the poor. The newly elected national convention also put an end to the monarchy, executed Louis XVI in January, 1793, and declared France a republic. They abolished slavery in the French colonies, prohibited imprisonment for debt and provided more economic opportunity for the commoner. Great estates were confiscated and the land sold to poorer citizens on easy terms. They also set maximum prices for bread and other basics and threatened with the guillotine any merchants who profiteered at the expense of the poor.

It is not coincidental that the significant defections from the revolutionary cause on the part of Philippine's male relatives occurred just at the start of this radical period. Her father had compromised his good standing as an elected member of the municipal council as early as 1790. When he was asked to compose an oath which would be taken by the new National Guard in a public ceremony, he drew up a formula including the statement "Supreme power belongs to the King." Although Duchesne, under pressure, rewrote the oath and modified this statement, he lost public support and withdrew for a time to his newly-acquired country home, safe from the revolutionary atmosphere of Grenoble.

Philippine's brother-in-law Jean-Joseph Jouve complained that his

---

[7]Chagny, "Grenoble: Les structures sociales d'une ville de province," in *De pain et d'espérance*, pp. 93–96.

mercantile interests were suffering and became an active sympathizer with the counter-revolutionary insurrection in Lyons in 1793. Philippine's sentiments were clearly with him. She felt that Jouve distinguished himself during the seven-week siege and she sympathized with his plight afterward:

> In order to save life and fortune, he was obliged to take refuge with his family in the mountainous district after the surrender of the city. . . . Here he experienced great suffering and poverty in his efforts to bring up a growing family.[8]

Her conservative cousin Camille Jordan also abandoned his former support of the Revolution. He, in fact, was one of the leaders of the 1793 insurrection in Lyons. Jordan was twice exiled for his counter-revolutionary activity.

Philippine's uncle Augustin Périer, made fabulously rich as an administrator of the Company of the Indies, had been a staunch supporter of the Revolution in 1789. He even held the elected office of commandant of the National Guard at Lorient, but a "violent reaction" set in against him at the start of the Revolution's second phase. He was one of about twenty thousand people suspected of counter-revolutionary sentiments who were murdered during the bloody Reign of Terror.

Augustin's brother, Claude Périer, was the most reactionary of Philippine's relatives. In the 1780s, in fact, the wealthy Périer had requested a small "charitable subsidy" from the municipal government of Grenoble which he planned to use in a new hardware manufacture. Périer's "charitable" plan had been to give work, over eighteen hours a day of it, to pauper children between the ages of eight and twelve.[9] Eighteenth-century France, in fact, had a number of such "charitable houses" for children. One of the best known was a lace-work factory in Sassenage. It employed four hundred poor girls, many orphaned, and compelled them to work long hours during a five-year "apprenticeship." The girls were given no pay. Poor food, crude living conditions and training in a skill was the charity they received.[10] Périer's atti-

---

[8]*Biographical Sketch of Mother Aloysia Jouve*, Religious of the Sacred Heart Archives, St. Louis, Missouri.

[9]Kathryn Norberg, *Rich and Poor in Grenoble, 1600–1814* (Berkeley, California: University of California Press, 1985), p. 166.

[10]Chagny, "Grenoble: Les structures sociales d'une ville de province," in *De pain et d'espérance*, pp. 106–108.

tudes, therefore, would not shock all of his contemporaries. He regularly employed poor children among the workers at his cloth manufacture at Vizille, a practice which became common in the industrialized cities of nineteenth-century Europe. Périer, we will recall, was very involved in the first revolutionary events of Grenoble and Dauphiny. He personally hosted the preliminary assembly of the Provincial Estates in his magnificent chateau in Vizille. But by the second stage of the Revolution, Périer had well distanced himself from the revolutionary process. In fact, he could save his own neck only by making several well-timed "patriotic" gifts.[11]

This account of the role of Philippine's relatives during the opening years of the French Revolution indirectly illuminates our view of Philippine herself. She heard rumors about the Revolution during her family's periodic visits to her monastery of St. Marie. She sympathized with the personal tragedies caused by the Revolution: Jean-Joseph Jouve's loss of fortune, the murder of her uncle Augustin Périer, her father's temporary fall from grace. Her relationship with her uncle Claude Périer remained always affectionate. She was shocked and saddened upon hearing of the king's execution. But Philippine understood little of the Revolution's significance for France. She was not a woman who engaged in discussions of politics, a topic which fell outside the proper domain of a woman of her class.

Philippine's attitudes and activities both compare and contrast with those of the Duchesne and Périer men. The men of her family were aggressive leaders. They would not remain indifferent before either a royal or Jacobin government with which they disagreed. They joined the fray. Their entrepreneurial undertakings demanded a spirit of adventure and of risk. These attracted them to ventures beyond France's own borders. These same qualities characterized Philippine, but they found expression in her charitable activity, her religious commitment and her desire to go to the missions.

There is yet a more pronounced contrast between Philippine and her male relatives. The men in Philippine's family limited their commitment to the Revolution to the extent that it aided those within the circle of their own social class or those slightly beyond its borders. To replace the absolute monarchy of the king with a limited monarchy was as much of a revolution as they could fathom. Government needed to be in the hands of certain sorts of men, they thought. To extend full rights to "unenlightened" men, not to mention women, seemed to

---

[11]Norberg, *Rich and Poor in Grenoble*, p. 174.

them simply contrary to the best interests of France. They were largely blind to the overwhelming social and economic disparities in France. While they made periodic charitable contributions, these were like applying small bandages to a body in need of radical surgery. Some of these charitable works, in fact, served to maintain the status quo. They were uncomprehending when the discontent of the poverty-stricken majority led to the revolutionary confiscation and redistribution of property, to the enactment of laws which "hurt" the prosperous classes and to unprecedented violence. Not surprisingly, they could not prescind from the presuppositions and interests inculcated in them by their own class and culture. Just as significant numbers of the world's privileged today manage to turn a deaf ear to the voice of impoverished and socially disenfranchised peoples, so too were many of the prosperous of Philippine's time unable, or unwilling, to understand the revolutionary demands of poor people then.

Philippine's ignorance of the larger issues at stake during the French Revolution betrays the very success of the education she received as a girl in the eighteenth century. She never questioned the status quo and she remained unaware of the deep social and political implications of the Revolution. On the other hand, Philippine's outward reach hardly knew bounds. The circle of charity and missionary activity which she drew, as the next chapter shows, did not revolve around her own security and interests. On the contrary, it was inclusive of others, people of her own background, but also people foreign to her own world, such as the American Indian and the materially poor of both France and the New World. Without being actively engaged in the Revolution or even aware of its long-term significance, she had imbibed something of its rhetoric of equality and rights for all. Although her activity was confined, in one sense, to the "womanly" domains of charity and religion, it crossed beyond boundaries which held the Duchesne and Périer men fast.

3. THE CHURCH DURING THE REVOLUTION

The Revolution most directly affected Philippine's life through its virulent attacks against the Catholic Church. Her shock and sorrow at the closing of many convents, the exile of priests, the continued suppression of the Jesuits and the eventual prohibition of public Catholic worship are the sympathies we would expect of a devout Catholic woman of her background. She little understood the circumstances which prompted these violent attacks. But the attacks are much less surprising when placed in their historical context.

The Church into which Philippine was born was a privileged and powerful force within French society.[12] Many bishops, archbishops and cardinals enjoyed immense incomes ranging from 100,000 to even 400,000 *livres* per year, much of it derived from lands they possessed in dioceses they never even visited. These figures become meaningful when we put them beside the seven thousand *livres* which the resident bishop of an unimportant diocese might receive and the three hundred *livres* which was the pay of many parish priests. The great prelates profited from vast lands which the Church had accumulated over centuries. In some poorer, southern districts, this amounted to four percent of the land, but it comprised thirty percent of, for example, Picardy and over sixty percent of all the land in the Cambrésis.[13]

But it was the Church's privileges more than its wealth which angered many people. The Church was exempt from all taxes, a privilege acutely resented in this time of financial crisis. Not only did the Church not pay taxes, it collected its own, known as the tithe, which averaged one-fifteenth to one-tenth of the harvest on all land under cultivation. The fact that the tithe was not fairly distributed among the clergy, with parish priests receiving very little indeed, angered peasant tithe payers even more. They were often quite attached to their priests and resented the distant and arrogant Church prelates, people they associated with the privileged nobility.

Nor is this a surprise since, of the 130 bishops in France on the eve of the Revolution, fully 129 of them were from the nobility. A contemporary at that time satirically divided all bishops into two classes, those who "administered the sacraments" and those who "administered provinces." As to their worldliness, when Cardinal Loménie de Brienne was proposed for the archbishopric of Paris, Louis XVI laconically remarked, "No, the Archbishop of Paris must at least believe in God."[14]

The Church had earned enemies in other ways also. Protestants had lost many of the concessions they once enjoyed. Theirs was a precarious existence in a clearly Catholic world. Many intellectuals resented the Church's control of the educational system. The Jesuits

---

[12]See Gerald R. Cragg, *The Church and the Age of Reason, 1648–1789* (New York: Penguin Books, 1970), pp. 193–208, for a discussion of the French Church at this time.

[13]Cragg, *The Church and the Age of Reason*, pp. 201–202.

[14]Cragg, *The Church and the Age of Reason*, pp. 203–204.

had made enemies of a powerful religious movement known as Jansenism. Jansenists emphasized human dependence upon God and the necessity of grace for humans to be able to do good works. The Jesuits were not content to oppose them with mere theological argument. They were instrumental in their rigorous repression by Louis XIV in 1715. The Jesuits also angered people by urging them to obey the king and to support papal interference in matters which many of the French, including the Parliaments, powerful bishops and cardinals, considered to be national affairs.

The aggressive and often acrimonious attacks made on the French Church in the eighteenth century were not simply attacks on "religion." Rather, they were attacks aimed at an entire structure of power and privilege. The Church had become an intricate part of that structure. Its authority was considered by many people to be as arbitrary and absolute as had been that of Louis XIV, the Sun King. When men opposed to the Church's power and privilege took the lead in the Revolution, they exacted swift retribution.

The first punishments reflected the vehement resentment inspired by Church wealth and privilege. In November of 1789, the Church's vast lands were confiscated and sold. In the spring of 1790, the old monastic orders were secularized, a fact which shocked Philippine and the other nuns of her convent. But many people resented these orders for their association with vast lands, ancient privilege and noble lineage. Congregations engaged in works of education or charity such as Philippine's, were spared for the time being. Virtually all male religious soon deserted their houses. Women religious tended to resist the local authorities and remain in their houses for as long as possible.

In an attempt to regulate the income of the wealthy Church hierarchy, the leaders of the Revolution decided to make the clergy salaried employees of the state. And to reduce interference from Rome, they decreed that all priests and bishops were to be elected. These measures naturally angered the wealthy bishops, but they also alienated many simple country folk who objected to the state's control of the humble parish clergy. Few bishops and only half the regular clergy supported the new legislation. The rest were labeled as "refractory" and either went underground, hiding in convents or the homes of sympathetic Catholics such as the Duchesnes, or sought asylum in other countries. In fact, Philippine's own Visitation monastery was eventually closed in 1792 on account of "making common cause with the refractory priests." Two weeks later the prohibition was extended to all women's congregations engaged in the work of schools and hospitals. For awhile, all Catholic worship was absolutely forbidden in France.

The Church of Philippine's day was in a situation of "persecution." Innocent priests were exiled, imprisoned or even murdered. Nuns engaged in the nurturing ministries of education and health care were forced out of their religious communities. Intolerant demagogues prohibited public worship, attempted to abolish Christianity and establish in its place the worship of Reason. Philippine spoke painfully of the "persecution" the Church suffered at the hands of the Revolution.

With hindsight, however, it is evident that there was ample provocation for this persecution. Institutions have a tendency to ally with powerful groups, to amass wealth and conserve their own ideology and privileges. Simply put, the Church of Philippine's time fell victim to this human tendency. The hostile persecution it suffered during the Revolution was the price it paid for its former privilege and power.

In the Christian program, however, suffering, in itself an experience of evil, can also be the spring of positive good. Suffering becomes meaningful whenever it inspires love and gives birth to works leading toward the transformation of our world. The story of the persecution of the French Church in the eighteenth century would be incomplete without a recognition of the numerous individuals, Philippine Duchesne among them, who gave meaning to the Church's suffering by selflessly reaching out to others, both those victimized by religious persecution and those victimized by an equally insidious form of persecution, that of poverty and want. It is to the story of Philippine's response to such suffering that we now turn.

IV.

Philippine's Revolutionary Years: 1792–1804

Philippine had no idea of the tumultuous years which awaited her upon her departure from the monastery of St. Marie. During the next twelve years, she would change her place of residence repeatedly; initiate a variety of charitable works, some of which were dangerous and all short-lived; experiment with several religious lifestyles; disconcert her family; and finally, anger and alienate her former Visitation sisters. These difficulties were a constant lesson to her in letting go of securities, even the one to which she was most attached, her desire to be a religious. These years were Philippine's apprenticeship to a lifetime dedicated to the service of others, particularly the poor and dispossessed.

1. RELIGIOUS LIFE AT HOME[1]

Philippine's first inclination upon leaving the Visitation monastery in 1792 was to go to Italy where her former novice mistress, Eugénie de Bayanne, had become superior of a monastery. Her father, however, flatly refused this request. So she spent a few months in Grenoble with the Périers, and then went to her family's country house in Grâne for Christmas. Internal political violence threatened families such as the Duchesnes. France was also at war with a coali-

---

[1]The years 1792 to 1804 are one of the most interesting, yet least studied periods in Philippine's life. Significant research is yet to be done drawing on family correspondence, the history of the Visitation order, archival materials in Grenoble and other primary source documents. Such research will establish more precisely the dates, location and exact nature of Philippine's diverse activities during this fascinating period.

The area of Philippine Duchesne's home in Grenoble.

tion of European countries—principally Austria, Prussia and Great Britain—who feared France's revolution would spread beyond its borders and into theirs. The Duchesne country home had become a refuge for other relatives too, including Philippine's cousin, Julie Tranchand.

Julie Tranchand had also been a Visitation nun, but at another monastery. Philippine and she decided to devise their own style of religious life within the Duchesne home. Their order of the day included early risings, set times for personal meditation, fasting, regular recitation of prayers, and other monastic practices. The Duchesne family had hardly bargained on such holiness in their household and they did not appreciate it. Eventually, their criticisms of Julie's and Philippine's ascetic lifestyle led the two to modify their regime.

Philippine's homemade religious lifestyle may strike many modern readers as unique, owing to the special circumstances of the French Revolution; however, Philippine and Julie were actually part of a long tradition of women's religious life. From the earliest years of the Christian Church, pious women have dedicated themselves to lives of prayer and service outside regular religious orders. This particularly female phenomenon has involved mostly single and widowed women. They have generally had more freedom than married women to follow their own rule of life. Catherine of Siena is one of the best-known examples. Her family also objected to her private religious practices.

In Philippine's time, women's religious congregations were still following a basically male model of religious life. Most of their rules were written by men and they had less freedom even in the internal administration of their convents than do many women religious today. Philippine tended to be quite rigid with herself concerning compliance with rules. This reflected not only the nature of religious life then, but her own personality which inclined toward both the spirit and the letter of the law. Some of her superiors tried to soften her enthusiasm in this regard. The years Philippine spent outside of religious life, then, are especially significant. She had no set rule or routine to follow, just a vision. The varying situations in which she found herself led her to modify her self-styled religious routines to respond better to the work at hand. Rather than follow directives, she had to initiate each new undertaking. Rather than continue the same routine, she had constantly to adapt her work and her prayer. The skills she cultivated during this period of searching were of inestimable value for her future role as a pioneer missionary on the American frontier.

2. CHARITABLE ACTIVITIES: 1793–1801

So despite Philippine's own desire to belong to a regular religious order, the ban on religious life in France forced her to experiment with other religious lifestyles for a period of twelve years, from 1792 to 1804. Until 1801, she was living outside of religious cloister. These years opened Philippine to the world and its problems in a way the monastery never could. Her awareness of social problems eventually prompted her to make choices about her life which were unpopular with her family and her former monastic sisters. Philippine's first such decision was to abandon the family house at Grâne. Apparently, life at home attracted her not in the least and she left just a few months after her arrival. She wrote later:

> The decree which obliged all religious women to return to secular life obliged me to go back to my family. My heart was never attached to this sort of life and it was a land of exile for me, a foreign land, and Sion, my true country [i.e. religious life], remained the goal of my desires and of my costliest efforts.[2]

Life at home was too sedentary for her active temperament and in Grenoble, with the closing of schools and orphanages, high unemployment and poverty, there was work to do. Although she could have lodged with her wealthy cousin Josephine or other relatives, Philippine instead found a like-minded companion and moved to a section of town more suited to her new life of charitable works.

At age twenty-three, Philippine was living on her own for the first time, away from the security of both her family and the convent. She remained on cordial terms with her relatives and also visited them for short periods. But, determined as ever not to forsake her ideals, Philippine persisted in following her own routine of prayer and meditation. Her principal work during this time was caring for priests either imprisoned or in hiding. Ironically, many of these priests were now in Philippine's former monastery which had been converted into a prison. Her visits to these "enemies of the state" jeopardized her own situation in

---

[2]Philippine Duchesne, *Histoire de Sainte Marie d'en Haut*, hereafter referred to in the text as *Story of Saint Marie*, Religious of the Sacred Heart Archives, St. Louis, Missouri. An extensive translation of this manuscript can be found in Callan, *Philippine Duchesne*.

Grenoble despite the protection afforded by her prominent family. She risked her life caring for them during the typhoid epidemic of 1794. The indigent of Grenoble were the other group which received her compassion and care. She spent long hours with the sick and the dying. She repeatedly defied the revolutionary government and endangered herself by leading refugee priests to minister to them. One of her sisters wrote:

> Every day, from early morning, after fulfilling her spiritual duties, Philippine would visit the sick, for whom it was difficult to procure spiritual aid in those unhappy times. She would search out the faithful, proscribed priests in their hiding places and then guide them through a thousand dangers to the bedside of the dying. It would be impossible to recount all the heroic acts of charity which she performed under similar circumstances.[3]

Philippine was part of a large, spontaneous movement of women's charitable activity in revolutionary France. She intensified the risk of her own work when she organized a group of these women into the "Ladies of Mercy." The group was forcibly disbanded for almost a year during the Reign of Terror, which began in 1793. They had been judged guilty of lending aid to refractory priests. The Ladies renewed their work only after the fall of Robespierre in July, 1794.

In her *Story of Saint Marie*, Philippine recounts that she lived for two years in her parents' country home, probably referring to the years 1795 to 1797. Her mother had become seriously ill in 1794. Philippine returned both to care for her and to help raise her nine-year-old sister Mélanie. Philippine's father was away in Paris on political business when Madame Duchesne finally died in June, 1797. He had recently been chosen a member of the Council of Five Hundred to represent their department of the Drôme. The writings of the Duchesne women at this time paint an attractive portrait of their family affections. In a last letter to her absent husband, Madame Duchesne wrote:

> Death would have been too sweet if I had the satisfaction of having you, my best friend, with me in my last moments. I

---

[3]Louis Baunard, *Histoire de Madame Duchesne* (Paris: Librairie Poussielgue Frères, 1878), p. 41, translation mine. See also the translation of Baunard's biography by Lady Georgiana Fullerton, *The Life of Mother Duchesne* (Roehampton: n.p., 1879).

die in sweet peace, leaving to my children the best of fathers,
and to you affectionate and respectful children who will do
all in their power to make up to you for my loss.

This is just one of the occasions on which Philippine had the experience of holding the dying in her own arms. Her sister Euphrosine
wrote:

That daughter who had formerly left her to follow God's call,
was her most faithful nurse during her entire illness. Day and
night she was at her bedside, caring for both body and soul;
nor did she leave her until she had drawn her last breath.

The strong bonds of affection uniting the Duchesnes, however,
were sorely tested by Philippine's commitment to her charitable projects. Her mother's death and her father's absence from their country
home freed Philippine, according to her own account, to leave there in
search of her own religious lifestyle alongside other like-minded
women.[4] She returned to Grenoble almost immediately. Her relatives
tried to dissuade her from the risks she was running, risks they felt
went beyond the sensible norms of conventional charity. But Philippine's religious search and charitable work could never be merely conventional for, as she insisted to her relatives, she saw Christ himself
incarnate in the poor:

Let me alone; it is my happiness and glory to serve my divine
Saviour in the person of the unfortunate and the poor.

Philippine's personal losses were just beginning in these years.
The loss of religious life at St. Marie and her mother's death were
losses imposed upon her. But her personal choices during this period
also reflect her ability to let go of securities. When her mother died,
she immediately dispossessed herself of the property she had inherited
in exchange for a yearly income. This income gave her the independence and support she needed to continue her charitable works full-
time. The decision sharpened tensions with her family. She even had
to defend herself before her sister Amélie:

---

[4]*Histoire de Sainte Marie d'en Haut.*

It was never my intention to abandon you without some compensation. You will be fair-minded enough to believe that one single motive has always guided me. My plan was laid long before I owned any property; and after a great misfortune brought me an inheritance, I planned to enjoy it by sacrificing it, keeping for myself only the hope of heavenly riches.

Religious orders were still banned in France and charitable projects were the only way Philippine felt she could pursue her dream of a life of service. She was hardly the type to wait at home leading the life of a comfortable landed lady.

The continuing influence of her father, however, is striking given Philippine's strong-headed character. When she was twenty, he had prevented her from making her vows in the Visitation order. When she left the monastery at age twenty-three, he kept her from joining a religious order in Italy. Now at age twenty-eight and financially independent, she still acquiesced to his request to live for a time with her grandmother Duchesne in nearby Romans.

But the experience proved so disastrous that, far from restraining Philippine's plans, it proved her very liberation. Her grandmother was a cranky, spoiled and eccentric old lady accustomed to ordering everyone around in the rudest of tones. Philippine had a head-on collision with the woman and was subsequently ordered to leave the house. It was a liberating experience because it gave her a valuable insight into herself and her own headstrong nature. In a letter to her sister Amélie, she wrote:

> I am still at Romans. It is not as easy to leave as I had thought it would be. I have let slip several opportunities, not wishing to leave Grandmother alone, and now I have no means of getting away. . . . Grandmother has expressed herself in no uncertain terms regarding my departure—it will make her quite happy. I had a pretty lively scene with her as a result of some representations I tried to make to her. I did not succeed in calming her wrath against either her tenants or her house-servants. From the conversation I gained only my own dismissal, and that in very pointed language.
>
> In seeing the changes which the years have wrought in our grandmothers, I cannot but make a few sad reflections. Their blood flows in our veins, and already we feel in ourselves flashes of their fiery impatience. Let us try to control

ourselves now in the first stages of this defect, which increases with age and may become incorrigible. Let us try not to be exacting with others, but rather to pass over in silence those thousand little annoyances which tend to embitter us. For we know that no one is perfect in this life and we must put up with the defects of others.

Ironically, her failure to get along with her grandmother also freed her from her father's desire that she live there. The advantage of her situation was hardly lost on her as she wrote to Amélie:

The reception I got from Grandmother and the dismissal she gave me were the first incitement to put my project into action. Far from being angry at the reception she gave me, I regard it as a real favor, for it wards off the reproaches Father might have made me for refusing to carry out his wishes, since she herself refused to have me around.

Her first such project, which ended in failure, was to join a group of nuns who had regrouped at the convent of Saint-Marcellin. Her cousin Julie Tranchand and several other Duchesne relatives who had belonged to Visitation convents were already living in common life there. Philippine never had any intention of staying with them. By her own account, the leisure time in Romans had rekindled her "old desires." This must refer to her overriding desire to return one day to religious life at St. Marie.

The period she spent at Saint-Marcellin is shrouded in mystery. In her own words, it was a time of trial. At least two factors help explain Philippine's stormy experience there. First, her difficulties with the other sisters probably stemmed from the fact that they followed a modified religious rule. It was calculated not to draw down any revolutionary wrath on the women, who were, after all, defying revolutionary orders. As we will see later when Philippine did return to St. Marie, she had no tolerance for half-way measures in religious life and guarded no silence on the matter. Her grandmother's blood did flow in her veins!

On a more personal note, Philippine also underwent an exacting interior experience at Saint-Marcellin. In a difficult passage of a letter which she wrote to her sister Amélie, she describes a conversion she had during a retreat there. The letter explains her decision to leave the convent, the impossibility of authentic religious life in revolutionary France and her intention to return to independent charitable works in

Grenoble. In this context, it seems quite likely that her conversion experience refers to her letting go of her very desire for religious life:

In the retreat I made there, I tried to strip myself of all overeagerness in desires, of all attachment to my own views, of all merely human sentiments. But how could human sentiments have part in a resolution that forced me to overcome those very sentiments and to lift myself above nature in order to correspond to a higher, stronger attraction? Stripped then of self, I sought to know the divine will, and I made up my mind. Few people understand what I am talking about, and few will refrain from blaming me. I excuse them because of their motives and beg them to act in the same way toward mine, if they cannot praise them.

Her family and friends might be expected to look askance at her decision to leave a convent to undertake private works in "the world."

Two paragraphs later, Philippine refers explicitly to giving up the security associated with religious life:

Formerly I looked forward without imprudence to a life of security in religion. Now all is changed; my plans are no longer the same, for it seems impossible to follow my desires, as there is no religious order in existence in France. . . . I have found a companion somewhat older than I and free like myself. She has a little revenue which, with some work added, suffices for her own support and that of a very good young woman who has been in her service for ten years and whom we shall continue to keep. We are just about to rent an apartment.

Religious life was not the only security which Philippine was forsaking. Although she continued to respond to her father with all the filial affection expected of a gentlewoman and to defer to his desires whenever possible, Philippine was choosing her own path in life. Her father objected both to the danger involved in her chosen work and to its religious nature. She begged Amélie to plead her cause before him, to assure him that her good works involved no danger. But she also accepted that, given his irreligious temperament, he would never understand her choices. Although she regretted the pain this caused him, she resigned herself to carry this sorrow to her grave. Philippine pursued her course independent of her father's wishes.

The last work in which Philippine engaged during this nine-year period of wandering outside of St. Marie was educating poor boys. She lured them from the streets with food and clothes and finally managed to assemble a group of fifteen or twenty. They were, she says, a real trial to her patience, a fact Philippine seems to have enjoyed in retrospect. Their rowdiness in her house provoked her neighbors. She was embarrassed at their eagerness to greet her on the street. A number of the boys' parents, moreover, were angry with Philippine for teaching the boys not to work on Sundays. It is worth noting that "education" for Philippine meant that they "learned the entire catechism, their prayers, and some hymns." Although her educational goals might strike us as somewhat narrow, they were certainly more affirming of the dignity of her students than those of other free schools in Grenoble. These sought mainly to teach the "lazy poor" to work, sometimes by making them labor from early morning until late at night.[5] Attitudes toward the poor in the eighteenth century, in fact, ranged typically from patronizing to cruel.

3. HISTORY OF ATTITUDES TOWARD THE POOR IN GRENOBLE

Philippine's attitudes toward the poor and sick to whom she ministered during her years of charity were, in one sense, quite conventional. Charitable works were expected of women of her position.[6] During her first years, moreover, she ministered primarily to priests, representatives of one of the most conservative institutions in France. Her care of the indigent frequently involved bringing them priests, and her education of poor children entailed teaching them their catechism. These works were in line with the traditional assumption that the poor, by virtue of being poor, were especially in need of religion. And Philippine's charity was also typical of her class in another way: it was supported with income she did not earn.

But her attitudes were also quite new. We can fully appreciate this only when we examine the history of attitudes toward the poor. Philippine recognized their human dignity in a way which radically departed from the conventional assumptions of her class. This striking shift in

---

[5]Norberg, *Rich and Poor in Grenoble*, p. 165.

[6]Abensour, *La femme et le féminisme avant la révolution*, pp. 177–81; and Smith, *Ladies of the Leisure Class*, pp. 136–38.

attitude is especially relevant for today's Church which seeks not only to serve the poor, but to learn from them and to be poor itself. The attitudinal change underway throughout France can best be illustrated by focusing on Philippine's own town of Grenoble.

Seventeenth Century:[7] Throughout most of the seventeenth century, Catholic charitable associations in Grenoble shared the common assumption of the well-to-do that poverty went hand-in-hand with sin and vice. The central work of the Company of the Holy Sacrament, for example, was locking beggars up. The poor, they thought, tended by their very nature to be thieves, vagabonds, fornicators and prostitutes. So they confined the poor to workhouses and submitted them to compulsory religious instruction in an effort to extirpate their vice. The paternalistic benefactors of such institutions considered their almsgiving to be not only a public duty to eradicate the social evils they blamed on the poor, but also a personal obligation: charity to the poor was necessary for the salvation of souls, the souls, that is, of the rich. For example, the Brothers of the Company of the Holy Sacrament said to their patrons:

> When one gives coins to a pauper, one is God to that pauper and he in turn is God to you, for he opens the gates of Heaven to your soul.[8]

Alms of grain, bread, wine and salt were dished out to the poor upon an aristocratic landowner's death so that they would pray for his soul.

Early Eighteenth Century:[9] By the eighteenth century, charitable-giving had become both less paternalistic and less religiously inspired. Successful merchants, industrialists and lawyers were replacing the aristocratic class as the major charitable givers. Their enlightened religious beliefs led them to doubt that there was any relation at all between their charity and salvation. Even though Grenoble's economic prosperity would easily have afforded an increase in charity, the records show that all religious and charitable donations were on the decline. Claude Périer, for example, left in his will a token twenty-five *livres* to each of the convents in Grenoble, while leaving a staggering seventy thousand *livres* to each of his dependents.

---

[7] See Norberg, *Rich and Poor in Grenoble,* pp. 11–80; and Chagny, "Grenoble: Les structures sociales d'une ville de province," in *De pain et d'espérance,* p. 104–106.

[8] Quoted in Norberg, *Rich and Poor in Grenoble,* p. 33.

[9] See Norberg, *Rich and Poor in Grenoble,* pp. 159–257, especially 239–57.

This new class of merchants, industrialists and lawyers vigorously opposed the policy of confining the poor, even if they were homeless. It was expensive and inefficient. The poor to these men were not so much a moral evil in need of compulsory religious instruction: they were a distasteful economic affliction.

Pre-Revolutionary Years:[10] Historians often associate the years immediately preceding the Revolution with a terrific outpouring of pamphlets decrying the plight of the poor. In Grenoble, just two writers concerned themselves with this problem, the abbé Reymond, a liberal priest known for his attacks on the ecclesiastical hierarchy, and Achard de Germane, a lawyer and the director of Grenoble's poor house, the General Hospital. Both men continued to blame the poor for their poverty and shared the mistaken belief of their contemporaries that there was work enough for all who wanted it. Their views are typical of the upwardly-mobile and well-to-do in Grenoble in the eighteenth century. Poverty was disdained as a defect and begging considered a crime.[11] Says Reymond:

> Of all the ills of society, the greatest is a host of beggars. . . . A pernicious penchant for idleness which enervates and corrupts lay at the root of poverty, and begging was just one manifestation of the pauper's laziness.[12]

Achard de Germane derided false beggars who, "covered themselves in rags to inspire pity, whose excuse is usually a sick husband or wife and children dying of hunger." These ploys "are only ruses to deceive the sensitive man, and alms are nothing but the reward of laziness."[13] The poor, in his view, deserved to be punished. Their laziness created a scarcity of labor, driving wages up and bringing hardship to rural landowners and urban manufacturers, and high prices to the rest of society.

Achard advocated that alms and all direct relief of poverty be curtailed. The able-bodied poor should be removed from the poor

---

[10]See Norberg, *Rich and Poor in Grenoble*, pp. 257–66.

[11]Chagny, "Grenoble: Les structures sociales d'une ville de province," in *De pain et d'espérance*, p. 101.

[12]Abbé Reymond, *Le Cahier des curés du Dauphiné* (Lyons, 1789), p. 147; and *Le Droit des pauvres* (Geneva, 1781), p. 8; both quoted in Norberg, *Rich and Poor in Grenoble*, p. 258.

[13]Achard de Germane, *Essai sur les moyens locaux les plus assurés et les moins dispendieux de faire cesser le fléau de la mendicité à Valence sans que les pauvres tant citoyens qu'étrangers soit moins secourus* (Valence, 1789); quoted in Norberg, *Rich and Poor in Grenoble*, p. 261.

houses and other institutions and forcibly taken to the countryside where, he mistakenly assumed, there was plenty of work. After 1768, beggars were no longer locked up in the poor house which he directed. They and other social undesirables—girls of low morals, the insane, syphilitic, scurvied and other contagiously ill persons—did continue to be incarcerated, however, but in another institution established outside the city walls.[14] At the root of Achard's plan was an almost religious belief in self-interest and the forces of a free market. Self-interest would make the poor work and induce the rich to cease their harmful almsgiving. He wrote:

> It is necessary to stimulate the wealthy citizens . . . and to tempt their self-interest, which is the motor of all men. . . . How blind men are; they prefer to give alms and diminish their fortune. . . when they could enrich themselves by offering a salary instead . . . Man has need only of the enlightenment of personal self-interest; if my system is followed, I dare to conclude that in fifteen or twenty years a regeneration of society will occur![15]

Achard's blind refusal to see that the poor were poor due to low wages and lack of employment, and his buoyant belief in self-interest as a solution to all societal ills, has been a popular theory among the wealthy of other historical periods as well. He also blithely ignored the fact that, just as today, the majority of the poor in the eighteenth century were women and children.[16]

The consequences of such attitudes for the poor were striking. They were less subject to forcible confinement, sermonizing or pater-

---

[14]Chagny, "Grenoble: Les structures sociales d'une ville de province," in *De pain et d'espérance*, pp. 101–107.

[15]Achard de Germane, *Essai sur les moyens locaux . . .* ; quoted in Norberg, *Rich and Poor in Grenoble*, pp. 263–64.

[16]For the eighteenth century, see Norberg, *Rich and Poor in Grenoble*, p. 266. Joni Seager and Ann Olson point out that, "Worldwide, the largest poverty groups are, first, women-headed households and second, the elderly (a greater proportion of whom are women because women live longer than men). Together these two groups represent an average 70 per cent of the poor in most countries of the world. Poverty is rapidly becoming feminized. The scattered statistics that are available tell the same story worldwide: in the USA, 78 per cent of all people living in poverty are women or children under the age of 18; in Australia, the proportion is 75 per cent; in Canada, 60 per cent of all women over age 65 live in poverty." See their book, *Women in the World: An International Analysis*, ed. Michael Kidron (New York: Simon and Schuster, Inc., 1986), p. 114, n. 28; see also p. 110, n. 19.

nalistic charity. But badly-motivated charity was better than none at all. Deinstitutionalization threw many of the poor back into the streets. Others who had received food aid were struck from the bread lists. In fact, all types of poor relief sharply declined in the city of Grenoble. The numbers of the poor, needless to say, did not.

Revolutionary Years:[17] The outbreak of the Revolution pushed the problems of the poor back into the consciousness of the well-to-do. After fifty years of benign neglect of the "lazy poor," the wealthy Grenoblois once again embarked on an active policy of poor relief. The poor themselves were the catalysts of this change. They recognized the extent to which their rights were being overlooked by a largely middle-class dominated revolution. They drew the attention of the wealthier Grenoblois through bread riots and the threat of violence. In 1790, bread cost more in Grenoble than anywhere else in France. Between January and October of 1794, the price of bread rose from thirty-seven *livres* the *quartal* to seven hundred *livres*. A worker who earned twenty francs in one day would pay eighteen francs for just one pound of bread. Under these conditions, the starving poor became a threat to the status quo. The affluent responded by liberalizing entrance procedures to the poorhouse and by increasing the city's bread distribution.

Charity, they knew, was a cheap alternative to violence. The municipal council itself admitted that its distribution of grain aimed "to prevent public disorder" and to "assure public tranquility."[18] When starvation and the shortage of bread threatened riots in 1793–1794, Claude Périer paid out 24,000 *livres* to troops brought in to maintain order. His donations of grain to the city were made coincidentally when the poor house's Bureau of Directors, of which he was a member, was about to be purged. Charity, at whatever price, was and remains vastly less costly to the status quo than genuine reform.

The improved situation for the poor of Grenoble was short-lived anyway. A severe financial crisis crippled the poorhouse. The wealthy were still reluctant to support it and its main source of income, a market tax, was lost when the middle-class leaders of the revolution suppressed it. The bread lists could not keep pace with the increased hardship of the poor. Women and children continued to make up the majority of the poor in France after the Revolution. The hardest hit group were single women, who received even less poor relief than they had before the Revolution.

---

[17]See Norberg, *Rich and Poor in Grenoble*, pp. 267–94.
[18]Quoted in Norberg, *Rich and Poor in Grenoble*, p. 289.

Furthermore, the temporary increase in poor relief halted abruptly in 1795. There was a relatively good harvest around Grenoble, conservative elements came back into control of the city, and, most importantly, the poor ceased to be a critical threat to social stability, although their misery had increased. Their situation would significantly change only in the nineteenth century when workers began establishing their own mutual aid societies, independent of aid from the wealthy.

4. PHILIPPINE'S ATTITUDE TOWARD CHARITY AND THE POOR

It is in the context of these attitudes toward the poor that we see just how new are Philippine's own views. Superficially, her charitable activity was entirely compatible with the assumptions of her own class. Women of the leisure class were expected to extend their caring hands to the needy. It was an ornament of good breeding. Her good works were supported by the superfluity of her family's wealth and they often touched either priests or the specifically religious needs of the poor.

Nevertheless, her charity represents a new appreciation of who the poor are in at least three ways: she recognized their inherent dignity as human beings, she discerned the special presence of God in their midst, and she was aware that charity was much more than an ornament—it was her life's calling.

Her appreciation of the dignity of the poor perhaps tells us more about her as a woman than it does as an individual. There were very distinct differences between the charitable activities of men and women in the eighteenth century. Men controlled all the large charitable institutions and most donations, and set the official policies toward the poor. Women's charity tended to have much smaller repercussions. A woman, moreover, would never voice the sort of disdain for the poor heard from some of her male contemporaries, as a leprosy on society, vessels of sin, villainous by nature and deserving to be locked up. These were not womanly sentiments.

But the limits of women's charity brought them certain privileges. Philippine's care for priests and the poor was personal. She visited them in prisons and entered their homes. She got to know them as persons. Just one of many examples is the occasion Philippine came upon a woman close to death. Since the area was too dangerous for priests to enter, Philippine brought the woman to her own apartment, laid her in the bed Philippine shared with her companion and then sought a priest for the woman's spiritual care. Philippine and her companion remained at the dying woman's side all through the night, caring for her physically and praying for her. The woman died in Philippine's arms.

Sociologists and psychologists often point out that the best way to overcome fear and prejudices regarding other groups, be they the very poor, the homeless, or people of another race, is to draw close to them. Such contact allows one to discover the commonality of human experience and to overcome fears, fears which are usually built on imaginary foundations. Women such as Philippine, who undertook charity by visiting the poor and sick, by entering into their neighborhoods and homes, meeting their families and friends, seeing their surroundings, caring for them in their dying moments, had a privileged opportunity to enter into and understand the worlds of these "other" people. The men directing charitable policy in Grenoble, on the other hand, betrayed the very distance they kept from the poor in the condescending policies they used to guide their charitable institutions and in the pamphlets they wrote which dismissed the poor as a lazy, pernicious and vice-ridden lot.

But Philippine's appreciation for their dignity went even further. She not only likened them to Christ; she discovered Christ in them. Her sister, probably unconsciously, couples Philippine's care for the sick and dying with Philippine's frequent attendance at mass. Philippine discovered Christ in the poor and suffering, just as she found Christ in the eucharist. Referring to the night Philippine cared for the above-mentioned dying woman, her sister wrote:

> As a matter of fact, nights like this were very frequent for Philippine, whether she spent them at the bedside of the sick or assisted at the holy sacrifice [of the mass], which could be celebrated only furtively, under cover of darkness.

Eucharist and the poor are both Christ's body for Philippine: a real presence of God in the world. This is a far cry from a eucharistic spirituality, or any spirituality for that matter, which separates religion from life, a God in heaven from humans on earth. The eucharist, for Philippine, was related to nurturance, God's nurturance of people, and people's for each other.

Christ for Philippine was above all the suffering Christ, who suffered for love of others. On any number of occasions, when she wanted to express her gratitude to God, she would do so by drawing close to the poor and suffering. She remarked once concerning a poor sick man whom she visited daily during this period of her life, "he represented my good Master by his sufferings."[19] God was present in a privileged manner for Philippine in suffering humanity, that is, the poor and the sick. Her attraction to them is a radical departure from attitudes reflected in Grenoble's charitable institutions at this time.

Finally, Philippine's care for others is significant because it was not simply one concern among many: a social duty incumbent upon her as a well-to-do lady. Rather, she chose to dedicate her life to such work. She left her family's country house and gave up social life in Grenoble precisely to have greater freedom of action. She devoted her inheritance to the needs of others. Her commitment to charity and to her own religious practices became the main focus of her life. In this light, "charity," as the word is employed today, seems almost too light a description for her radical dedication.

In recent years, theologians and Church documents have spoken a great deal about the relationship between charity and justice. The works of charity include providing assistance to the poor, caring for the sick, visiting the imprisoned and extending aid of all sorts to the downtrodden. In Philippine's time, as today, doing the works of charity was considered the duty of all Christians. It was particularly expected of affluent women. Philippine and her wealthy cousin Josephine were models among women dedicated to the works of mercy. Neither their culture nor their Church expected them to analyze the *causes* of suffering or poverty in their society. They did not attempt to critique the structures in their society which fostered inequalities nor did they try to change those structures. They engaged in the works of mercy little aware of their relation to the works of justice.

It is only recently that the Church has called attention to the integral connection which exists between charity and justice, to emphasize that the love of neighbor expressed in charitable works cannot exist apart from doing the works of justice.[20] Charity addresses immediate needs. To do justice is to work to change the structures which perpetuate hunger, poverty and other social evils.

The call in Philippine's day was simply to do the works of mercy. These she did with all the energy and personal conviction she could

---

[19]*Histoire de Sainte Marie.*

[20]See, for example, Congregation for the Doctrine of the Faith, *Instruction on Christian Freedom and Liberation*, no. 57; and also no. 68.

muster. She recognized the human dignity of the poor in a way new for her society. Far from disdaining them, she discovered God incarnate in their suffering. Her service to them was a life's call. One can only wonder about the conviction with which she would have pursued the works of justice were she alive today.

5. THE PROMISE TO FRANCIS REGIS

In 1801, Philippine was still in Grenoble involved in her charitable works. One day she was strolling up the hill to her old monastery of St. Marie with some former Carmelites. While speaking to them of the place she so loved, Philippine realized the strength of her desire to return to Visitation life there. Just a few days later, in fact, she resolved to do all in her power to re-establish religious life in the abandoned convent. How she went about this is hardly a tale of saintly inspiration and easy success. On the contrary, like the establishment of most religious orders and institutions in the past, her story is laced with the earthy reality of human planning, persuasion and stubborn persistence.

It begins with a vow she made in honor of St. Francis Regis, the French missionary to the poor. The content of her promise is worth repeating since it plays an important role in her later life. With the permission of her confessor, she promised that if she were back in St. Marie within a year, she would have a novena of masses offered at Regis' tomb, fast and receive communion on his feast each year, establish an oratory in his honor in the convent, and ensure that twelve poor people receive religious instruction. In short, Philippine made a deal with God and St. Francis Regis.

At its best, this sort of contract reflects the fact that Philippine felt she had a very real relationship with God and St. Francis, one that involved both give and take on their part and on hers. But these kinds of contracts also have negative aspects as well. Many years later when Philippine was beset by failures and burdened by her inability to keep her side of the above bargain, she would be overcome by scruples. She feared that her failures reflected God's displeasure with her and that they were related to her inability to fulfill the promise she made to Regis at this time.

Philippine's later doubts about God's love for her and her scruples about not keeping her promise to Regis reveal the frailty of her very human striving for perfection. It is ironic that someone who left her family, friends, country and worldly goods behind, who gave gratuitously of herself throughout most of her life, should come to doubt that God could act in any less generous manner with regard to herself. The doubts and fears which appear in her later years with regard to the promise to Regis are simply one more indication that Philippine's holiness can never be understood apart from her very human experiences.

6. THE RETURN TO ST. MARIE

Philippine did not use her vow to Regis as a replacement for her own efforts in obtaining St. Marie. She embarked on a complicated process of persuasion and politicking to achieve her end. She describes this and subsequent events in her *Story of Saint Marie:*

> With my intentions placed in such good hands [those of Francis Regis] I felt new courage and I began to take action. I consulted, or had others consult, the administrators of the diocese as to the proper course to take in order to get possession of Saint Marie. . . . One of the vicars general was Father Brochier, a man of wide experience and animated by the spirit of God. I set great store by his approbation, foreseeing even then that many people would blame our enterprise and that it was wise to have the support of highly respected authorities.

"Not by bread alone. . . ," but not without it either! Philippine had to rally the support, sometimes with great difficulty, of Brochier, her own confessor, her father, the former superior of the monastery, the former confessor of the monastery, the prefect of Grenoble, the vicars general and others. Her family's influence proved of great help and finally, on December 10, 1801, the building of St. Marie was leased to her for eight hundred francs per year. Philippine was also responsible for the extensive repairs which needed to be done.

Originally she intended to have the monastery signed over to the former superior of the monastery and to other religious the superior judged suitable. Philippine naively expected many of the nuns to return and be willing to contribute to the repair and re-establishment of the monastery. By an accidental turn of events, however, the legal papers for leasing the building were made out in the singular, to be signed by one person alone. Philippine made the critical decision to sign the building over to herself. This was just one of many acts which convinced those around her, especially the other religious, that she was re-establishing the monastery of St. Marie under *her* own terms.

Philippine herself protests in her *Story of Saint Marie* that this is not true. Concerning this particular incident she says that her impatience at delays, the need to prevent others from bidding on the building at a lower price and the distance of the superior caused her to sign the papers herself. But she also notes that the gossip of other religious who had got wind of her plans and did not entirely approve of her course of action was another incentive for her to sign the papers herself. In fact, throughout her lengthy *Story of Saint Marie* it is clear that Philippine anticipates opposition to her plans. She becomes more painfully aware of the wide extent of this opposition as her story proceeds. She believes that she is merely, and consistently, defending the proper form of religious life. And while the reader may or may not agree with her assessment, one is hard put to disagree with the conclusion of the religious who opposed her, including her superior on most occasions, that Philippine's own convictions about religious life—enclosure, holding goods in common, praying the Office, religious dress and other matters—were so specific as to admit no other way. But with the building signed over to herself, her relentless way of pursuing her own ideals regarding religious life and with a few key male ecclesiastics siding with her in various disputes with the other religious, Philippine's position at St. Marie was hard to challenge. The storm between Philippine and her former Visitation sisters erupted even before any of them had moved back. Here is her own account of the events which followed after the monastery was leased to her:

> I went home and began to pack my things and dispose of what I would not need. I remained indoors in order to avoid meeting the people who were displeased with me. All the former religious of the house were. They said I was rash in going to live in a building that was falling in ruins and from which I might be expelled again. They accused me of acting without consulting anyone and of sacrificing all to my own selfishness. "Has she the means on which to support the religious who have lost all their revenues? We do not want to starve to death. We have made a vow of poverty, but not of begging our living. We will not return to our convent until we can be sure of the same security as we had before." All these remarks were made with ill-temper and repeated in the same spirit, so I considered it useless to make any advances toward these women, as they were angered by the least sug-

gestion of a return [to St. Marie]. It was enough for my peace of conscience that the door was now open to them and that both the ecclesiastical and the religious superiors had been consulted.

Philippine moved back to the monastery just a few days after acquiring it. She was accompanied by Madame Faucherand (a former nun at St. Marie), a twelve-year-old girl, and an "out sister" (a sister charged with contacts with outsiders coming to the monastery). Philippine set about the grinding tasks of cleaning and repairing a building which had been long abandoned while she awaited the arrival of her former superior and the other religious.

From her return to St. Marie in December, 1801, until the end of August, 1802, Philippine encountered constant opposition to her ideas about religious life at St. Marie. She asked her ally and adviser, the vicar-general Father Brochier, to compose a Rule for them. Although it was exteriorly less strict than their former Rule, the other nuns objected to its demands. Philippine writes:

This Rule, from which I had hoped such great things, produced the worst effect. The religious criticized it loudly, especially the article on all things being held in common, which they found simply impossible. They had no scruple about retaining the ownership of all their belongings, yet they raised an outcry about the overthrow of the [previous] Rule because the order of the day was not exactly as it had been formerly and the election [of the superior] was slightly different. "Our former Superior is alive," they said; "why speak of electing another?" They did not consider the fact that there was no question of a superior for the religious who were still dispersed, but only for those who would come to the convent, which must have a head. Another article of the Rule answered all their objections, as it expressly stated that as soon as circumstances allowed, all the proposed changes would give way to strict observance of the former Rule. . . .

The majority [of the former religious] did not come to celebrate the feast of St. Francis de Sales with us at Saint Marie, but went instead to a private oratory, and after mass assembled "to protest against what they called the measures taken by Madame Duchesne." They then acquainted some of the vicars-general with that protest. I was in complete ignorance of what was going on. . . .

Even the return of the former superior, Mother de Murinais, did not ease the situation. One of Philippine's first acts after acquiring the monastery was to notify the former superior and invite her back to what Philippine termed "her," that is, de Murinais', "home." But the superior was suspicious of Philippine's dealings. She wrote back to her sarcastically, pointedly congratulating Philippine on the success of what de Murinais considered to be Philippine's *own* project. De Murinais hesitated to return at all, being warned by most of the former religious against such a move. Faucherand was struggling with mental problems. She too began to criticize Philippine, to such an extent, in fact, that Philippine even feared being physically attacked, something Faucherand had apparently not spared others on previous occasions. Soon, reports Philippine, Faucherand lost her mind, but hurt Philippine only by leaving the monastery. Philippine's two other companions also began to think about leaving. At this critical juncture, de Murinais finally decided to return, bringing with her three other sisters. Philippine's account continues:

Certainly things were better than before, but they in no way came up to my expectations of a religious institution. We had only Office in choir and meditation; there was no silence, no religious practices, no reading at meals, no *Benedicite* and grace in common, no cloister, no uniformity of dress, nothing. There was not even question of introducing these gradually. They all said they were just making a trial of it, for they had not made up their minds to persevere even in so easy a manner of life. What each one brought with her showed that; they had left their belongings elsewhere and had brought just about enough for a month in the country. In the depths of my heart I experienced much bitter anguish. . . .

Two religious who had some pupils offered to join us, and Mother [de Murinais] accepted them. In a conversation in which I took part and in which I insisted on the necessity of uniformity of dress, they said that *I wanted everything my way and did as I pleased, but that they also would do whatever they pleased.* . . .

So the household was composed of a superior who, in order to attract subjects, accepted all types of character, or rather yielded in turn to each of several religious who were doing each as she pleased, and of some young girls who were boarding pupils. . . .

I realized that wills were unstable. Often there was such

coldness toward me, I foresaw the breakup of the community. I did not want to have the least thing with which to reproach myself for having contributed to this, but everything tended that way. . . . It was pointed out to these women, and they realized it themselves, that discipline was absolutely necessary in the house, so they got together, both outside the convent and inside, to compose a rule, never having accepted that of Father Brochier. The superior showed me a copy, though they had asked her not to do so. I made a copy of it and showed it to Fathers Rey and Brochier, as it contained the vaguest kind of statements which gave not the slightest hope of making for stable union. There was no single purpose, no holding possessions in common, no cloister; one could come and go at will. They both advised me to keep out of the way as much as possible and to contribute to the upkeep of the house only as much as each of the others did, and said that as a result they might all move out and a better order of things be established later on. I followed their advice. . . .

And, not surprisingly, they did all eventually move out, the superior included.

After learning of their imminent departure, Philippine began to consider the possibility of associating St. Marie with another religious order:

There are several circumstances I consider remarkable in all these events. All the former religious of the Visitation came for a reunion at Saint Marie on July 2, the feastday of the order. I found the spirit so different from what I had formerly known, and the will to return to the cloister so undecided, that alone and prostrate before the blessed sacrament with the utmost agony of soul I said to Him that on that very feast of the Visitation I must make the sacrifice of the order. When my handkerchief was saturated with blood, I could not remain in the church, and I had to leave our Lord all alone.

It is not easy to know what to make of Philippine's account. There is little doubt that what she said was true regarding the looser religious life of the convent, the reluctance of some of the religious to return to cloister, their hesitancy about putting all their goods in common, and their resistance to Philippine herself. But Philippine's resolute and

uncompromising character clearly played a central role in the unfold-
ing of this drama. This is a woman who had said of her first entrance
into religious life:

> The day I entered St. Marie On High I took the resolution
> never to fail on a single point of rule . . .

And were that not daunting enough, she continues:

> . . . and indeed I do not recall ever infringing a single one.

Such self-demanding people can themselves be mystified by the
"laxer" standards of others and consequently be quite difficult to live
with in community. Furthermore, it should be recalled that the religious returning to St. Marie had been living outside the monastery for
nine years. What each experienced during those years, how it conditioned her view of a return to the cloistered life, are questions that
might not have occurred to someone as single-minded as Philippine.
There was never much doubt as to the outcome of this struggle: Philippine's radical vision of religious life held the day at St. Marie.

Grenoble had been rife with gossip ever since Philippine obtained
rights to the monastery. The public took a dim view of her disputes
with the other religious. On August 27, 1802, Philippine was left with
just three companions: an Ursuline nun, a sister who did domestic
work within the monastery, and the latter's blood sister who likewise
helped in the house. There were just six or eight pupils in the school
run by the monastery. She wrote:

> I was crushed. I was a subject of scandal. Gossip had it that I
> had driven away the religious, that I would not yield in
> anything, that no one could bear to live with me, that Fathers
> Brochier and Rivet with their high-flown ideas were the only
> ones who took my part.

In fact, Brochier became ecclesiastical superior of the group and
Rivet's own sister joined the nuns and became superior. The boarding
school prospered in spite of the negative gossip. Eventually, the little
group heard of the Ladies of the Faith, a religious society recently
organized under the direction of Father Joseph Varin. Philippine and
her companions were anxious to join them.

Varin and another priest, Father Roger, soon came to visit St.
Marie to evaluate its suitability for association with the Ladies of the

Faith. It was 1804. Philippine had heard very positive remarks about the new society and its young superior, Madeleine Sophie Barat, and was eager for Varin's approval. Philippine's first encounters with him are again revelatory of her determined and fiery temperament. Varin and Roger arrived on July 30, 1804, the eve of the feast of St. Ignatius. Philippine wrote in her *Story of Saint Marie:*

> After mass next morning they went through the whole house. I took my place directly behind Father Varin so I could hear all he might say and note any least sign he might give of satisfaction or disapproval. But there is no knowing the thoughts of these people who are so completely self-controlled, and I who am not of this type, began to be not a little irritated.

By the following day, Philippine was sure that the two had been swayed against them by the negative gossip in Grenoble. She continued:

> Well, the morrow dawned. Madame Rivet and I went again to see the two priests after mass. Father Varin spoke to me again of *Holy Indifference and of the slowness* with which the works of God are accomplished. I think I answered him that, on the contrary, Holy Scripture represents Him as *racing with giant strides*, and I followed this up with the statement that had St. Francis Xavier acted with such deliberation before undertaking good works he would never have accomplished them nor done so much in so short a time.

Philippine was wrong about Varin's impressions of her. He appreciated her assertive spirit. When he shared his opinion of St. Marie with Madeleine Sophie Barat, the superior of the Ladies of the Faith, he said:

> You will find someone in this house. . . were she alone and at the remotest corner of the world, you should go after her.[21]

---

[21]Jeanne de Charry, *Histoire des Constitutions de la Société du Sacré-Coeur,* 2 pts. in 5 vols. (Rome: Typis Pontificiae Universitatis Gregorianae, 1975–79; part I, 2nd ed., 1981), pt. I, vol. II, *Textes,* "La Mère Barat raconte les débuts de la fondation de Grenoble," p. 67, translation mine. Two volumes of this work have appeared in English translation, *History of*

He described Philippine as a "generous, great-hearted person," and added, referring to his previous indecision about accepting the Grenoble convent, "I won't hide from you it is she I have principally in mind when I balance the reasons for and against your journey."[22] St. Marie was accepted as part of the new society and Sophie Barat planned her own trip to Grenoble to meet these women, especially the one who had so captured the interest of her friend Varin.

---

the Constitutions of the Society of the Sacred Heart: pt. I, vol. I, *The Formation of the Institute* (Sussex: St. Richard's Press Limited, 1975), trans. Barbara Hogg; and pt. II, vol. I, *The Definitive Constitutions and Their Approbation by the Holy See* (n.p.: n.p., n.d.), trans. Barbara Hogg.

[22]Joseph Varin, *Lettres à Sainte Madeleine-Sophie Barat (1801–1849)*, ed. Jeanne de Charry (Rome: n.p., 1982), letter 44, p. 115; Barbara Hogg, trans., *Letters to Saint Madeleine-Sophie Barat (1801–1849)* (Rome: The Secretary Birds, 1982), pp. 82–83.

V.

The Society of the Sacred Heart

Sophie Barat arrived at St. Marie on December 13, 1804, just three years after Philippine's return to the monastery. She had never seen a cloistered monastery, but her biggest surprise was surely her first meeting with Philippine Duchesne. Without any warning, Philippine threw herself prostrate on the ground and kissed Sophie's feet. She then got up and greeted Sophie's traveling companions as if nothing out of the ordinary had occurred. Reflecting on the experience later, Sophie said:

> I reached the door and when it was barely opened, I saw someone running to meet me who then prostrated herself at my feet. I was twenty and some odd years old then and God knows how I looked . . . Anyway, this person was Madame Duchesne . . . and I still blush when I recall that she wrote in her journal regarding our meeting: "How beautiful the feet of those who come in the name of the Lord." There you have an example of her spirit of faith![1]

Philippine was thirty-five years old. After years of change and turmoil in her own life, she was about to come under the spiritual direction of Sophie Barat, ten years her junior and the superior of one small religious community in Amiens, France.

---

[1]"La Mère Barat raconte les débuts de la fondation de Grenoble," in de Charry, *Histoire des Constitutions*, pt. I, vol. II, p. 67; translation mine.

1. SOPHIE BARAT AND THE SOCIETY
OF THE SACRED HEART

Sophie Barat was born in 1779 in Joigny, France, a small Burgundian town on the left bank of the Yonne River. Her parents were of modest means and had two children older than Sophie, Louis, eleven years her senior, and Marie-Louise, nine years her senior. Sophie never went to school. But from age seven to twelve, she learned at home the same lessons which her brother Louis taught in the boys' school in Joigny. She therefore received an education significantly beyond that given to most girls of her time. A few years after Louis became a priest and moved to Paris, he asked his parents to send Sophie along too. Since childhood, she had wanted to be a religious. Louis recognized her acute intelligence and had ideas of his own about what innovative program of studies would prepare her to be an excellent religious. When she was about sixteen she joined him in Paris. She had already studied ancient history, the classics of French literature, Spanish, Italian and possibly some Latin. It is difficult to determine the exact level of her learning in each of these areas. In Paris, her brother guided her through a demanding program which included mathematics, Latin, reading the Church Fathers, theology and biblical studies. She may have learned a smattering of Greek, or even Hebrew.[2] Serious and austere himself, Louis attempted to make the child over in his own image, an image he found eminently suited to religious life. The price Sophie paid for her education was the sacrifice of her legitimate childhood needs for play and affection. Louis tried to kill all spontaneity in the child, teaching her instead to control her every act. Merely glancing out of the window while at study, he said, was an offence to God. Years later, Sophie would have to struggle hard to overcome the scruples and fears he had helped create in her. But her hard won success would be an invaluable asset to her in guiding the austere likes of Philippine Duchesne.[3]

Sophie met Father Joseph Varin, superior of the Fathers of the Faith in France, when her brother Louis entered the same order. Varin was inspired by his charismatic predecessor, Léonor de Tournély, founder of the Fathers of the Sacred Heart. Both men sought to re-establish the suppressed Jesuit order in France and to revitalize Catho-

[2]de Charry, *Histoire des Constitutions*, pt.I, vol. I, pp. 167–72; Hogg trans., *Formation of the Institute*, pp. 119–23.
[3]Mary H. Quinlan, "Saint Madeleine Sophie Barat's Doctrine of the Interior Life" (unpublished manuscript).

lic life in France. They envisioned an apostolic women's order parallel to their own which would help in this work. When Varin met Sophie, he persuaded her to forgo her desire to be a cloistered Carmelite nun so that she could use her remarkable education and personal gifts to join in the new foundation of an active religious order. He convinced her of the importance of a women's institute imbued with devotion to the Sacred Heart and dedicated to the education of young women.

Sophie and three other women made their first religious consecration before Joseph Varin on November 21, 1800, in Paris. The institute they were joining was known as the *Dilette di Gesù*, a group founded in Prague in 1799, which then moved to Italy. It was the female counterpart of Varin's group, the Fathers of the Faith. As superior of the Fathers of the Faith French mission, Varin wanted to establish a community of the *Dilette* in France. Sophie and her companions moved almost immediately to Amiens, where they and two other pious women took over a girls' boarding school. Sophie was named local superior of the *Dilette* in December, 1802, when she was just twenty-three years old. But by the time she set out for Grenoble two years later, all ties with the *Dilette* had been severed and the new group, known now as the Ladies of the Faith, consisted solely of the small community in Amiens. In 1806, just about a year after Philippine had joined their society, Sophie Barat was elected Superior General of the Ladies of the Faith. In autumn of the same year, they chose a new title for themselves, Daughters of the Sacred Heart of Jesus, before changing it finally in 1815 to Society of the Sacred Heart of Jesus. Only then did the religious begin to identify themselves publicly as women devoted to the Sacred Heart.[4] Sentiment against groups such as the Jesuits, who had actively promoted this devotion and who were associated with royalist tendencies, had finally abated. Within Sophie's own lifetime, under her remarkable leadership, the little society would grow to more than three thousand religious on four continents.

2. DEVOTION TO THE SACRED HEART

Catholic devotion to the heart of Jesus extends well back into the Middle Ages and has changed dramatically in meaning as it was inter-

---

[4] de Charry, *Histoire des Constitutions*, pt. II, vol. I, pp. 18–22; Hogg trans., *The Definitive Constitutions*, pp. 13–15. Pt. I, vols. I and II of de Charry's study contain a fascinating account of these early transformations in the religious society.

preted by different groups in different ages. In one period it served to emphasize the humanity of Christ as opposed to his divinity. In the later Middle Ages, the physicality of Christ, especially his bodily suffering, was stressed as central to human redemption. Accordingly, the blood which flowed from his heart and the physical heart itself were important motifs in Christian piety. The devotion to the Sacred Heart acquired widespread popularity in the seventeenth century after a French Visitation nun, Margaret Mary Alacoque, received a revelation from God. She said God wanted Christians to honor his heart of love and to receive the eucharist as an act of reparation for impieties he suffered, especially in the blessed sacrament. In the fifty years following her death in 1690, about seven hundred confraternities of the Sacred Heart were formed in France.[5]

By the time of Philippine Duchesne and Sophie Barat, devotion to the Sacred Heart had multiple meanings. These ranged from a concentration on Christ's physical heart, a devotion which repels many people today, to an emphasis on the intangible qualities symbolized by his heart, such as love, generosity, compassion and forgiveness. To speak of the "heart of Jesus" in this latter sense was to speak implicitly of all these other qualities. To be "devoted" to his heart meant to open oneself to growth in love, generosity, compassion and forgiveness. Reparation for acts contrary to Christian piety and love of the eucharist were also integral components of this devotion. The devotion to the heart of Christ so pervaded eighteenth- and nineteenth-century France, in fact, that it even took on certain political connotations. Some French nationalists, anti-royalists and enemies of the Jesuits, for example, associated it with the political views they opposed.

For Sophie Barat, the heart of Jesus represented the whole person of Christ, whom she associated with the aforementioned intangible qualities of love, generosity, compassion and forgiveness. When she employed the words "heart of Jesus" and "Sacred Heart," she was not referring to a statue or picture of Jesus pointing to his physical heart, although devotion to his physical heart did play a role in her spirituality. She was referring to Christ himself. The heart of Jesus was the symbol and source of God's love and compassion for the world.[6] This was who God was for her.

---

[5] de Charry, *Histoire des Constitutions*, pt. I, vol. I, p. 25; Hogg trans., *Formation of the Institute*, p. 19.

[6] See Helen Rosenthal, " 'Union and Conformity with the Heart of Jesus' in the Spirituality of Saint Madeleine Sophie Barat," Diss. St. Louis University 1985, pp. 31–69, especially 60–65, for a fuller discussion of this topic.

The Constitutions which Joseph Varin and Sophie Barat composed for the Society of the Sacred Heart of Jesus state that the one aim of the order is "to glorify" the heart of Jesus. This is accomplished in two ways. First, the members are to conform their own thoughts and feelings to those of Jesus. Second, they are to work for the sanctification of others, "embracing every means in their power of spreading the worship of the Sacred Heart."[7]

Since love of the heart of Christ, for Sophie Barat and Joseph Varin, implied taking on Christ's attitude of love and compassion for the world, this devotion meant more than a comfortable, even sentimental relation between the individual and God. While more individualized aspects of this devotion, such as reparation for the sins of others, sacrifice, and love of the eucharist were certainly important, it is worth noting that "glorifying the heart of Jesus" was much more than a personal religious attitude. It implied a complete consecration to the service of others.[8] Personal contemplation, in which the religious could begin to identify with Christ's thoughts and feelings, was the starting point.[9] But the personal transformation brought about in contemplation did not stop there. It impelled one to work for the sanctification or transformation of others too. In modern language then, the task of spreading "devotion to the heart of Christ" involved cultivating the qualities of love, generosity, compassion and forgiveness in oneself and in all those with whom one came into contact.

3. THE APOSTOLIC WORK OF THE SOCIETY

The means available to these nineteenth-century women for this task of transformation are significant. The opening of their Constitutions points out that they were to consecrate themselves to the sanctification of others "as far as it is possible for women." This refers less to the long tradition in Christian society of women as morally weak char-

---

[7]"Abridged Plan of the Institute" [composed in 1805], no. 4; and "Summary of the Constitutions" [composed in 1820], no. 343, in Constitutions: Society of the Sacred Heart of Jesus (Rome: Tipografia Poliglotta della Pontificia Università Gregoriana, n.d.).

[8]"Constitutions of 1815," no. 158, in Constitutions: Society of the Sacred Heart of Jesus; and see the profound theological study of Dominique Sadoux and Pierre Gervais, La vie religieuse: Premières Constitutions des Religieuses de la Société du Sacré-Coeur (Paris: Beauchesne, 1986), pp. 120–21.

[9]"Abridged Plan of the Institute," no. 5.

acters than it does to other ecclesiastical and societal barriers. The first
of these was the Church tradition, dating back to papal legislation of
1566, which required that women religious be cloistered to be considered "true religious."[10] Cloister necessarily limited the type of apostolate which religious women could undertake.

Second, the cultural assumption that women were the prime religious and moral educators in the home encouraged many women religious to assume the same role within the larger "family" of French
society. They ran schools for children, were addressed as "Mothers"
and prepared young girls for the task which would await them as wives
and mothers in their own families. Sophie Barat wholeheartedly em-
braced this assumption. She felt that by educating young women who
were the future moral educators of their families, religious women
could help re-establish Catholicism in France. Just as a wife and
mother could transform the moral tone of her household, so religious
women, it was argued, could transform the moral tone of France.
Consequently, the Society of the Sacred Heart's main work was the
education of young women. In the boarding schools, established primarily for well-to-do girls, the nuns would be able to provide the girls
with an integral formation. The education of poor children, equally
important but less viable in a boarding school, was undertaken in day
schools referred to as "poor schools."[11] The establishment of schools
for women was particularly significant in France, where there was a
shortage of schools for women of all classes.[12]

The phrase "as far as it is possible for women" to sanctify others
also recalled, even if unconsciously, the presumption that women were
inherently less suited to lead souls to God. This historical prejudice,
already discussed in chapter one, was even subtly apparent in the
friendly relationship between Joseph Varin and Sophie Barat. For example, in a letter to the young woman encouraging her in her first
efforts to be superior, Varin used a Latin adjective referring to Sophie,
but he left it in the grammatical form reserved for men. Then, antici-
pating her correction of his Latin, he writes, "But that is precisely the

---

[10]de Charry, *Histoire des Constitutions*, pt. II, vol. I, p. 99; Hogg trans., *The Definitive
Constitutions*, p. 84. De Charry's profound study goes on to show how the Society of the
Sacred Heart succeeded, with Church approval, in adapting the traditional practice of enclosure to allow for the needs of their active apostolate. The religious were withdrawn from "the
world," but did not follow a strict interpretation of "cloister."

[11]"Abridged Plan of the Institute," no. 6.

[12]Mary H. Quinlan, "Education in the Thought of Saint Madeleine Sophie" (unpublished manuscript).

point, I do not want you to be 'feminine' and so I say '*esto vir,*' be a man."[13] She would hardly object to such a comment having, like most women, internalized these cultural assumptions about women and men. Both she and Varin assumed that effective leadership depended on possessing qualities they identified as "masculine."

For Philippine, the work of educating boarders and poor children was simply a continuation of her former apostolate as a Visitation nun. It is interesting to see how the Society's *Constitutions of 1815* clearly reflect the then current cultural assumptions about rich and poor, and about women as the religious and moral educators of the family. According to the Constitutions, religion is what both wealthy and poor girls really needed to be "educated." For example, concerning the boarding school, which educated girls primarily from affluent families, the Constitutions say:

> Let [the religious] reflect that girls educated in their houses [i.e. the convent schools] are destined in the ordinary course of Providence, to become wives and mothers of families.
>
> Incalculable good can be done by a truly Christian wife and mother who is solidly virtuous and devoted to all her duties. Many men living in forgetfulness of God and of the faith may be withdrawn from evil and won back to virtue by the example and care, the wisdom, the gentleness, and the prayers of a thoroughly Christian wife.
>
> It is certain, at any rate, that the order and regularity of family life, the peace and good behavior of servants and, above all, the earliest education of children depend principally upon the mother of the family, and that it is through her that the knowledge, love and practice of religion are transmitted to the next generation. Many other good effects besides these will be produced in the world by the example of her virtues and her life.[14]
>
> Religion should therefore be at once the foundation and the crowning point of the education they intend to give, and consequently the chief subject taught; the rest is only accessory, but yet necessary in its degree, since their object is to form those who, for the most part, are called to live in the

---

[13]Varin, *Lettres*, ed. de Charry, letter 2, p. 5; Hogg trans., *Letters*, p. 21.
[14]"Constitutions of 1815," nos. 171–73.

world, which they should edify without offence, and whose customs they should know and follow in all that is not contrary to the rules of the gospel.[15]

Apart from religious instruction, these girls were "only to be taught what is necessary to be known by persons called to live a Christian life in the world according to the requirements of their state and position." This included reading and writing, grammar, history, geography, arithmetic and, when requested by the parents and serving some useful (not vain!) purpose, they were also to be taught foreign languages.[16] Manual skills and a knowledge of domestic economy were also a part of the education fitting them for their future lives as wives and mothers.[17]

Such an education hardly responds to the expectations of most women today. However, within nineteenth-century France, the schools established by the Society of the Sacred Heart quickly earned a reputation for the solid education they provided. The girls learned all the secular knowledge that they needed. Much more importantly, the religious aimed to cultivate in each girl a devotion to the heart of Christ. In secular language, we would call this "character formation": the religious were vigilant in ensuring that each girl grow in her own capacity for love, generosity, compassion and forgiveness.

Even this formation, focused primarily on religious instruction, proved a threat to some of Sophie Barat's contemporaries. They felt that women were inherently incapable of understanding theological abstraction. Introducing women to the deeper points of doctrine and theology might shake their frailer religious faith. Nevertheless, Sophie Barat was committed to providing a strong formation in scripture and theology for the young women attending her schools. She wanted their faith to be informed by substantive, not sentimental, ideas. Her broad educational vision went beyond that of many Catholics of her day. For example, she wholeheartedly accepted non-Catholic girls in her schools. And to those who questioned her on this point, she forthrightly asserted: "We shall meet them again in heaven."[18]

The day classes provided for the poor both reflected nineteenth-

---

[15]"Constitutions of 1815," no. 176.

[16]"Constitutions of 1815," no. 188.

[17]"Constitutions of 1815," nos. 190–92. For a feminist critique of this sort of education, see Smith, *Ladies of the Leisure Class.*

[18]On these points, see Quinlan, "Education in the Thought of Saint Madeleine Sophie"; and "Saint Madeleine Sophie Barat's Doctrine of the Interior Life."

century assumptions and departed from them to a certain extent. Schools for the poor were not new to France. In Grenoble itself, free instruction had been provided the poor in its orphanage, the poor house and charity schools. The educators in these little schools sought to save the poor from their "natural laziness" and inculcate in them a love of work. The children often had to labor long and cruel hours.[19] Their benefactors sought to lead them down the road of salvation by teaching them religion.

Some of these assumptions are reflected in the education offered the poor in the religious society which Philippine was entering, although in a much more benign tone. The poor were associated with idleness: they were given manual work to overcome this vice. In the case of orphans, as we shall see in a later chapter, their labor was often the domestic work which would otherwise be done by hired help or by the nuns themselves. But the poor girls were generally treated with dignity and kindness. Sophie Barat was adamant on this point. Many incidents from her life illustrate her conviction that the poor were never to be condescended to or treated with any less dignity than that accorded prominent and wealthy individuals. On occasion, she had to chide some of the other nuns who did not grasp this point.[20]

From a modern perspective, however, it is apparent that there was generally no consciousness of the larger questions of justice surrounding the situation of the poor. The Constitutions are mute on this subject, a fact which partially explains the inadequate attention, until recent times, given by the Society of the Sacred Heart to the education of the poor and to questions of justice.[21] The language of the Constitutions seemed subtly to encourage among the poor an acceptance of their lot. Regarding classes for the poor, the Constitutions state:

As the eternal and spiritual good of their souls is the object aimed at, the utmost endeavour shall be made to teach them the catechism well, and to give them on the truths and duties of religion all the instruction suited to their age, capacity and station. *They shall be taught to know the excellence and merit of*

---

[19]Norberg, *Rich and Poor in Grenoble*, pp. 159–68.

[20]See, for example, Mary H. Quinlan, "The Return to the Original Inspiration of the Founder" (unpublished manuscript), pt. 2, p. 9.

[21]See Sadoux and Gervais, *Vie religieuse*, pp. 309–11, on this topic.

*poverty, and learn how to sanctify it by an esteem and love for it,
based upon the sentiments and example of Jesus Christ.*[22]
Some manual work, under supervision and guidance,
shall be provided for all during part of the class hours, *to
protect them early from the dangers of idleness,* and later on, to
procure them means of subsistence and of gaining a suitable
and respectable livelihood.[23]

Although the poor were to be taught religion almost exclusively,
complemented only by reading and writing and some arithmetic when
necessary,[24] it should be kept in mind that religion was the main focus
of the boarders' education as well, other subjects being taught only as
they were necessary to the girls' social background. Although "idleness" is not a danger mentioned regarding the more affluent boarders,
they too were given manual work to do, to protect them from *their* own
peculiar danger, "frivolity"![25]

The Constitutions go on to say that the poor had a special claim on
these religious, women who, after all, sought to cultivate a love of
poverty in their own lives. This rather romanticized notion of poverty
certainly made too little of the fundamental difference between the
poverty of the religious and that of the poor children: the poverty of
the religious was voluntary, something they chose for themselves; that
of the poor children was involuntary, something life circumstances
imposed upon them. And as the "Summary of the Constitutions,"
composed in 1820, recognizes, the vowed poverty of the religious, who
lacked nothing essential, in no way compared to the abject poverty of
children who had made no such life choice.[26] Poverty not chosen is
rarely loved, and few people today would even argue that it should be.

That the Constitutions even allude to the distinction between
voluntary and involuntary poverty is in itself notable in the nineteenth
century. There was not the same hope or expectation of significant
economic change for the poor as there is in many societies today. In
keeping with the common assumptions of their culture, these
nineteenth-century religious did not suggest change in the status quo
separating the rich from the poor. Rather, they focused their energy on

---

[22]"Constitutions of 1815," no. 204, emphasis mine.
[23]"Constitutions of 1815," no. 206, emphasis mine.
[24]"Constitutions of 1815," no. 205.
[25]"Constitutions of 1815," no. 190.
[26]"Summary of the Constitutions," no. 350.

providing the poor with the habits and skills necessary to lead a digni-
fied life within their own class. In many cases, this education no doubt
spared the girls from the especially wretched and dehumanizing conditions rampant in the industrialized cities of Europe. These poor
schools, moreover, provided literacy training to girls who would otherwise never learn to read.

While discussion of the structural changes necessary for the cre-
ation of a more just society is absent, the gospel imperative of a "preferential option for the poor" did find its way into the Constitutions of the
new religious order. The poor students were to be favored by the
religious. The "tenderest charity," say the Constitutions, "should be
reserved for those whose poverty makes them specially attractive."[27]
"This work for poor children . . . is incomparably dearest to the Heart
of Jesus." The religious chosen for this work will therefore consider it
"an enviable mark of preference."[28] In fact, the latter has not always
been the case in the history of the religious order which Philippine was
joining, despite Sophie Barat's strong commitment to the poor. Philippine followed her superior's lead on this point. Philippine's lifelong
dedication to the children in the Society's poor schools and her unflagging defense of the poorer foundations made by the Society in the New
World make her stand out in her new religious family.

4. PHILIPPINE'S FIRST YEARS IN THE SOCIETY

Sophie Barat remained at St. Marie, the second convent in the
new religious society, for a year in order to inculcate in each of the
religious there the spirituality and educational philosophy of the Society of the Sacred Heart. Seven novices made their vows on November
21, 1805, just before Sophie had to leave to attend to business in
Amiens and elsewhere in the growing Society. Meanwhile, the nuns
continued their work in the boarding school, which now had seventeen
pupils, and the poor school, which had twenty.

Philippine's multiple responsibilities during her first years in the
Society are typical of the activism which would mark the rest of her
life. In 1806 she was secretary to the superior, head of the boarding
school and teacher for the older children. She was also charged with
ordering all the material necessities of the school and convent. She

---

[27]"Constitutions of 1815," no. 208.
[28]"Constitutions of 1815," no. 215.

cared for nuns and students alike when they were sick. This was an especially arduous task in times of extreme contagion. Although Philippine was relieved of some of these duties in 1807, her life was hardly sedentary. The boarding school alone already had sixty pupils. Philippine maintained this same pace of activity until she left Grenoble for Paris in 1815.

Throughout this period, Philippine complained frequently of her excessive activities and her desire for more time for prayer. Here we encounter one of the paradoxes of Philippine, for throughout almost all of her life she was overworked and complained of it. As early as 1807 we have evidence of her correspondence with Sophie Barat requesting relief from some of her many duties.[29] She longed to spend more time in prayer. Such requests continued for over forty years. Ironically, however, the few times in her life in which Philippine lacked activity, for example, the period she spent with her family in 1792 upon first leaving St. Marie and then again at the end of her life, she was unhappy and felt useless. Clearly, Philippine was a woman who thrived on activity. Much of the work she took on in her life she had created for herself. She was quick both in identifying needs and in doing something about them. It is indicative of her aggressive, independent and strong character.

One is therefore tempted to question her constant complaints about lack of time for prayer. Did she really desire more time for solitude and contemplation, or was her best "prayer" during this period what she could actively do for others? A penchant for activity can also serve to fill the time in which one would have to take a hard look at oneself. But Philippine's case fits neither of these situations. Her life consistently bears out that she genuinely desired more time to be in solitude with God.

A good way to determine real desires is to see what activities drop when time constraints are pressing. If one values work, friends, family, prayer and sleep, for example, which of these falls by the way when time becomes limited? In Philippine's case, her two great attractions were clearly her time for prayer and her dedication to her work. Rarely

---

[29]For the original French, see Madeleine-Sophie Barat and Philippine Duchesne, *Correspondance: Texte des manuscrits originaux*, pt. I, *Période de Grenoble (1804–1815)*, ed. Jeanne de Charry (Rome: Tipografia Poliglotta della Pontificia Università Gregoriana, 1988), letter 20, pp. 82–83. Seventy-nine of the letters in this volume are from Sophie Barat to Philippine, only two (letters 10 and 12) having been preserved from this period from Philippine to Sophie Barat. A second volume containing the rest of the correspondence between the two women and English translations of both volumes are forthcoming.

was either sacrificed for any reason. When she was overworked, which was the case throughout most of her life, she chose simply to pray at night and to sacrifice her sleep. "Night adoration," as it was called, was a popular devotional practice for religious in the nineteenth century. For Philippine, the deep silence of night held the additional attraction of a long period uninterrupted by the demands of her work.

Philippine's affective style of prayer, her manner of loving God, was a good counter-balance to personality traits which marked other aspects of her life. For example, the severity she usually reserved for herself was sometimes felt by others too. Despite her constant struggle to control her rather judgemental temper and grow in kindness and patience toward those around her, Philippine's aggressive and irascible nature still sparked on occasion. Sophie Barat was quick to catch this on meeting Philippine. What she wrote to Philippine in February, 1807, after she had left Grenoble, was repeated many times:

> Now do endeavor to acquire the virtues so necessary for drawing hearts to Christ: meekness, humility, affability, evenness of manner, which is the fruit of patience, and above all that love of Jesus which I so desire to see in you. . . . Meditate frequently on these words of [the fifteenth-century spiritual treatise] the *Imitation*: "My son, the more you renounce self, the more you shall find me." . . . Again I recommend very specially to you a kind and gentle manner toward others, and I beg you to use it also in dealing with yourself.[30]

Writing again in March, 1809, Sophie said:

> Grasp this fact clearly: our Lord, in His goodness, wishes you to become a great saint. He brought you into this little family just to give you the means of doing so. . . . I know you cannot correct yourself suddenly. How could you become meek, stripped of all attachment to your own judgement, etc., when the contrary faults have been rooted in your character for so long?[31]

It was in prayer that Philippine addressed herself to these failings and in which she expressed the more affective and tender aspects

---

[30]*Correspondance*, pt. I, letter 31, pp. 112—13.
[31]*Correspondance*, pt. I, letter 31, pp. 112–13.

of her personality, a side which did not always show in her human relations. Her own descriptions of her prayer indicate that it was entirely unlike a "willed" effort, the fulfillment of one more duty which she forced upon herself. Rather, she says that it was a very felt experience, what could be called affective prayer rather than discursive or intellectual prayer. It is not surprising that someone as active and self-demanding as Philippine would find such an experience restful. She herself tells us that she had great difficulty undertaking meditations which required elaborate reasoning. Nor is it surprising that she especially loved prayer at night, with its suggestion of intimacy. Philippine's style of prayer responded to personal needs of intimacy and closeness which she experienced only minimally in most of her personal relationships.

Remaining in adoration before the eucharist is another religious practice which is foreign to many people today. Philippine's night adoration before the eucharist could be mistaken for a passive, even superstitious faith in the magical powers of a material object. Any type of religious practice or prayer performed solely out of habit or duty, rather like checking in at a time-clock, risks devolving into an empty ritual. But none of Philippine's descriptions of her night adoration indicate that it was a mechanical, shoulder-to-the-plough religious act, a ritual performed only out of habit. Her own accounts indicate that these hours of prayer were dynamic encounters, experiences of God's love for her and hers for God. She felt both the joy of God's presence and the pain of God's absence. Her own character was molded and affected during these nights.

On the other hand, Philippine's enthusiasm for long hours of prayer at night also forms part of an ascetical tendency which betrays both her radical generosity and her severity with herself. Sophie Barat discerned both these tendencies in Philippine and for years struggled to modify Philippine's spiritual and corporal austerities. Sophie's first difficult task at St. Marie was adapting the convent to the spirit of her new religious society. This proved to be an important challenge for Philippine.

While the interiority cultivated in the former Visitation monastery was quite in accord with the contemplative dimension of the Society of the Sacred Heart's spirituality, there were certain other practices which had to fall by the way. Sophie Barat moderated some of the exterior mortifications engaged in by the sisters. She feared that through frequent repetition such penances "should become a mere form and no longer have the same value in the eyes of God." She even restrained her brother Louis when he recommended such practices to the nuns during a retreat.[32]

Sophie Barat wasted no time in removing the cloister grilles at St. Marie. The order of day became less fixed and many formalities were dropped. The poverty and austerity which the nuns displayed in their contacts with students and parents were also modified, although inside the cloister, they were maintained. Instituting these changes was a delicate task for the twenty-five-year-old superior. She followed Varin's advice in adapting the religious practices at St. Marie:

> . . . when one takes over a task already begun, there is obviously much to reform, patience and much prudence are needed far more than zeal. You must go gently, begin by winning their hearts, the rest will follow without noise or clamor, even the details.[33]

Philippine, inclined to a strict interpretation of religious life, was not always pleased with such changes. Sophie Barat's removal of the cloister grilles is a case in point. Sophie did this to facilitate the nuns' work of education. She believed that the nuns should be close to the people with whom they worked, that any austere signs which might put others off should be removed. Years later, in negotiating for papal approbation of the Constitutions, she continued to insist that the Society's houses be exempted from having grilles. "How many countries there are where we could not deal with them!"[34] In a conscious following of Ignatius of Loyola, Sophie Barat wanted the religious to work for the salvation of others:

> We should not retire behind four walls like the Orders of solitaries, where we would only work in secret.[35]

---

[32]de Charry, *Histoire des Constitutions*, pt. I, vol. I, p. 319; Hogg trans., *Formation of the Institute*, p. 225.

[33]Varin, *Lettres*, ed. de Charry, letter 54, p. 138; Hogg trans., *Letters*, pp. 95–96.

[34]Letter to Eugénie Audé, May 28, 1826. All translations of Sophie Barat's letters to Eugénie Audé, unless otherwise indicated, are my own. The letters are to be found in the Religious of the Sacred Heart Archives, Rome, Italy.

[35]Quoted in de Charry, *Histoire des Constitutions*, pt. I, vol. I, p. 280; Hogg trans., *Formation of the Institute*, p. 197.

But for Philippine, this change was a shattering loss and she complained to the new superior. Years later, Mother Barat recalled the
scene:

> When Mother Duchesne saw the first grille fall—I had or-
> dered it to be removed—she hid herself in her room to weep.
> I noticed her sadness and asked her what had caused it. "Oh!
> Mother, my beloved grilles!"

Mother Barat's response was pointed:

> Your grilles, my dear, don't talk to me about them. Our aims,
> our action cannot be shut up like that inside a grille. . . .[36]

Years later, when Philippine was living on the American frontier, Sophie could not resist driving her lesson home: "I ask you now," she
wrote, "where would you be with grilles—in Louisiana?"[37]

Philippine's spirituality was often guided by the axiom "the
harder, the holier." It was a delicate task for Sophie, ten years her
junior, to guide Philippine toward a more practical and healthy spirituality. Philippine, for example, continually requested the most menial
tasks and the most uncomfortable places to sleep. She sprinkled her
food with bitter herbs to spoil its taste and was eager to perform other
corporal austerities. Her night vigils weakened her health and hampered her work on the following days. Philippine's religious practices
and her writings reveal what might be called "a spirituality of suffering." Writing to her sister in March, 1805, about her disappointment
regarding a canceled visit, she said:

> There is no need for me to tell you how much I should have
> enjoyed seeing you in the midst of your dear family. . . . But
> you realize, dear Sister, that my vocation is a consecration to
> sacrifice and to privation of natural joys.

Of course, such language was common in nineteenth-century spirituality. Sophie Barat used it too and, superficially, some of her com-

---

[36]Quoted in de Charry, *Histoire des Constitutions*, pt. I, vol. I, p. 279, and pt. I, vol. II, p.
68; Hogg trans., *Formation of the Institute*, p. 196.

[37]Quoted in Margaret Williams, *The Society of the Sacred Heart: History of a Spirit, 1800–
1975* (London: Darton, Longman and Todd, 1978), p. 45.

ments might strike the reader for their negativity. She counseled Philippine in August, 1806:

> [The soul] would not live without suffering, and in its work for Jesus it asks only suffering as a recompense.[38]

And in May, 1807, she wrote:

> Remember, my dear daughter, our Lord calls you to carry his cross. Have you forgotten these words he has so often whispered in the depths of your heart: "You must become a victim, you must be immolated for love of Him"?[39]

But Sophie Barat never recommended suffering for suffering's sake. In her last remark above, for example, she was encouraging Philippine to accept difficulties in life over which there was little control. Sophie had a very positive appreciation for the central role suffering plays, like it or not, in *all* human lives and the positive growth it can bring in those able to embrace life's experiences as they come. She knew that the attempt to live well brought its own troubles and suffering. For example, in a frank description of religious life and the solitude it involves, she wrote to Philippine in March, 1805, that it was

> . . . a solitude dreaded by nature and the senses—complete self-renunciation, absolute detachment. . . . You realize, of course, that I am not referring to any new sacrifices you should make. You might think so and wear yourself out with uneasiness. . . . For you the "cleft in the rock" [where God calls you] is this: to acquire the spirit of humility and meekness, the spirit of prayer.[40]

In other words, Philippine had her work cut out for her in simply dealing with her own human failings. Fabricating additional sacrifices and austerities was pointless. Sophie wrote to her:

> A large portion of [the Cross] is reserved for you, but be courageous and ready to accept it willingly, without asking

---

[38]*Correspondance*, pt. I, letter 14, p. 56.
[39]*Correspondance*, pt. I, letter 19, p. 77.
[40]*Correspondance*, pt. I, letter 2, p. 9.

for it. You will have crosses that come from yourself, but there will be others that may seem more painful.[41]

Like Philippine, Sophie was also attracted to night adoration. In fact, during the early years of the congregation, she wanted to make perpetual adoration an integral part of the Society's religious practice.[42] But Sophie's and Philippine's attitudes also contrast in significant ways. Sophie disapproved of night adoration, for example, whenever it interfered with their work for others. In fact, the whole thrust of the Constitutions on the subject of the nuns' health stresses that it is a gift from God, to be carefully preserved so that they may be fit to serve others.[43] Sophie wrote to Philippine in February, 1807, on the subject of Lent:

> Take care of your health and do not weaken yourself by fasting. I beg you to take six hours of sleep, otherwise I shall take from you that extra hour of nightly adoration and you will go to bed at the hour of rule. You understand I gave that permission only because my brother [Louis] asked it for you. No I will not allow you to take only five hours of sleep—with all the hard work you have to do. Be reasonable and be satisfied with what I have allowed. Must I tell you again that I have a scruple even about that?[44]

Not surprisingly, Sophie's brother Louis delighted in Philippine's ascetical tendencies. Sophie often opposed him when he urged Philippine toward greater austerity. Joseph Varin, who had helped free Sophie from some of her own scruples, used all his considerable influence over the young superior also to restrict Philippine's austerities. Sophie Barat was convinced that austerities served no end whatsoever if they did not issue in practical, concrete results which benefitted others. In the language typical of her time she wrote to Philippine in July, 1807:

> If after some months of secret prayer with your divine Spouse you do not become more humble, more obedient,

---

[41]*Correspondance*, pt. I, letter 5, p. 17.

[42]See, for example, *Correspondance*, pt. I, letter 80, p. 210.

[43]"Constitutions of 1815," nos. 157–68; and see *Correspondance*, pt. I, letter 21, pp. 85–86; and Sadoux and Gervais, *Vie religieuse*, pp. 281–84.

[44]*Correspondance*, pt. I, letter 17, p. 71.

more patient, I shall withdraw the permission for night adoration.[45]

Even in Lent, Sophie restricted Philippine's penances. She asked her instead "to sacrifice" her night prayer.[46] She reprimanded Philippine for denying herself communion and forbade her to do any penance during Easter week. On the contrary, she was to receive daily communion, a privilege often not allowed to religious in the nineteenth century.

In short, much of the spiritual guidance which Sophie Barat offered to Philippine consisted in tempering Philippine's austere inclinations, encouraging her toward gentleness with both herself and her sisters, and teaching her that self-imposed suffering and sacrifice were wrong when they harmed either one's work or one's disposition.

5. THE FRIENDSHIP OF PHILIPPINE AND SOPHIE

Sophie Barat remained at Grenoble for a year in 1804–1805, a few months in 1806, a month in 1808, from late 1809 through most of 1810, and again from May, 1812 to September, 1813. During those periods and through their frequent correspondence Philippine and Sophie grew to be close friends. In fact, it was one of the most important personal ties Philippine ever developed in her life. It afforded Sophie an influence over Philippine which few people ever had.

Their friendship was never entirely reciprocal. Despite the ten years separating them in age, the younger Sophie always held a dominant position in the relationship. This is especially evident in the first years of their friendship. Philippine suffered acutely during Sophie's absence. Sophie had constantly to assure Philippine that her feelings for her were strong and enduring. For example, when Sophie left Grenoble for a short stay in Lyons in 1805, Philippine wrote to Sophie asking her to promise not to leave her alone in her struggle for spiritual progress. Sophie responded in April, 1805:

You know me very superficially if you need such a promise to count on. Our Lord, who gave you to us, has set no limits to this charge but that of death. Until then, if I can help you I

---

[45]*Correspondance*, pt. I, letter 21, p. 87; and see letter 68, p. 191.
[46]*Correspondance*, pt. I, letter 9, p. 32.

shall do so with all my heart. I do not belong to myself but to
you. Everyday shows me this more clearly, so no more fears
on that score. Read that sentence again, if you like, and never
come back on the matter. . . . [47]

When Sophie left Grenoble in 1805, Philippine felt her absence so
keenly that Sophie was compelled to reproach her for wanting the
"milk" of her novitiate days.[48] In the sentimental language reminiscent
of the nineteenth century, Philippine wrote to Sophie in April, 1806:

> It is well that I must wait a while for the pleasure of talking to
> you. . . . I would not like to have nuns knocking every in-
> stant at the door and wishing to speak to their Mother. I
> should want her all to myself.[49]

Although such language is not surprising in its nineteenth-century
context, it is evident that Philippine's affection for Sophie was colored
by a certain infatuation. Sophie saw that this might distract Philippine
from her love for God. For example, Philippine was jealous when she
was not chosen as Sophie's traveling companion to Poitiers in July,
1806. Sophie wrote to her three weeks later:

> Have you not said more than once since my departure:
> "Yes, Lord, you really had to deprive me of this friend
> whom I love in all truth for you, but who is, I admit, a
> human support. I must lean on you alone. Be, then, my one
> and only friend. I want no other since you are so good as to
> be content with me and even to seek so persistently the love
> of my poor heart."
> Of course, you have believed up to now that my bits of
> advice helped you and that no one else, perhaps, would take
> so keen an interest in correcting your faults or would put up
> with you, seeing how much patience and courage this calls
> for at times! Now, thank God, you realize that this is not
> true. . . .
> I have so great a desire that you should love your Jesus
> that I disregard myself; I only long to enkindle in your soul

---

[47]*Correspondance*, pt. I, letter 4, pp. 12–13.
[48]*Correspondance*, pt. I, letter 8, pp. 24–25.
[49]*Correspondance*, pt. I, letter 12, p. 46.

the confidence and love I myself should have for him, in order that you may love him for me. . . . Pray for me, but do not let your mind dwell on me for any other reason but this act of charity.[50]

Philippine even entered a long period of spiritual desolation after Sophie's second departure in July, 1806. Toward the close of 1807, she went so far as to request a transfer to Poitiers in order to receive spiritual direction again from Mother Barat. Sophie refused her request. In the spring of 1808, when another nun, Emilie Giraud, was transferred from Grenoble to Poitiers, Philippine once again had to struggle to overcome her feelings of being overlooked.[51] This, no doubt, was a contributing factor to a sharp disagreement between Philippine and Emilie, about which Philippine angrily wrote to Emilie shortly after the latter's departure.[52] Only in late 1808 did Philippine finally write to Sophie that she had overcome the pain of their separation.[53] When Philippine left for the New World in 1818, never to see her friend again, she had clearly grown beyond the "milk" of her novitiate days.

The disequilibrium marking this relationship, in which there was deep affection on both sides, is not altogether surprising. Sophie was an extraordinarily talented and charismatic figure. Her gifts allowed her to see into the character of the hundreds of women she counseled. She strengthened their gifts and helped free them from many less savory aspects of nineteenth-century spirituality, such as its undue negativity about the human condition and a sometimes vacuous sentimentality. Philippine's relationship with her was central to her own personal and spiritual growth. She continued to struggle with her own irascible temperament and her inordinate love of spiritual and corporal austerities. But Sophie had undoubtedly helped her mature into a freedom regarding such practices which Philippine might never have attained on her own. It is not surprising, then, that Sophie remained a key figure throughout Philippine's life. Their vast correspondence, marked by keen affection and mutual respect, broke down toward the close of their lives. In this later chapter of their friendship, to be

---

[50]*Correspondance*, pt. I, letter 14, pp. 51 and 54.

[51]See *Correspondance*, pt. I, letter 25, pp. 96–97; and letter 26, p. 99.

[52]See *Correspondance*, pt. I, letter 28, pp. 103–104.

[53]See *Correspondance*, pt. I, letter 29, p. 105. The subject is again raised in July, 1810; see letter 37, p. 127.

examined below, we will note again that their relationship was colored by a certain dependency on Philippine's part.

But the bond between the two women was more than just that of a "spiritual mother" and a "spiritual daughter," as they said in the nineteenth century. Sophie Barat recognized some of her own dreams and desires in the radical, other-centeredness that inspired Philippine. When Philippine shared with her superior her desire to be a missionary, Sophie not only approved enthusiastically, she identified with her. Mother Barat's responsibilities as superior of a fast-growing religious congregation had led her to the reluctant realization that she would never be able to realize her own missionary dreams.[54] Years later, as superior of thousands of religious on four continents, Sophie lived vicariously through Philippine and other friends her dream of being a missionary. The fact that each could participate in the joys and difficulties of the other throughout the better part of almost fifty years, usually far away from each other, is the truest testimony to their friendship.

---

[54]See *Correspondance*, pt. I, letter 9, pp. 28–31.

VI.

New Worlds, New Cultures

In 1815 Philippine was called to Paris to attend the order's Second General Council. Each of the now five houses in the Society was to send its superior and one representative to meet with the Mother General, Sophie Barat. Philippine, as the longest professed religious in her community, was designated by Mother Barat to represent the community of St. Marie.[1] She set off for what she thought would be a short trip to Paris. In fact, she would never see her hometown of Grenoble or her much-loved St. Marie again.

1. PARIS: PREPARATION FOR AMERICA

It had been two years since Philippine and Sophie had seen each other. In the interim, they had both been through trying times. Philippine had lost her father. Sophie, with the help of Varin, had been struggling against terrific odds to establish her fledgling congregation on a firm footing. In fact, since the two women had first met in 1804, the order had weathered several serious storms of internal division.

One of the Council's most important acts was its unanimous approval of the Constitutions. Joseph Varin had been working on these for years. It had required constant consultation and collaboration with Mother Barat to draw up a set of rules which captured the order's contemplative spirit, responded to the needs of its educational apostolate, and also suited the Church authorities who had the final word about approving the Constitutions. Philippine pointed out admiringly at this time the circumspection with which Varin, known for his au-

---

[1]de Charry, *Histoire des Constitutions*, pt. I, vol. I, p. 547; Hogg trans., *Formation of the Institute*, p. 388.

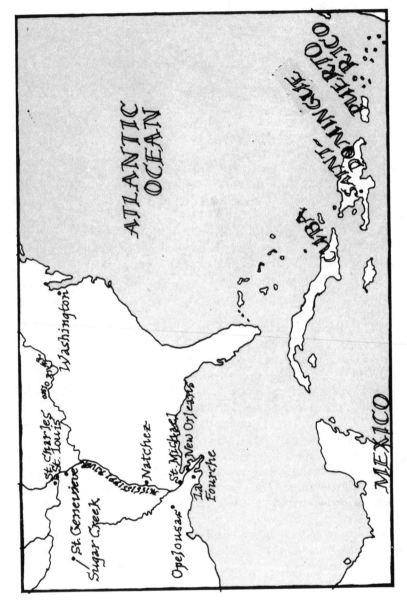

The Southeastern United States and Caribbean Islands of the time of Philippine Duchesne's arrival in the New World.

108

thoritarian, even imperious manner,[2] was able to relinquish formal authority over the order once the Council had accepted the Constitutions. The Superior General, Mother Barat, was left solely in charge, although Varin continued to exert a strong informal influence over the order through his contacts with her. Varin, along with Sophie's brother, Louis, had just become a member of the recently re-established Jesuits.

The Council also decided that the growing congregation needed to open a new house in Paris. It would be the residence for the Superior General and provide a central novitiate for all of the congregation's houses. They asked Philippine, known for the practical know-how with which she had managed repairs at St. Marie, to oversee the details. So after the Council closed in December, 1815, Philippine remained in Paris. She and two other religious set to work cleaning and repairing the house on Rue des Postes. The work was heavy and hard. It was a full three months before the place was habitable enough for them to move in on March 27. Within a few days, other sisters joined them, including Octavie Berthold, a novice from Grenoble who would later accompany Philippine to the New World. Even then, Philippine did not return to St. Marie. Rather, she became assistant and secretary to her friend, Mother Barat, and was treasurer both in the Paris house and for the general finances of the Society.

In spite of the joy this must have given her, Philippine was sad to leave the stability and prayerful solitude of the Grenoble monastery. She was a woman of strong attachments to places. The paradox noted earlier, feeling called both to the cloistered life of a Visitation monastery and to the mission frontiers of the New World, never entirely disappeared in Philippine's life. Although leaving places always took a high emotional toll on her, the life she chose was by nature filled with movement and departures. From Paris, she wrote her farewell to the community of Grenoble:

> . . . I am very tired of my worldly life [in Paris]. All the beauties of St. Sulpice are of less value to me than the quiet of our own chapels. I long for the day when we can secure a little corner for lodgings in our own little convent and I shall see no more of the streets of Paris.

---

[2]See de Charry, *Histoire des Constitutions*, pt.I, vol. I, p. 503; Hogg trans., *Formation of the Institute*, p. 357.

But lest we be too taken by Philippine's yearning for solitude from the streets of Paris, it is worth pointing out that she somehow managed to familiarize herself with all the well-known churches and places of pilgrimage in Paris before the rules of cloister were finally enforced! And even then, she continued to struggle with her constant desire for more solitude and her tendency to take on more work. Just a few years later, when Philippine arrived in America in 1818, she made an insightful comment regarding her activism in a letter to Sophie Barat:

> See how I reach out to many activities when I have not even a firm foothold yet; but desires are unruly when one realizes what needs there are. . . . [3]

Indeed, in Paris, at the same time she was writing letters about yearning for the "quiet of our own chapels," she was also pleading with Sophie Barat to send her to the New World. The streets of Paris would seem tame beside some of the scenes awaiting her on the American frontier.

Early in their relationship, Sophie Barat had enthusiastically encouraged Philippine to pursue a missionary vocation.[4] But she was too good an administrator to think that a struggling order could simply pack off a few nuns and set up shop in a new land. She was not swayed by Philippine's exuberant and impulsive pleas to be sent to "the heathen." To just such a demand in 1808 she replied:

> It is simply astonishing that a woman of upright intention and sane judgement like yourself could have concocted any such scheme, fixed her will on it, and then could believe it to be the will of God. What does it amount to? Simply abandoning a solid and lasting good to go in search of one that is uncertain. . . . [5]

But the situation of the congregation had changed by 1815. In Paris, Philippine continued to pester her superior about a foundation in the New World. In 1816, Sophie wrote to another friend in the order:

---

[3]The French edition of the correspondence between Philippine Duchesne and Sophie Barat after 1815 is soon to be published under the care of Jeanne de Charry. Where relevant, I will simply indicate the date of letters written after 1815.

[4]See de Charry, *Histoire des Constitutions*, pt. I, vol. II, "La Mère Barat raconte les débuts de la fondation de Grenoble," pp. 68–69.

[5]*Correspondance*, pt. I, letter 27, p. 101.

Can you believe it—Philippine is always thinking about her mission overseas, and my brother [Louis] has almost smoothed the way for her. In spite of the terror such a venture causes me, we shall, perhaps, see it carried out. I tremble to think of it. Pray about it, but do not talk about it, lest people get excited and lose their heads. We live in an age in which it does not take much to upset people.

In fact, Louis' intervention was key. Although he knew little about the missions, he was naturally disposed to favor Philippine's extreme inclinations. On his own initiative, he had contacted William Dubourg, the bishop of Louisiana in North America. The large diocese of "Louisiana" at that time extended from the Mississippi to the Rocky Mountains.[6] Dubourg, born in Saint-Domingue, had been raised in France. It was during a visit there in 1816 that he and Louis Barat met. Between them, without even consulting Mother Barat, they arranged that Philippine would go to work in Dubourg's vast diocese. Louis Barat's rather cavalier manner gave Philippine tremendous hope that the Mother General's will would be swayed. She was probably not offended in the least by his remark to her about the unsuitability of women for the missions:

Now you will need three generous religious to accompany you. But they must be great souls, and among women great souls are very rare. That thought may discourage you, but you have sighed so long a time for your savages and with such constancy, it is probable that God will make an exception in your case and not require you to be a wholly great soul.

Louis' meeting with Dubourg was indeed influential in starting a process. Within a few months, the bishop called on Mother Barat herself. He knew of Philippine's long desire to work with the Indians. In the territory of his own diocese, there were many Indians, but no one to work among them. He presented so convincing a case to Mother Barat that she accepted his invitation to send a group of her religious. They would begin their work in the burgeoning river town of St. Louis. Straightaway however, her chief advisors, including Varin, ral-

---

[6]John Rothensteiner, *History of the Archdiocese of St. Louis, In its Various Stages of Development from A.D. 1673 to A.D. 1928*, 2 vols. (St. Louis, Missouri: Blackwell Wielandy Co., 1928), vol. I, p. 249.

lied against the new foundation. For one, they claimed that Philippine
was too valuable to Sophie in Paris to leave her at this time. When the
naturally temperamental Dubourg returned to meet with Mother Barat
in May, 1817, he was understandably chagrined and angry to learn that
she had changed her mind. Just this once, Philippine's impetuosity
played to her advantage. She boldly interrupted their conversation,
knelt dramatically with clasped hands before her friend Sophie and
begged her to let her go. The Mother General paused, reflected a
moment and finally acquiesced. She told Philippine that she would
begin at once the search for other religious to go with her.

Philippine began immediately to prepare for the journey, a most
complicated affair in the early nineteenth century. She studied English, little aware of the obstacle it would be for her throughout her
life. There were financial matters to be settled with her family. Her
vow of poverty meant that she relinquished final authority over reve-
nues from her inheritances, but she still had to regularize how these
funds would be transferred to the Society, or to her relatives when the
congregation felt their need was greater. In fact, the money from her
inheritances and other gifts made by her wealthy relatives proved a
significant source of income for the Society both in France and later in
America.

Provisions for the journey, which in those days could easily last
two or three months, were another matter. This was a one-way trip.
There would be no hotel or friend's home awaiting them on the other
side of the ocean. Like emigrants before them, they faced the harsh
task of deciding what to take with them and what to leave behind in
starting their new life. There were the obvious necessities such as
clothing and household supplies, but also seeds for sowing, religious
books and objects for their personal use and missionary work, and an
unending list of items unavailable on the American frontier. Exteriorly,
Philippine was as busy as ever during the next eight months. Her loyal
friend and cousin Josephine helped in every way possible, using her
influence to obtain their passports, running countless errands and generously acquiring provisions for the nuns.

Interiorly, Philippine, now forty-eight years old, was adjusting to
the prospects of beginning a whole new life. Setting out for America
was more than an adventure. It was the fulfillment of a lifelong dream.
Neither the grace nor the gravity of the moment escaped her:

> Ordinarily [God] gives one outstanding grace to a soul, and
> this becomes the source of many others. In my case that
> signal grace was my return to St. Marie and membership in

the blessed Society of the Sacred Heart. This was far beyond anything I had hoped for. And still—in spite of the fact that I have profited so poorly by all the instructions and the examples of solid and sublime virtue I have received—still God in His goodness is opening to me a new career that calls forth all my gratitude and overwhelms me with confusion when I think of it.

But new beginnings imply endings. The arduous process of saying good-bye had a special poignancy in this woman who so loved specific people and places. Her farewell letter to the nuns at St. Marie, with whom she had lived for over ten years, is revelatory of both her rougher edges and her exaggerated self-effacement:

When I look into my own soul, I cannot find any reason for expecting you to remember me. I know full well that I deserve to be forgotten, and I really ought to desire this very thing. For if you remember me, you must inevitably recall all the faults I committed—faults that were prejudicial to an institution for which I would willingly give my life, faults I repent of most sincerely. But when I think about the charity which is the bond of union in our holy Society, I am not surprised at your thoughtfulness, and I beg you to add this kindness—pardon for all my past faults and prayers that I may avoid such conduct in the future. You must be as merciful to me as God Himself is.

Paradoxically, only the radical choice of leaving everything and everyone she had ever loved behind her could adequately satisfy her need to express her love. The strength of her conviction diminished the sorrow of these months. In the midst of her complicated preparations and her feelings of loss, she experienced an uncharacteristic inner peace and at-oneness. She expressed her conflicting sentiments in a farewell letter to her sister Amélie:

I know your heart well enough to realize that my going would cause you sorrow, but I was also sure enough of your courage and faith and of the judgement you would pass on the motives that inspire me. . . . I also knew that my decision to go to America would not alter in the least the tender intimacy with you that has been a joy in my life and now adds to the costliness of my sacrifice. Surely, exposing one-

self to danger is nothing in comparison with giving up a
tender and holy friendship. But no—that friendship will continue, will even grow stronger and increase just because of
the detachment, and God, who is always generous, will give
us graces that will make its value infinite. My prayers will be
with you always, and if God blesses my efforts, you and your
family will have a large share in the work of our inspiring
mission. God has drawn me to it through years of attraction
and has granted me this great grace after many, many
prayers. In bringing it about, the guidance of Divine Providence is evident in so admirable a manner that all holy souls
see in it the finger of God.
. . . . Now good-bye, my dear Sister. Our friendship is
too strong to be affected by distance. I shall always love you
tenderly.

And to Josephine she wrote:

When my thoughts revert to what I am leaving in France —
all that is dear to me—I put them aside, being intimately
convinced that, as I have desired only one thing—to answer
God's call and abandon myself to His Providence—so the
voyage and the trials ahead will never be as great as the help I
may confidently expect from Him.

2. THE VOYAGE

Philippine left Paris with three other religious on February 8,
1818. Her traveling companions and fellow missioners were Octavie
Berthold, thirty years old, a Swiss convert whom Philippine had
known both as a postulant at St. Marie and then as a novice in Paris;
Eugénie Audé, twenty-six, another young religious Philippine had
known in the Parisian novitiate;[7] and Catherine Lamarre, forty, a religious from the Society's convent in Cuignières, founded in 1808. The
little group would pick up their fifth member, Marguerite Manteau,
also forty, at the convent founded in Poitiers in 1806, on their way to
the Bordeaux seaport.

---

[7]See Ruth Cunningham, *The Untold Story: Eugénie Audé, R.S.C.J.* (1986, published pri-
vately), for an account of Eugénie Audé's life.

Present to see Philippine off were many of her relatives, Father Varin, Mother Barat and a number of other religious dear to her. Always projecting a strong exterior in times of sorrow, Philippine managed to control her emotions as she parted company forever from the people she loved. One of the nuns present at the farewell scene described it several days later in her journal:

> The moment of separation was very painful for us all. As for Mother Duchesne, she did not shed a tear, though we know how deeply she felt it all; for she is naturally so affectionate. Seeing Mother Octavie crying as she said good-bye . . . Mother Duchesne took her gently by the arm and led her out of the house. The carriage was waiting and there was no time to lose.[8]

The five religious had been chosen carefully for the new foundation. Philippine, Octavie Berthold and Eugénie Audé were all "choir religious," and addressed formally as "Mother," while Catherine Lamarre and Marguerite Manteau were "coadjutrix sisters" and addressed as "Sister." Choir religious at this time were charged with the teaching duties in the schools and assumed all the governing roles in the congregation, while the sisters usually dedicated themselves to the important practical tasks involved in managing the schools and convents. Catherine Lamarre and Marguerite Manteau additionally had experience teaching at the primary level. The mix of skills was important to the group's success in the New World, but the peculiarity of this system merits further comment.

Although many women who entered religious orders felt a vocation specifically to one of these two roles, the distinction was based also on social class. Women who entered with more education were usually accepted as choir religious and those who entered with less were assigned as sisters. These distinctions often reflected the nuns' economic backgrounds rather than their innate talents as teacher or cook. In these early years of the Society, aptitude rather than social background sometimes dictated the assignment of someone as either a choir religious or a sister. But social and educational background were also factors and they assumed ever greater importance as the Society grew.

---

[8]*Relation du 16 février* (Paris, 1818). Religious of the Sacred Heart Archives, Amiens, France.

Increasingly, the coadjutrix sisters represented a kind of servant class within religious life.

To a certain extent, religious life mirrored the class structure of society in general. In the nineteenth century, such a two-tiered system was generally taken for granted and accepted without question in Europe. Philippine, in fact, was surprised upon reaching America to find that some people there found the division distasteful. A few years later, Sophie Barat wrote to Eugénie Audé about two "ladies," meaning choir religious, and one "sister" that she was sending to join the nuns in America. The sister, she added, "is a gem: she will be of as much use to you as a lady."[9] Nor does it escape the eyes of modern readers how often choir religious are referred to in the correspondence individually by name while the sisters are designated collectively as simply "the sisters." Such practices and social attitudes are reflections of the period's biases.

In the journey to the American frontier, there is no doubt that the balance struck between Mothers Duchesne, Berthold and Audé and Sisters Lamarre and Manteau was vitally important to the congregation's success. The practical know-how of Sisters Lamarre and Manteau, in addition to their experience with younger children, mentioned but sporadically in the sources for this book, were invaluable assets on the frontier. It is obvious in retrospect that the same healthy mix of talents and personalities could have been achieved without such a two-tiered system, a system abolished only in 1964, long after it had outlived its original purpose.[10]

Philippine received a personally difficult blow, one she should have expected, just before her departure. Mother Barat designated her superior of the group. Philippine was true to character when she received the obedience. One of the nuns present recorded:

On the eve of the departure, our Mother General assembled us all and gave Mother Duchesne her obedience as superior of the mission band. She dreaded this office and believed she would never be able to bear it. She certainly had not foreseen, when begging for the foundation, that she would be placed at its head. She submitted to the burden, however,

---

[9]February 1, 1826.
[10]On this topic, see Sadoux and Gervaise, *Vie religieuse*, pp. 245–49.

realizing, no doubt, that it would offer her more opportunities for suffering.[11]

Sophie Barat was just as true to her own character, however, in adding her own advice about Philippine's opportunities for suffering. She urged her to accept the penance of her own new life circumstances rather than seeking out others. Sophie wrote to Philippine after her departure from Paris, but before she had arrived at Bordeaux:

> Now, my dear daughter, enter more and more fully into the designs of our loving Lord. Try to grow each day more worthy of His work by laying a deeper foundation of humility in your soul, for out of this will spring gentleness and forbearance with the souls entrusted to you. I am happy about your love for them, and I know you will do all in your power to lessen the sacrifice they have made. . . .
>   Take care of your health. The hard penance of the position of superior, which you have always dreaded so much, must replace all other penances. . . .

Aware of the difficulties of governing a religious community from overseas, Mother Barat also gave Philippine many of the powers which would normally belong only to the Mother General. Philippine would be able to make new foundations, receive women wishing to enter the congregation, determine the work of each nun and dismiss those found unsuitable to the Society's mission. As clear as this mandate seemed, however, Philippine was often hampered in her governing of the communities in the New World. As subsequent chapters will show, a variety of factors account for this. They include Philippine's own governing style, the character of some of the religious in the New World, the intervention of bishops and other ecclesiastical authorities, and Sophie Barat's continuing involvement in the new foundations from her post in France.

The group arrived in Bordeaux on February 13, 1818. Since rough seas delayed their departure, they decided to make a directed retreat with Louis Barat who was in Bordeaux at the time. Philippine found herself in desolation, beset by fear as she launched into the unknown. She wrote to Sophie Barat:

---

[11]*Relation du 16 février.*

Although God sustains my courage and even the intensity of my desires, still, when I arrived here, my soul was in a state of anguish, hard and dark. . . . My companions, too, have had their moments of weakness. I realized this and tried to be of help to them, knowing full well my own wretchedness. All this only makes it seem more astonishing that God in His goodness should have made choice of us.

And lest we think that saints easily find their way out of such spiritual difficulties, she wrote to Sophie later in the same retreat:

We are all steadfast in our resolutions, but God has begun sending us trials. The retreat goes rather badly. I am hard as flint. My head is in a whirl. You can have no idea of the many details and anxieties connected with a trip of this kind—they never end.

They finally set sail on March 21, 1818. The desolation that Philippine felt lasted the entire seventy-day voyage. She was physically exhausted, depressed by the dreaded duty of being superior, and tried by the vicissitudes of sailing the high seas. Once during their voyage, they were stopped by a pirate ship from Buenos Aires, but on learning that the ship was American, the pirates allowed them to sail on unmolested. Philippine wrote the following graphic account to Sophie Barat toward the end of their long voyage:

We are nearing the end of our journey in fairly good health. As it is summer, we are able to sail the whole length of the coast of Cuba. . . .
    For fifty-two days we saw only sea and sky. It was May 11 before we actually caught sight of land in the distance, the island of Caicos, one of the Lucayas belonging to England [at the southeast end of the Bahamas chain]. . . . There was great rejoicing on board at the sight of that Lucaya island, for land is far more attractive than the sea.
    The ocean holds such terrors at times that I was more than once on the verge of writing to beg you not to send another person out here until you received assurance that all is well with us and that such a sacrifice would be of real worth. . . . I am thoroughly convinced now that people who have been to Louisiana [the Mississippi Valley] generally speak only of what is attractive, lest they should discourage

anyone from going there, and that is Father Martial's [Dubourg's vicar-general, traveling with the nuns] line of conduct. But I owe you the truth, and I shall not hide from you either the perils of the sea or my own cowardice.

A storm at sea is really a terrifying sight. The roaring of the deep mingled with the crash of the tempest would drown both thunder and the booming of cannon. Add to this ear-splitting din the rolling of the vessel in the midst of great waves. The shouting of the sailors as they encourage themselves at their work has a tragic, a lugubrious effect. But their silence is even more dismal, and still worse is the sight of the captain pacing the deck in deep thought. A vessel tossed violently in an angry sea gives one some idea of the confusion of Judgement Day. The sky and the stars seem to disappear suddenly behind mountains of water. The sea, nearly black during the storm, gapes wide, revealing its bottomless depths, then suddenly closes. The waves sweep over the deck and are hurled out to sea with a new rolling of the boat. Twice during the night the high waves burst open the portholes and flooded our berths. The bending masts, the sails furled or torn, the steering wheel abandoned, lest the boat be too strained—all this is very terrifying unless one sees God in the storm.

The odor that permeates the whole ship is another trial, the confinement, the stench from the hold that is so nauseating and that can be avoided only by going on deck for fresh air—and one cannot always go there, especially in bad weather or when the sun is very hot. At night men sleep there; in the morning they are getting up. Besides, we cannot leave our little holes too early because people dress in the common room.

But if I have realized regretfully that many of our nuns could not endure the terrors of the sea, I have lamented still more over the great number who could not survive the stifling atmosphere of the cabins, the hard, narrow berths, the continual noise. In addition to the handling of the rigging and cordage, which often goes on at night, there is loud talking as if it were daytime. Eating and drinking go on in the common room, where two of us sleep [Philippine and Marguerite Manteau] and which adjoins the cabin occupied by the other three.

Seasickness is a wretched malady, affecting both stomach and head. One is utterly good for nothing; connected thought is impossible. One can scarcely drag from one's dull heart the least little prayer of love. I could only repeat the "*Ita, Pater,*" and "My God, I have left all things for You." And if in this condition one asks for a little water to drink or a cup of tea, it is often brought five or six hours later. If one can take only broth, what they bring is made from cabbage and is covered with grease, and sometimes it is made from spoiled meat. It is a mistake to say one should eat when one is sea-sick. For several days I could take only a little broth once or twice in twenty-four hours, and this only if I remained flat on my back, but I was quite well after that. Eugénie [Audé] and Marguerite [Manteau] were either more courageous or in better condition for the trip, for they have suffered less from this illness. For two or three days we were all so ill, we could not help each other at all, and the steward had to take care of us. . . .

The ship made its way through the gulf of Mexico toward the mouth of the Mississippi and their landing destination in New Orleans. The nuns were fascinated by the sights of this new world, fireflies and foliage unlike that of their native France, huge rocks crowding the channel and even a few crocodiles. They saw sweeping southern plantations with their majestic homes and the black slaves whose labor made such wealth possible. Eugénie Audé gives a moving account of the nuns' landing in America on May 29, 1818, which was, coincidentally, the feast of the Sacred Heart that year:

It was with the deepest emotion that we set foot on this soil which is for us, in the eyes of faith and the designs of God, the Promised Land. Mother Duchesne's heart could not contain its sentiments of gratitude. In spite of the marshy ground she knelt and kissed the very soil. Her eyes were wet with tears, tears of joy, the kind Father Varin desired for us. "No one is looking," she whispered to us. "You kiss it, too." If only you could have seen her face! It was radiant with joy. . . .

Philippine and her companions stayed in an Ursuline convent for their first six weeks in the New World. As she approached the convent, she saw Indians for the first time. It gave her an idea of the condition to which they had been reduced by the arrival of Europeans. They were begging. Philippine offered them something and noted that despite the sadness of their faces, they still showed strength.

The Ursuline nuns could not have been more gracious to the newly-arrived religious. They nursed Philippine through an illness which, out of self-mortification, she had been keeping to herself. The doctor thought it was scurvy, although Philippine disputed this. But more trying and boding ill for the future was the fact that she received no letters from Bishop Dubourg. And she heard that their school was not, as agreed upon in Paris, to be in St. Louis at all. She learned this from Mr. John Mullanphy, a rich man from the St. Louis area passing through New Orleans, and someone into whose unhappy debt she would fall on several occasions in the future.

The religious departed New Orleans on the steamboat *Franklin* on July 12, 1818, six weeks after their arrival. The trip by steamboat up the Mississippi cost about one hundred dollars per person, an enormous sum in those days. The Ursuline sisters insisted on paying it as their contribution to the new foundation. The dangers attached to river travel at this time ran the gamut from bursting boilers to epidemics that decimated the ranks of the passengers. But Philippine and her companions survived the forty-day journey without incident. On August 21, 1818, they arrived in St. Louis.

3. THE FIRST FOUNDATION: FROM ST. LOUIS TO ST. CHARLES

The town of St. Louis had been founded in 1764 by Pierre Laclede. In 1818, it was still just a frontier trading post, consisting of four long streets surrounded by farms and prairies. But its location at the confluence of the Missouri and Mississippi rivers made it an attractive location for settlers. Its population was less than 4,500 when Philippine arrived.[12] Just two years later, after bitter controversy, the territory of Missouri was admitted into the Union as a slave state.

Philippine had still not heard from Dubourg when they landed in his city. He told her he had indeed written to her on June 24, that is, about four weeks after the nuns' arrival in New Orleans. But the letter

---

[12]James Primm, *The Lion of the Valley* (Boulder, Colorado: Pruett Publishing Co., 1981), p. 107. I am grateful to Carol S. Verble of the Missouri Historical Society for this reference. See also George R. Brooks, "St. Louis in 1818," in *Philippine Duchesne and Her Times* (St. Louis, Missouri: Maryville College, 1968), pp. 1–12.

had not reached them. Dubourg had been expecting them in St. Louis and arranged for them to stay temporarily with a French Catholic family whose home was on Main Street. The couple, General Pratte and Émilie Labbadie, would be among a number of St. Louisans to befriend the nuns and help them during subsequent years.

Philippine's fears about not remaining in St. Louis were soon confirmed in her conversations with the bishop. He had decided since their agreement in Paris that they would start a school in St. Charles, a village about twenty miles from St. Louis on the other side of the Missouri River. Philippine contested this choice. On her side were a number of St. Louisans who highly respected the education offered by the Religious of the Sacred Heart in France and wanted such a school for their own children on the frontier. The bishop would hear nothing of it. He also rejected Philippine's request to found a school in St. Genevieve, a town near St. Louis which the nuns had visited on their trip up the Mississippi. When the bishop offered Florissant as a compromise solution, it was Philippine who said no. Building prices were exorbitant there and the population was sparse, making it an even less attractive choice than St. Charles.

But worst of all and also contrary to their agreement in Paris, the religious were not to work among the Indians. Dubourg had decided that the education of the English-speaking American children and French-speaking Creole children was more important. Philippine submitted to his will and, on September 7, she and her four companions reluctantly set out for St. Charles. In her first letter to Sophie Barat from St. Charles on August 31, 1818, she referred to the village as "a tomb in which [the] enterprise for the Society would be buried." Mother Barat was also chagrined at the bishop's decision:

> We cannot help regretting that your bishop has put you in a place so unsuited to our purpose. He should have gotten you a house in St. Louis as he promised.[13]

This was but the first of many disappointments which would mark her life in the New World.

The village of St. Charles, Missouri had been founded as a trading place of Indians and white men in 1769, the year of Philippine's birth. It lay twenty miles northwest of St. Louis on a high bluff overlooking the Missouri river. Dubourg argued that it would become one of the

---

[13]July 9, 1819; quoted in Cunningham, *Eugénie Audé*, p. 23, and see p. 24.

most important cities in North America, serving as a center not only of American trade, but of world trade. Although Philippine saw it as the most remote of all the places she had seen on the frontier, she painted a tactful picture of the bishop's decision in a letter to Sophie Barat on September 12, 1818, just a few days after her arrival:

> Having made the rounds, either in spirit or in person, of St. Louis, St. Genevieve, Florissant, and St. Charles, we are now settling down in the last named place, which seems to put us as far away from you as is possible in America, because of the many halts and detours one must make in order to get here. Bishop Dubourg, who looks very far into the future, considers this place quite important, as it is the largest village on the Missouri, about twenty miles from its junction with the Mississippi. American settlers from the eastern states are constantly pouring into this section of the country—restless people, who hope St. Charles will become a great commercial link between the United States and China, for the Upper Missouri rises not far from another river that pours its waters into the Pacific Ocean at a place where the crossing to Asia takes just two weeks.

Philippine, like so many other European immigrants, shared Dubourg's ignorance of American geography. St. Charles is situated well in the eastern half of the United States. The seemingly convenient river trip to which she referred would involve over four thousand miles of travel on three rivers, the Missouri, the Snake and the Columbia, in addition to some overland travel! As to the distance to Asia, if her own voyage from Europe took her seventy days, one could hardly count on a two-week trip from the western coast of America to Asia.

Their first lodging in St. Charles was a home they rented, at a rather high price, from Marie Louise Beauvais Duquette. It measured about twenty-eight by thirty-eight feet and consisted of one large room with three small rooms on each side. Their new home served as their sleeping quarters, common room, kitchen, chapel and school. One of Philippine's first acts was to install a picture of St. Francis Regis, the French missionary and preacher to whom she had entrusted the welfare of St. Marie and her mission to the New World. At this point, she was still able to keep her promise to him. In fact, she wrote to Sophie Barat to remind her of the novena of masses which had to be offered at the saint's shrine in La Louvesc.

Just one week after the nuns' arrival in St. Charles, the religious opened the first free school west of the Mississippi. Within just a few more weeks, they had opened yet two more schools, a day school for girls able to pay about three dollars a month, and a boarding school for girls from wealthy St. Louis families. The boarding school opened with just three boarders. They lodged with the five religious in their already cramped quarters. The education was elementary, adapted to each group's needs, and included reading, writing, counting and, of course, the foundations of Christianity. In just a month the free school had over twenty children. Not surprisingly, Philippine herself took charge of it, leaving Mothers Audé and Berthold each at the head of the other two schools.

The first year at St. Charles was an exacting trial for the nuns. They supported themselves from the income of their boarding and day schools. But the boarders were few and the fees the religious charged in the day school were insignificant. The only "prosperous" aspect of their work was the size of the free school. Besides running three separate schools, the five nuns had to occupy themselves with myriad other chores facing settlers on the frontier. They dug a garden, gathered and carried manure to fertilize it, watered their one cow and cleaned its stable.

Philippine's biographers have made a good deal of the physical hardships the nuns endured on the frontier. They have drawn in part on Philippine's own accounts in constructing their narratives. In her letters to friends and relatives in France, she speaks of the scarcity of eggs, butter, fruit, vegetables, oil and even bread. In a particularly well-known passage, she complained also of the cold. In mid-December she wrote:

The Missouri is almost frozen over, and it is so cold that the water freezes beside the fire, as does the laundered linen hung there to dry. Neither doors nor windows close tight, and no one here knows how to make a foot warmer; besides, it would cost at least twenty-five or thirty francs.[14] A little stove cost us 250 francs. We have logs, but they are too large, and there is no one to chop them for us and no saw with which we might cut them ourselves.

---

[14]During most of Philippine's life, five French francs were worth about one United States dollar of the same period.

There is no doubt that Philippine and the other nuns suffered in St. Charles. It should be kept in mind, however, that her perspective was that of a French woman accustomed to a well-heated home, relatively plentiful food even in the convent and domestic help. Their home in St. Charles had fireplaces, which was the typical source of heat for most settlers. In fact, as harsh as her life on the frontier was, it was no harsher than that endured by many of her neighbors. The nuns' home was comparable in size. Their work around the house and in the garden was not more than was expected of most pioneer women. Indeed, it was less than that borne by many.[15]

Biographers of saints, moreover, have a tendency to emphasize the sufferings and sacrifices endured by their subjects. So it is worth noting that Philippine herself, in her letter of February 15, 1819, to Sophie Barat, remarked that that first winter in St. Charles was a gentle one. The Reverend Mr. Salmon Giddings, a contemporary of Philippine's and founder of the First Presbyterian Church in St. Louis, left an even more precise description of that winter:

> The winter of 1818–19 was very mild and exhibited a singular contrast with the two or three preceding. The mean temperature of January was nearly thirty-nine degrees: the weather continued mild during the month of February and the thermometer on some days rose to seventy-two degrees. At St. Louis, the Mississippi remained open during the whole season.[16]

This account of the relative mildness of that first winter in no way detracts from Philippine's own report of a December day in St. Charles when the laundry froze. It is rather a reminder of the ease with which the stereotypical "saintly" experiences of great figures can be exaggerated. In the process, the lives of saints become removed from the context of ordinary human life. The physical hardships Philippine endured on the American frontier were genuine trials—trials she suf-

---

[15]Fascinating accounts of pioneer women can be consulted in Joanna L. Stratton, *Pioneer Women: Voices from the Kansas Frontier* (New York: Simon and Schuster, 1981); see especially pp. 57–76 on the workload of pioneer women.

[16]Louis C[aleb] Beck, *A Gazeteer of the States of Illinois and Missouri* (Albany: Charles R.and George Webster, 1823; reprint New York: Arno Press, 1975), pp. 199–200. I am grateful to Carol S. Verble of the Missouri Historical Society for this reference. See Stratton, *Pioneer Women: Voices from the Kansas Frontier*, pp. 89–106, on settlers' experiences with the seasonal adversities of midwestern North America.

fered along with thousands of other settlers. She and her companions suffered from shortages of food, an overload of work and an intensity of cold to which they were unaccustomed. France, with its quiet chapels and familiar customs, was but a memory for Philippine now.

4. CULTURAL DIFFERENCES AND RACIAL PREJUDICE

There were other difficult realities trying Philippine and her sisters in America. First was the loneliness of being in a new culture. Philippine depended on letters for her personal support, but the voyage between Europe and America could easily take three to six months, meaning that an exchange of letters sometimes took up to a full year. The distance separating her from Josephine, Sophie Barat and other significant friends was not merely spatial then, but temporal as well.

She was also confounded by the new language. Dubourg had once remarked that learning English would be an impossibility for anyone fifty years of age or older.[17] Philippine was proving his point in her own person. Although the majority of the children in the poor school at St. Charles were Creole and all knew French, there was no escaping the necessity of knowing English. Shortly after their arrival in St. Charles, Philippine wrote:

> We have just received our first postulant, Mary Mullen. . . .
> She understands only English, and I despair of ever speaking to her or of really understanding her. To read English and understand what one reads is not so difficult, but the pronunciation staggers me.

Moreover, with the passing of years, English gradually overtook this area of the New World and became the dominant, and essential, idiom. Philippine's inability to master it proved a painful liability throughout her life. The two younger choir religious, Eugénie Audé and Octavie Berthold, were both more able in this area.

They were also, evidently, more naturally attractive personalities to Dubourg, the children in the school and their parents. Philippine is ever the rugged realist in these matters. She recognized and accepted her limitations without losing herself in self-pity. She never considered giving up and going back to France. Her single-minded determination,

---

[17]See letter of Philippine Duchesne to Sophie Barat, August 31, 1818.

combined with her tendency to think little of herself, simply led her to search for tasks she felt were more suited to her abilities. During their first year in St. Charles in 1819, she wrote in letters to Mother Barat:

Knowledge of English is bringing Mother Octavie forward. The Americans are quite proud of her. Their national pride seems to make them scorn those who do not speak their language, so English is a real necessity. I simply despair of ever speaking it. Eugénie hesitates, too, but she has enough to do with the French-speaking children. She is venerated by them. From all this you will realize that God has not bestowed on us the gift of tongues. Perhaps He wants His missionary nuns to sanctify themselves on failure.

As to Octavie and Eugénie, they are running in the way of perfection, and the little good we accomplish is due to them. In them you will have two superiors, and if you cannot replace me by an English-speaking religious, Octavie could take my place. We shall soon have more American children than French-speaking Creoles. What good am I without a fluent use of English? I feel this with our postulant. For her good and that of the others I would gladly see myself in the lowest employment in the house. What is more, you know me. The nuns are afraid of me, and a superior should put everyone completely at her ease. . . .

Equally as important as the language was comprehension of the new culture, or cultures, which Philippine met in America. She was just beginning to catch on to the "idiosyncrasies" of her new world, such as the egalitarian spirit of the frontier inhabitants. She wrote to Sophie Barat regarding the free school that the nuns had to "be careful not to call this a 'poor school,' for that hurts the feelings of the parents and keeps the children away." The phrase was commonly employed, apparently with less offence, in France. Philippine also asked permission to accept small payments from parents who otherwise would not allow their daughters to attend the free school. In 1828, almost ten years after her arrival, Philippine was still mystified by the egalitarian bent she found among settlers. Referring to the tiered system of education which the Society of the Sacred Heart employed, she observed that it was "repugnant to the American spirit to have two different class regimes in the same institution." Ever a French woman, Philippine continued to reflect many of the assumptions of her own social class.

But lest the theme of egalitarianism in America be over-enlarged, Philippine was also getting her first taste of another reality on the American frontier—racism. References to "Creoles," "Americans," "negroes," "mulattoes," "mestizos" and "savages" punctuate her letters back to France. Philippine's curiosity as to the divisions among racial groups on the frontier indicates that these particular prejudices were foreign to her own experience. In one of her first letters back to France, written from New Orleans, she comments on her shock at the patent prejudice against blacks on the American frontier. When she realized that one of her own religious sisters was ready to adopt this racial bias, Philippine was furious. In a passage which, curiously, has not heretofore been published, she wrote on June 7, 1818:

> Here is a quite astonishing incident, one which has indeed moved me. These ladies [the Ursulines of New Orleans] wanted to have all our laundry done at their own expense and by their Negresses in order to help us in every way possible. I had Catherine [Lamarre] do just the soaping. She was doing the wash in the same shed [as the Negresses]. After several quarrels, she came to tell me that she did not like being with these Negresses, and that here the whites did not mix with them. I answered her that they have the same soul as she; that they have been redeemed by the same blood and received into the same Church; and in view of the fact that she and we had come for the Blacks, that if she did not want to keep company with them, it would be well to avail herself of the ships about to return.[18]

Alongside many Europeans of a similar background, Philippine's attitudes about blacks were certainly benign.

Another letter, written October 8, 1818, shortly after her arrival in St. Charles, again reveals her curiosity about racial differences in America. In this letter, she evidently acquiesces in the conventions of prejudice in the New World:

---

[18]Religious of the Sacred Heart Archives, Rome, Italy. I am grateful to Sisters Jeanne de Charry and Maureen Aggeler for this reference. My translation of this and subsequent letters retains the capitalization of the French transcriptions.

[St. Charles] is situated on the Missouri, which is frequented only by those trading with the Indians who live not very far away from here, but I have not seen any little savage girls since we came here, only a mestizo girl who is promised to us as a domestic or postulant, according to her aptitudes. Against this race there is not the same prejudice as there is against negroes and mulattoes. Bishop Dubourg has said positively that we may not admit them to the boarding school or free school, and he has appointed a separate day for the instruction of the colored people; otherwise, he says, we should not hold the white children in school were we to admit the others. He told us of an experience he had in the college in Baltimore, which shows that prejudice against people of color cannot be overcome in this country. He consulted the Archbishop of Baltimore on the matter and was told that this prejudice would have to be maintained as the last safeguard of morality and manners in this country.[19]

Dubourg's and Philippine's feelings regarding the propriety of interracial contacts are, in light of the last line quoted above, ambiguous. Philippine lacked abolitionist sensitivity: she played no role at all in the burgeoning anti-slavery movement, a movement in which prominent Catholics were conspicuously absent even during the Civil War. Her numerous remarks regarding the Indians, "the savages" as she frequently called them, are tinged by the superiority Christian missionaries subtly betrayed in their attempts "to civilize" native Americans. Often in her letters, Philippine commented on the specific strengths and weaknesses she perceived in each of the many racial groups populating this new country and her remarks often concluded with rather sweeping generalizations.

Such comments must be placed not only in their nineteenth-century context, but also in the context of all her writings and her actual deeds regarding these groups. For example, she once observed of mestizos that they "seem to inherit the worst faults of both Indian and white parents." Although Dubourg told her not to accept them in the schools, a few mestizo children were admitted to the school in St. Charles and other schools later founded by the congregation. Several

---

[19]This adapted translation is based on Callan, *Philippine Duchesne*, p. 277, but corresponds more closely to the original French. See also Philippine's letter to Sophie Barat of February 15, 1819.

mestizo women entered the congregation itself and Philippine would have been happy to receive Indian girls too, had there been any vocations. Years later in the convent in St. Louis, Philippine opened a special Sunday school for mulatto girls who were otherwise excluded from the schools.

But perhaps the most illustrative examples of Philippine's moderately progressive position vis-à-vis women of color are her attempts to associate them with the Society of the Sacred Heart. Soon after her arrival in America, she suggested that a type of third order be formed, which would be open to black women wishing to enter religious life. She wrote to Sophie Barat on November 28, 1819:

> A holy and wise ecclesiastic from New Orleans presented several young men of color, skilled craftsmen, to form a sort of third order attached to the order of the gentlemen of St. Lazarus. He has had the bishop make a similar proposal to us regarding some girls of color who wish to enter religious life. It seems to me that the rank of commissionary sisters could suit them perfectly, and, with this title, they could render services just as important as the lay sisters, who will be difficult to find among the whites, all being equal here, and with our two good sisters [Lamarre and Manteau] growing old.[20]

Philippine's readiness to accept blacks into the Society apparently surprised no one who knew her. A full year earlier on November 19, 1818, Sophie Barat felt it important enough to raise the issue, forbidding Philippine to mix blacks and whites in either the schools or the order itself:

> Do not be so foolish as to mix the whites with the blacks: you won't have any more students. The same goes for yourselves: no one will enter the order if you accept black subjects among the novices. We'll see what we can do for them. The important thing is that you win confidence in the beginning and thereby draw to yourselves both subjects and students.[21]

---

[20]Translation mine.

[21]Translation mine. On August 6, 1825, Sophie Barat responded to Eugénie Audé's request regarding the "admission of a negress for the cookery" as follows: "I permit it [since] it seems to be a necessity."

In light of the prohibitions of both Dubourg and Barat, it is at least plausible that Philippine had entertained the notion of mixing the races both in the schools and the order itself. But the incorporation of black women into the Society as "commissionary sisters"[22] or under any other terms never became a reality in her lifetime. She did occasionally ponder the issue. In 1830, she wrote to Joseph Rosati, then bishop of St. Louis:

> We had a visit recently from one of our mulattoes from St. Ferdinand [a school the nuns had opened]. She longs with her whole heart to enter with us, but we may not accept her as a religious. This has suggested to me the idea of offering our house out there for the use of colored girls, either like the Sisters of St. Martha or like the St. Michael nuns in Paris, who were founded for girls whose parents complained of them. Many of these girls, being strongly urged by grace, wanted to become nuns. A very edifying community was established for them, having its own rule, but occupying a separate building within the same enclosure. Could not we, too, gather together colored girls who want to leave this world and set aside for them one or two of our own nuns until they would be able to continue on their own as a community or congregation according to their special calling?

Philippine's concerned remarks and attitudes regarding people of color also reflected the worldview of many well-to-do French immigrants. They took for granted a certain social hierarchy which separated classes, and in this case races. It would not occur to them to criticize the lack of social mobility available to groups lower in the given hierarchy.

Her comments regarding blacks, made with reference to the nuns' need to hire servants, are a case in point. The nuns sorely needed domestic help if they were to manage three schools including a boarding school. Yet servants for hire were practically unavailable on the frontier. The white settlers and the few free blacks refused outright such work, a fact which baffled the French Mother Duchesne. She

---

[22]There were white "commissionary sisters" loosely associated with the order. These women made a promise of obedience and took care of many of the tasks outside of the convent on behalf of the cloistered religious. I am grateful to Sr. Marie Louise Martinez for this information.

attributed the settlers' reluctance to work as servants to their "false pride." In fact, as Benjamin Rush, a Philadelphia physician, professor and one of the signers of the Declaration of Independence had observed in 1787, settlers on the American frontier accepted work as servants only when forced by extreme necessity.[23] The nuns were, not surprisingly, often without servants and continued to haul their own water, keep the garden, care for the animals, do the cooking, laundry, cleaning and other domestic chores, in addition to running the three schools. They got a little help from the orphans they accepted, but not enough.

This provides the background to Philippine's comment regarding the controversial admission of Missouri as a slave state into the Union in 1820:

> At present the laws of the state are being drawn up. The most disputed point and the one that has caused the greatest conflict concerns the admission of slavery. It seems that all those who now own slaves will be allowed to keep them and that the children of their slaves will belong to them, but there can be no more African slave trade. We do not want slaves and we have no money to buy them, yet we scarcely know how to get along without them, especially as we are cloistered and do not go about. No one wants to hire out as a domestic servant; all want to be on the same social level. Up to now we have given a home to some young girls who are orphans and who have been placed with us legally until they are twenty years old. . . .

But the Society of the Sacred Heart did eventually accept slaves and even buy them. For example, in 1821 a wealthy widow gave the religious, then in Louisiana, a black family as servants. The superior of that convent, Eugénie Audé, purchased her first black slave, Frank, shortly thereafter. By 1833, this convent owned at least eight slaves,[24] and probably more. In 1830, the convent founded in St. Louis, with Philippine as superior, accepted a slave, Joseph, in lieu of tuition. The

---

[23]Benjamin Rush, *Thoughts upon Female Education, Accommodated to the Present State of Society, Manners, and Government in the United States of America*, in *Women, the Family, and Freedom: The Debate in Documents*, eds. Susan Groag Bell and Karen M. Offen, vol. I (Stanford, California: Stanford University Press, 1983), p. 77.

[24]See Cunningham, *Eugénie Audé*, pp. 33 and 57.

same convent purchased a black couple in 1834. Given the fact that slaves accounted for about fifteen percent of the Missouri population throughout Philippine's life in America,[25] the slaves that the nuns owned were few indeed. And within the parameters of the degrading institution of slavery, the situation might be considered a good one for the slaves in question.

Liza Nebbitt, for example, who spent most of her life at St. Michael's convent and raised her children there, is a well-known slave in the order's history precisely because she was so loved by the religious. Although Liza was never officially associated with the order nor could be, the nuns allowed her to take a vow of charity each year on Pentecost, a ceremony which they all attended. When they began to have high-quality photographs taken of some of the nuns, they made sure Liza's picture was taken too. She shared the same affection for the religious and became particularly close to several. When she died, a biography as long or longer than those written for deceased religious, was circulated among the order's convents.[26]

But the position of Philippine and the other religious regarding people of color and the institution of slavery itself was, in the final analysis, ambiguous. They were generally uncritical of the separate and lower status accorded to blacks and mulattoes in America. They said they did not want to have slaves, but in the very period in which slavery was being vehemently denounced by both black and white abolitionists, especially in Missouri, they in fact accepted owning slaves. Philippine explained in a letter to Sophie Barat in May, 1836, that the nuns could not handle all the manual work in the convent of St. Louis without the help of blacks.[27] Philippine and her sisters would have paid the concrete price of an increased work load for themselves had they renounced slavery absolutely. The assumptions of their own culture in the nineteenth century, however, kept this question from ever being raised.

It is instructive to return to Philippine's comment about Americans, that "all want to be on the same social level." Evidently, the "all" in question refers not to *all* people on the frontier: native Americans, mestizos, blacks, mulattoes, Creoles and "Americans." Rather, it re-

---

[25]Department of Commerce and Labor, U.S. Bureau of the Census, *A Century of Population Growth: From the First Census of the United States to the Twelfth, 1790–1900* (Washington, D.C.: Government Printing Office, 1909), p. 82, Table 20, and p. 140.

[26]I am grateful to Sr. Marie Louise Martinez for this information.

[27]I am grateful to Sr. Cora McLaughlin for this reference.

ferred to the group which refused to be hired out as servants and consisted primarily of whites of European extraction. They "all" wanted to be on the same social level with each other, but not with *all* the other people in America. The ideal of egalitarianism was a strong force in America, but it was not inclusive of all racial groups.

The ideal to which Philippine was most committed, education of the Indians, and for which she had paid the extreme price of leaving her native land and her loved ones, was precisely the ideal which most eluded her in America. This was the hardest disappointment of her life at St. Charles. She noted in a letter to a friend:

> As for real Indians, we never see them because the Americans from the East are pushing them out and making war with them. They are withdrawing further away. We would need Jesuits to bring them to us, as they brought them to Mother Marie of the Incarnation.

And she continued with a description of the deplorable situation into which many of the native Americans had fallen:

> We would attract them more quickly with liquor than with sermons. They will give anything they have in exchange for that. But in conscience no one should give it to them, seeing what a state it puts them in and how dangerous it makes them. God allows some faint light of religion to shine amongst them and bring about conversions, but these are very rare. Degradation is almost general amongst them, and the diversity of languages, the enormous distances in this country, the difficulty of travel, all combine to make it impossible for us to help them yet.

The "degradation" Philippine noted was, in her mind, in no way peculiar to the Indians. Rather, it typified the frontier situation. On October 8, 1818, she commented that the situation in St. Charles was improving in this regard:

> A few years ago, however, one might have witnessed conduct comparable to pagan bacchanalia: girls scantily clad, holding a bottle of whisky in one hand and a man with the other, dancing every day of the year and never doing any work. Now there is more exterior decency, but these people are as ignorant of morality as the Indians are. In our free school we

now have twenty-two children, and in proportion to the population this equals a school of one hundred in France. These children have never heard of our Lord, of His birth or His death, nor of hell, and they listen open-mouthed to our instructions. . . . Among the children who pay a little fee there is the same ignorance. . . . We have to combat worldliness as well as ignorance. Some of the boarding pupils have more dresses than underclothes or handkerchiefs. . . .

In fact, it was still Philippine's dream to be able to support Indian girls as boarders with the income from the paying boarding school. A boarding education was, she thought, preferable to a day school because of the integral formation the nuns could provide. In the case of the Indians, this was especially necessary due to the cultural differences separating Europeans from native Americans. Evangelization and education in the European missionaries' mind typically entailed a radical transformation of native American culture and religion. But any kind of education for the Indians was absolutely out of the question in St. Charles. They had work to do with other "savages." Philippine wrote to Mother Barat on October 8, 1818:

We complain to the bishop that we still have no savages, but he says, "Indeed you have true savages, and the good you do among them will be more lasting and have wider effect because of the influence of the rich over the poor."[28]

5. THE CLOSING OF ST. CHARLES

This was Dubourg's real educational aim. It is worth noting that his view was consistent with certain points made in the Constitutions of the Society.[29] But, as Philippine had foreseen, the boarding school at St. Charles could not survive. There simply were not enough children to provide the necessary revenue for the nuns' livelihood and the support of the free school. Poor schools, while not always opened alongside the boarding schools, were an essential part of Sacred Heart educa-

---

[28]Translation mine.

[29]de Charry, *Histoire des Constitutions*, pt. II, vol. I, p. 106; Hogg trans., *The Definitive Constitutions*, p. 89.

tion in France. They were naturally contingent upon a flourishing boarding school and were established whenever possible.[30]

Although Philippine was disappointed about not opening the school for Indian girls, her disappointment diminished with her growing attachment to the free school and to the people of St. Charles. The townspeople did all that they could to keep the Religious of the Sacred Heart in their town. Within the first few months of the nuns' arrival, they had already begun to discuss building a home for them. The impossibility of the financial situation pressed hard upon Philippine. She wanted to stay in St. Charles for the sake of the free school. She wrote to Sophie Barat on February, 15, 1819:

> If we were not so short of funds, we could do much good by educating several of these [poor] children at our own expense. But what can we do, with neither lodging nor provisions? We cannot remain in this house, where one room the size of the parlor in the Paris convent and six small rooms cost almost two thousand francs. The bishop was badly mistaken when he thought we could house twenty-five boarding students here. We cannot lodge ten, even with rolling up the beds every morning. The section north of the Missouri River can never send us boarding pupils who will pay tuition. The best we can do here is a day school run by a few of us, and it will not support the nuns. Pride tries to hide misery, but we see these poor, hungry children coming barefooted often in the coldest weather and wearing a single cotton garment—a very thin one, too—and nothing under it.
>
> You see, my dear Mother, that though we are forced to give up the boarding school here, it is heartbreaking to leave no help at all for these children, who could be nicely trained. In four months many have learned to read, to write, to know the whole of the little catechism, a number of hymns, and the prayers at Benediction.

Dubourg finally realized that the nuns' efforts in St. Charles were futile. Philippine argued for splitting the little community in order to salvage the free school in St. Charles. Just a few of the nuns could start a boarding school elsewhere where conditions were more propitious.

---

[30]"Constitutions of 1815," no. 203; and de Charry, *Histoire des Constitutions*, pt. II, vol. I, p. 153; Hogg trans., *The Definitive Constitutions*, pp. 124–25.

Dubourg initially approved of this idea enthusiastically, but he wanted the boarding school to be in Florissant. This was the locale Philippine had initially opposed because of the exorbitant costs of building there. But Dubourg now promised to help by providing a man to oversee the work of building there and by paying most of the costs. His promise was ironic given the fact that he was holding more than seven thousand francs of the nuns' money in his own possession while they were struggling in St. Charles. He had offered them no financial assistance then. Dubourg also repeated his own views of the educational needs of his diocese:

> You cannot fail to draw a large number of pupils for the boarding school [in Florissant], which is a more important work than you seem to realize, for it is from the education of the upper levels of society that reform must come, and they are just as ignorant as the lower classes. This seems the time to consolidate your establishment. For my part, I am quite decided on this point. If you are determined to follow *my advice* (I give no *orders* in this matter), then we must get to work and lose no more time.

But the bishop offered only one alternative to the untenable situation at St. Charles, namely Florissant, which cast his remark about "advice" and "orders" in a rather different light. Sophie Barat roundly opposed splitting the small community among two small villages, a move she felt would doom both foundations.[31] In fact, she generally objected to any foundation in small villages, preferring instead cities where the nuns' boarding schools were more likely to flourish.[32] When she heard of Dubourg's proposal, she wrote on July 27, 1819:

> What? Move from one little village to another? Go to such expense for what must always remain a mediocre institution? Why does your good bishop not station you in St. Louis? If you had but a little corner in that city, the hope of seeing you soon well established would encourage me to send out more religious. As it is, I candidly admit that I will send no one else until I know definitely the outcome of this move.

---

[31] See her letters to Philippine of March 19, July 9, and July 27, 1819.
[32] In addition to the letters cited in the above note, see, for example, her letter to Eugénie Audé of April 8, 1824.

Philippine counted little on Dubourg's promises of financial help, aware of his own debts in St. Louis and having become more familiar with the man himself. When the nuns saw the small plot of land which the bishop was offering them in the parish of Florissant, St. Ferdinand, and sensed that his promise of financial help was but tenuous, Philippine had second thoughts about the move. In February, 1819, she wrote in her *Journal:*

> Fear of expense which building at St. Ferdinand entails terrifies us, and we have begged the bishop to let us remain at St. Charles in the house the townspeople wish to build for us on the property they are willing to give us.

The proposed house in Florissant was initially estimated to cost fifteen thousand francs. Philippine and her companions had only 5,800 francs, the majority of which was in Dubourg's keeping. The situation had further degenerated by mid-March. Philippine wrote in a letter to Louis Barat:

> When I saw the contractor's plans and estimate for a convent there, I realized it was simply extortion—excessive expenditures that would bring ruin on us. I wrote to the bishop, refusing the services of the contractor and telling him that we had no other funds than those we had placed in his keeping. He replied that he had weighed the matter well and, being unable to assist us, he thought it best to drop the undertaking at Florissant. . . .

By the end of the month, the bishop was offering new advice *and* orders. Philippine wrote, ending on a characteristically kind note:

> The bishop came to make his retreat at Father Richard's house. He spent one whole day upsetting all our plans, as well as the desires of Fathers Richard and Acquaroni, who have simply exhausted themselves in their efforts to get us firmly established here at St. Charles. The bishop has in his keeping the sum of two thousand dollars, which was sent to him from France by Mother Barat for us at the time of our departure for America. He declares he will use it only at St. Ferdinand's and that he will borrow the rest of the money needed for the erection of the new building. He says we shall not have to worry about the details of the construction, as he

will have the pastor there superintend the work. . . . Bishop Dubourg added that he does not want us to divide, as our number is too small.

In the midst of all this trouble he has shown us more kindness and interest than ever before. He has read our Constitutions, found them full of wisdom, thanked us for having acquainted him with them, and said he preferred this Rule to that of any other order he knew. Finally, on leaving, he said graciously that he left his heart with us, that he had come here seeking rest for mind and heart and had found both. . . .

The nuns were compelled to close their convent and the three schools in St. Charles and move. It was almost a year to the day after their arrival when they departed on September 3, 1819. A woman quick to warm to people and places, Philippine took the closure quite hard, particularly the loss of the free school. For years she would struggle to re-open it. On July 29, 1819, a few weeks before leaving St. Charles, she wrote her friend Sophie Barat:

The dear Lord has favored us with a share of His cross. The greatest and undoubtedly the hardest to bear is the lack of success in our work here. If a saint had been in charge, all would have gone well. That thought makes the burden of my office all the heavier. Every day I see more clearly that I do not possess the qualities necessary in a superior.

Her biographer, Louise Callan, insightfully sums up this chapter of Philippine's life:

In spite of the very evident material factors that had conditioned the failure, she felt that its primary cause had been herself. She was not blind to patent facts nor to the almost hopeless circumstances in which she had worked for twelve months, but she was blind to the courageous leadership, the unswerving loyalty, the selfless devotion with which she had carried on that work. The struggle had been constant, even heroic, yet she was so alive to a sense of her own incapacity that she simply could not see things in any other light.[33]

---

[33]Callan, *Philippine Duchesne*, pp. 305–306.

VII.

Florissant and the Indian School

The religious began their new foundation in Florissant in true frontier fashion: they had no house. Since the lease on the Duquette home in St. Charles was up on September 6, 1819, Bishop Dubourg informed the nuns that they would have to move out even though the Florissant house was not yet finished. The real brunt of this misfortune was borne by Father Charles De La Croix, a Belgian priest. He found himself sleeping in a corn crib, relinquishing his own cabin on the bishop's property to the nuns until another could be built for him. These were the inauspicious beginnings of the Society's foundation in Florissant. Philippine and her companions would struggle for years to establish their convent and schools on a sound footing there.

Florissant had been founded in 1785 by French settlers who named it St. Ferdinand de "Fleurissant," or "flourishing," because of its luxuriant foliage. Although today the town is just one of many suburbs of St. Louis, accounting for only about one-fortieth of St. Louis' total population, in the early 1800s it lay fourteen miles northwest of that city and boasted a population about one-fourth the size of St. Louis.

1. THE FINANCIAL SITUATION

Philippine's fears about the costs of construction were amply realized. The initial estimate of fifteen thousand francs, about three thousand dollars, was already more than the nuns had, and the real costs of construction continued to rise. Without the generous aid of De La Croix, and of the pastor of St. Ferdinand's, the Trappist Joseph-Marie Dunand, building might have stopped several times. Dubourg was over-extended with his own construction projects of a seminary and cathedral. He consequently offered none of the financial assistance originally promised and asked both Philippine and Sophie Barat to have money sent from France, money which the nuns did not have. Philippine wrote to Mother Barat in July, 1819, that Dubourg was overwhelmed with embarrassment at the nuns' debt. They would have to pay it themselves. In October, 1819, Dubourg solved his dilemma by forcing Philippine to take out a loan of two thousand dollars from John Mullanphy, the wealthy Florissant resident whom she had met a year earlier in New Orleans.

Mullanphy, the wealthiest man in the St. Louis area, was an Irish merchant and trader known for his philanthropy.[1] A shrewd business-man, he had already made fantastic profits by cornering the cotton market in 1812, thus setting a precedent for later American business magnates. Mullanphy used some of his wealth to do good works. He helped to establish the first hospital west of the Mississippi, the church of St. Ferdinand in Florissant, and the convent, school and orphanage which the Religious of the Sacred Heart opened in St. Louis in 1827. He also paid for the medical treatment of many victims of the 1834 cholera epidemic.

Nevertheless, it is clear from Philippine's writings that Mullanphy was as shrewd in charity as he was in business. The two thousand dollars she was made to borrow from him in 1819 had still not been entirely repaid in February, 1821, when Philippine anxiously wrote to Sophie Barat concerning a letter she had received from Louis Barat:

> He [Louis] enclosed the triplicate of the note for 571 dollars, which I hastened to turn over to the man [Mullanphy] to whom we owed ten thousand francs. People say he had his eye on our house, holding the mortgage as he does and know-ing the extreme difficulty with which people like ourselves get any money. I prefer to reject such an idea as dishonorable to him and contrary to the goodness of God, whose Provi-dence toward us had been manifested in a thousand ways.

The scarcity of money on the frontier had made the situation desperate for people like Philippine, and inviting for entrepreneurs like Mul-lanphy. By March she had reason to believe the rumors were true:

---

[1]See Gilbert J. Garraghan, *Saint Ferdinand de Florissant: The Story of an Ancient Parish* (Chicago: Loyola University Press, 1923), pp. 69–74, for the following discussion.

In such a situation one cannot rest easy if one has debts. We still owe fifteen thousand francs, part of that sum being held under a mortgage which the creditor [Mullanphy] boasts about. Divine Providence will not allow him to foreclose on us—God has been on our side too often for us to fear that, but the man may act with us as with his other debtors. As no purchaser for our house has been found, it might bring him at auction just the amount we owe him, though it has cost us nearly forty thousand francs.

A brief respite came in the springtime when Mullanphy departed for France. Mother Barat, who realized Philippine was being charged ten percent interest, twice the going rate in France, paid Mullanphy off when he went to call on her in Paris. Philippine and her companions now had all the time necessary to repay their new and more friendly creditors.

During construction of their own house, the religious occupied the eighteen-square-foot, one-room log cabin which De La Croix had relinquished to them. They opened their boarding school at once, which increased despite the fact that their single room had to serve as both classroom and dormitory. The nuns had only the cabin's loft for their own living and sleeping quarters. It was almost four months before they moved into their new home, just in time for Christmas, 1819.

Their prospects brightened. By the spring of 1820 there were twenty pupils in the boarding school, the majority from the oldest and most influential families of the region. Within a year, there were also ten day pupils and, especially significant for the future of the Society in America, three novices and three postulants had entered to prepare for religious life. Although life physically continued to be one of genuine poverty and hardship, the nuns had relatively more food and fuel compared to their days in St. Charles.

Philippine could not always appreciate the progress they were making. Her descriptions of the situation, and her perceptions of herself as superior at this time lead to interesting speculations about community life on the frontier. She wrote to Louis Barat:

> I think the bishop's [Dubourg's] good judgement will make him approve of a change of superior. There is no one in the community who is not suffering. I will never gain the confidence of either the community or outsiders, but everyone trusts my two companions [Eugénie Audé and Octavie

Berthold], and they use this confidence to do good. . . . I am the least useful in the community, but I am happy to share the hard work. I wish I were put in just that kind of employment; then I would be content. It is heartbreaking, after such ardent desires, to see our success hindered or slowed up and to realize that I am the obstacle. Happy, too, would I be if, having no support from anyone on earth near me, I were deprived even of those consolations that really are too sweet for a life that is dying in Jesus Christ. That is what I desire. . . .

This letter was written in May, 1820, when the community had just lost three postulants and Philippine was still anxious about the debt for their house. On the other hand, the educational mission of the little community was off to a good start and they had finished construction of both their home and a day school. But as her last comment shows, she almost wished to be deprived of consolations so that she might better die in Jesus Christ. Her harsh judgements about herself are also contradicted by the opinion of some of the other religious. For example, less than a year later, when Philippine's three-year term as superior was up, Octavie Berthold wrote to Mother Barat begging that Philippine not be relieved of office:

What would we do without her? There are seven of us in her little family now. We love each other very much and our hearts are all one with hers. . . . Furthermore, she knows the country and the character of the people. Anyone else would be an apprentice, as it were, at all this.

It would be interesting to know the thoughts of the other religious, especially Eugénie Audé who, before long, would find herself in significant disagreement with Philippine on a multitude of issues.

Philippine's financial worries continued to weigh on her. She considered the original estimate of the house's cost, fifteen thousand francs, to be exorbitant. But it ultimately cost her and the other nuns a full forty thousand francs. She abhorred being in debt. From her arrival in St. Louis, she had felt that building in Florissant was a foolhardy move, but it was what Bishop Dubourg wanted. She admired him enormously. How Philippine chose to react to him in situations of disagreement is revelatory both of her own character and of her position as a woman in the Church.

On the one hand, she is frank and generous in her praise of the prelate. For example, in a letter of May, 1820, she pondered his deeds:

> In less that two years he has a cathedral built, a seminary founded and functioning, three or four schools in different sections of this immense diocese, all parts of which are visited at least from time to time by priests.

Especially typical is a letter she wrote in February, 1821, to her cousin Josephine thanking her for a gift of five hundred francs. Philippine was beside herself about the debt in Florissant, but she spiritualized the whole matter, making God's hand in the matter almost obscure all the human hands involved in the debacle. Even though she delicately avoided mentioning Dubourg by name, one can still sense her exasperation about the whole business:

> We are the grain of wheat dying in the earth; can we repine at such a destiny? But we are full of confidence and wholly animated with courage to persevere, hoping that someday our work will bear fruit. It matters little whether we taste of it in this life, provided only that we serve God's cause. He let it happen that when we arrived in St. Louis money was plentiful and the price of land and houses was excessively high. It seemed better for us to build here at Florissant. That was not my opinion, but I had to follow the opinion of others and borrow money to complete the building. And now the failure of the banks has caused the disappearance of the paper money which was practically the only currency here. We could buy lands and a house in St. Louis for nothing today, yet we must pay back the loan at a time when the money is worth ten times as much as when we borrowed it. These are the unexpected occurrences against which human prudence can offer no protection. But Divine Providence is with us, and we can count so trustfully on God, we shall stand firm at our post. So sincerely are we persuaded that God Himself wants us here, not one of us regrets her position. . . .

But Philippine was not always so sanguine. In matters of money, Dubourg seems to have stirred the anger of more than just Philippine. St. Louisans felt overwhelmed by his entreaties for aid, the Jesuits were angry on several occasions when he reneged on promised donations, and leery creditors kept a close eye. In 1823, Philippine, who frequently glossed over problems with individuals in her letters, leaving them unnamed for "holy charity," wrote the following lively lines to Sophie Barat about some money they had lost:

> I am really chagrined and humiliated to think you lost that note for a thousand francs. It happened as a result of the naivete of our Sisters. They had not been in New Orleans fifteen minutes when they gave a scrupulous account of all the money they had to the person interested [Dubourg]. That person wrote to me the same day, pointing out the "beauty" of our position, and saying that in consequence he was going to dispose of the one thousand franc note on Bordeaux. The same thing happened to the fifteen hundred francs Mother Eugénie sent me, in spite of my cleverness in hiding the money. We owed him that, however, so it was a matter of justice to pay him.

In the same letter, she twice refers to Dubourg as the "Seer" rather than by name, in a gently mocking, even sarcastic tone. One can smile imagining whether or not she felt remorse after writing this letter, but her points were well taken. The title "Seer" refers no doubt to his well-known tendency to paint rosy pictures of difficult situations, entice others to undertake them and then exit the stage himself. In Philippine's own case there were already numerous examples: his descriptions in France of all the work she would do with the Indians in the New World, his speculation that St. Charles would be a great crossroad for international trade (even then she had called him, perhaps facetiously, one "who looks very far into the future"), his thought that their home would easily accommodate twenty-five boarders when it could barely hold ten (and only had three!), and his optimism about how easy it would be to pay for the construction in Florissant. When Dubourg eventually left his diocese for France, he had become enmeshed in such a morass of misunderstandings with St. Louisans, and even his own successor Bishop Joseph Rosati,[2] that despite all his accomplishments in establishing Catholicism on a firm foundation in his diocese, one must conclude that his leadership style was wanting in several respects.

Philippine was enormously respectful of authority, especially ecclesiastical authority. Although she questioned Dubourg's judgement

---

[2]See, for example, Rothensteiner, *History of the Archdiocese of St. Louis*, vol. I, pp. 422–25.

and disagreed with him on a number of occasions, she remained loyal. An example well illustrates her position. In 1820, Dubourg cavalierly removed the pastor of St. Ferdinand, Joseph-Marie Dunand. Dunand had been one of just a few missionaries in the region from 1808 until 1818[3] when Dubourg himself arrived. Dubourg's removal of Dunand angered Dunand's Florissant parishioners and St. Louisans alike. Some of these people were already at odds with the bishop on other matters. Philippine, who resided in Dunand's parish, also felt Dubourg was wrong. She wrote to friends in France, where Dunand would return, to explain the situation, clear his name and smooth a path for him. However, since juridically Dubourg was within his rights and as bishop could remove whomever he pleased, Philippine acquiesced to his authority and supported it rather than voice any protest. Her loyalty to Dubourg in times like these, even when she disagreed with his choices, bought her a good deal of trouble. For years the association in St. Louisans' minds between Dubourg and the Society of the Sacred Heart contributed to the nuns' unpopularity among many people in that city. Voicing responsible dissent when authorities seemed to be in the wrong was not a particularly strong value in the frontier Church. On the contrary, Philippine's abiding loyalty to ecclesiastical authorities was considered an ideal in the nineteenth century, especially for religious women. And there is no doubt that Philippine's loyalty has contributed to her stature in churchmen's eyes.

The money problems which beset Dubourg, Philippine and others endeavoring to establish religious institutions in the United States were not peculiar to them. In 1821 the country itself entered a significant financial crisis. Numerous state banks collapsed, including the Bank of Missouri, and money was scarce. The effect was immediate on the fledgling boarding school in Florissant. By 1822 the religious were refusing to accept any more nonpaying students in their school. In 1823, only Philippine's fear that the children would lose their faith kept her from dismissing the students whom the religious had been supporting for free. The nuns' own poverty was preferable to that. The fast success of their boarding school, which enrolled twenty-two students within two years of its opening in 1819, was followed by a steady four-year decline. At one point in 1825, they had only four pupils.

Philippine was hardly passive during this crisis. When Mother Barat suggested in 1824 that they close the school, Philippine protested

---

[3]Rothensteiner, *History of the Archdiocese of St. Louis*, vol. I, pp. 217–23.

that the poorer people needed it. She suggested that they simply open a more modest boarding school, more in keeping with the poverty of that area. From that time forward, Florissant had two boarding schools, one costing nine hundred francs per year, and the other about 180 francs.

Philippine began to receive numerous invitations to found convents and schools in more promising towns and cities on the frontier. Two criteria stand out in her reflections on the suitability of a place for foundation. They were not always complementary and sometimes stood in open opposition to each other. First, Philippine tended toward financial realism. She weighed closely the precise terms of offers for foundations: whether or not they included land, a house and school, or required construction; whether or not the area was very populated, and so forth. If a site was offered even on good terms, but held little promise of paying students, which was the nuns' source of income for their modest life style and for their work with poorer children, she hesitated to consider it.

On the other hand, Philippine was especially drawn to places where the Society could be with and serve the poor. For example, of the various offers coming her way during these early years in Florissant, she was especially drawn to a mission at Portage des Sioux. It was a far northern parish where white traders frequently had children with Indian women and then abandoned both "wife" and children upon returning to their own Christian wives. Philippine wrote about it in 1821 to Mother Barat:

> [The white traders] do not know how to provide for the children born of these illegitimate alliances. They leave them with their mothers, and so the children of Christian fathers are brought up like little animals. Many of these traders, however, are rich; and if they knew where to place the children, they would certainly have them educated. . . .
>
> This seems to me the most useful kind of establishment we could found, and the easiest. It also resembles the work done by Marie of the Incarnation in Canada and is most closely conformed to the purposes that drew us to this country. I have no other desire than that of consecrating my life to this work, if God so wills.

This letter betrays the cultural imperialism which pervaded Christian missionary work among the Indians who, allegedly, raised their children "like little animals." Surely it was the behavior of married

Christian traders who impregnated Indian women and then walked away from their responsibilities which was "animal-like."

But the point here is that Philippine was willing to argue for a foundation that would have been difficult to support financially. Despite the trader's "wealth," this was a very uncertain venture. It would be quite likely that some of these same "Christian" fathers would again abandon their children, but this time to the nuns. The distance of Portage des Sioux from larger towns was another drawback. They would have no other paying boarders or day students. Surely they would find other mestizo children in need of education for whom they would have to care for free. But founding an institution specifically for mestizos responded to Philippine's initial vision of the congregation's work in the New World. Such children were regularly marginalized from the dominant white culture, and sometimes within Indian society itself.[4]

In cases such as this, Philippine allowed her personal attraction to work with the poor and marginalized to temper her financial realism. Her usual hard-headed calculation often took second place where the poor and dispossessed were concerned. Her concern for them took priority over the otherwise important value of building her works on a foundation of security. And it is especially significant that she wrote about her attraction to this foundation in the very same letter to Sophie Barat in which she expressed great anxiety about the financial straits of the Society in Florissant in 1821. It is also worth noting that Sophie Barat, more intent on administration than Philippine, usually reined Philippine in on such projects, recommending instead that the nuns strengthen existing foundations before branching out. In February, 1822, she wrote to Philippine that she did not approve of the proposed foundation among the Indians. She thought there were too many problems connected with the venture.

A rather romanticized notion of religious orders, from the early Benedictines to the Franciscans to congregations today, has held that only those which are truly poor succeed in establishing themselves within the Church. In fact, history is replete with short-lived religious orders which foundered precisely because they were too poor. And every major order which has succeeded either came into wealth unex-

---

[4]See, for example, James A. Clifton, *The Prairie People: Continuity and Change in Potawatomi Indian Culture 1665–1965* (Lawrence, Kansas: The Regents Press of Kansas, 1977), p. 324, for a discussion of mestizos within the tribe with which Philippine eventually lived.

pectedly through luck or donations or had simply to face the hard facts of making the books balance during its efforts to expand. Like any institution, a religious order can easily become so involved in its own survival that it forgets, rationalizes or pushes to one side, its initial vision.

As subsequent chapters show, Philippine admirably held in balance both the need to establish the Society on a firm financial footing in the United States and a radical commitment to the poor and dispossessed. She made choices which were not always to the advantage of the Society in terms of its exterior success. She was on the side of the poor. Her choices betray her basic disagreement with the arguments of Dubourg and others that "it is from the education of the upper levels of society that reform must come," that work among them is more valuable because "of the influence of the rich over the poor." Philippine was willing to choose for the poor—in terms of financial commitment, emotional energy and personnel—in ways which impinged upon the prosperity of the Society in general and her boarding schools in particular. This commitment, her willingness to take risks and live in insecurity on behalf of others in need, was not always appreciated. It sometimes drew criticism from some of her religious sisters, equally dedicated to the educational apostolate, who favored the establishment of "successful" schools, often among people more financially favored.

Philippine's refusal to resolve the tension of living in a world of both rich and poor has particular poignancy for our own world, a world in which the divide separating the rich from the poor continues to grow dramatically. In such a world, any philosophy of "reform from the upper levels of society," the "good influence of the rich over the poor," becomes a meaningless rationalization apart from radical, concrete and consistent choices to be on the side of the poor.

2. THE FOUNDATION AT OPELOUSAS

In 1821, Bishop Dubourg urged the nuns to found a convent and school in Opelousas, Louisiana, known also as Grand Coteau. He stressed the advantages of the place where "Mrs. Smith, a rich widow, offers us a house, lands, furniture, and money for traveling expenses." What he failed to mention were the isolation, underpopulation, difficulties of transportation and the limited availability of a priest there. He also neglected to inform them that Mrs. Smith expected to live with the nuns, reserving several rooms for herself for the entertainment of her friends, a condition the nuns would never be able to accept.[5] In a letter to Mother Barat in June, 1821, Philippine wrote:

> Bishop [Dubourg] dwelt at length on the advantages of such a foundation, which would procure for Lower Louisiana the good we have tried to do up here. . . . That section of Louisiana is rich and would furnish more pupils than this area does. . . .
>
> We all agree on the need of a second foundation, first, because a house in Lower Louisiana is necessary to support the one in Upper Louisiana; second, because the milder climate agrees with some temperaments; third, because when the expenses of the trip are repaid, we in turn could pay off our most unpleasant debt. . . .

In effect, Philippine was committed to maintaining the Florissant foundation despite its poverty and apparent failure. She argued to Sophie Barat that the new house in Opelousas would generate sufficient income for both foundations. It would also provide room for more of the young women asking to enter the Society, allow the nuns to double both the number of paying pupils and poor students and thereby further their mission of evangelizing people on the frontier.

The foundation was made in 1821, not by Philippine, who felt her English was inadequate, but by Eugénie Audé, whom Philippine then considered her "right arm."[6] Philippine early perceived that Eugénie possessed qualities which lent themselves to successful leadership:

> I thought that Mother Eugénie could do the most good because of her appearance, her virtue, her genial manner, and the ease with which she now speaks both English and French.

Dubourg made Eugénie and her companion, Mary Layton, the Society's first novice, leave early for Lower Louisiana to meet the two other Religious of the Sacred Heart on their way from France to the New World. Philippine opposed him on this, but he was the bishop. Dubourg gave the two religious only four days to prepare for their departure on August 5, 1821. As it turned out, the voyage from France

---

[5]Cunningham, *Eugénie Audé*, p. 32.
[6]Cunningham, *Eugénie Audé*, p. 28.

was delayed and the new Religious of the Sacred Heart whom they were sent to meet arrived about eight months later.

Several difficulties beset the new foundation in its beginnings: illness, a misunderstanding between Dubourg and the convent chaplain, and homesickness on the part of some of the religious. Eugénie's uncharacteristic silence in writing caused Philippine to worry that the young superior might be facing other problems too. Philippine decided to visit Opelousas in July, 1822. She discovered first-hand the disadvantages which Dubourg had failed to mention. In this instance also, Philippine spiritualized this turn of events, seeing God's hand first and Dubourg's second. She wrote to Mother Barat in September, 1822, from a stopover at a dingy inn during her trip South. Commenting on another priest's opinion of the new location she said:

> He thinks a foundation would have been better located in that fairly prosperous town Natchez [in southwestern Mississippi] on the great river [Mississippi] where there is continual traffic, than in a little hole like Opelousas, where we can never reach more than a very restricted circle. But we were just badly informed and God allowed it to happen in order to recompense the faith of Mrs. Smith and to save the souls of the children in those parts who are so idolized by their parents that they would never have had the courage to send them to school at a distance. There will be few day pupils, and one could hardly place a novitiate there because it is so inaccessible at any season and so difficult to provide for. One must lay in supplies in the spring by means of rafts, which cannot reach there at any other season, and the carrying charges are so high: the transportation of one medium-size clothes cabinet from New Orleans to Opelousas cost 120 francs, each chair cost five francs.

Nevertheless the school prospered under the able and talented administration of Eugénie Audé.[7] At the end of just one year it was out of debt. There were seventeen boarders and more on the way. Parents and priests in New Orleans, in part inspired by the good reputation of the school under Eugénie's care, begged the Religious of the Sacred Heart to make another foundation in their own city. Some people in the St. Louis area even claimed that the standard of the boarding

---

[7]See Cunningham, *Eugénie Audé*, pp. 31–42.

school in Florissant had declined since Eugénie's departure. Philippine denied that this was true.

Meanwhile and unbeknownst to Philippine, Eugénie was striving to establish the convent and school in Opelousas independently of Philippine's direction. This was ostensibly contrary to the will of Mother Barat. Sophie Barat had given full governing authority to Philippine when the religious departed for America in 1818. On November 23, 1821, she repeated to Philippine, "If the foundation at Opelousas takes place, I put you in charge of it as Provincial." Then, on February 10, 1822, Mother Barat wrote to Eugénie herself, who was already in Opelousas:

> I counsel you to refer all urgent questions to Mother Duchesne. She is, as it were, your Provincial. I have given her full authority, and if that title were in use among us she would certainly bear it. At least I have given her full powers. Have recourse to her in all ordinary cases and refer to me only the most difficult and those that can wait for months for an answer.

Nevertheless, Eugénie never relaxed her efforts to gain her independence from Philippine's authority. In March, 1822, for example, she wrote in her own inimitable fashion to Mother Barat:

> Oh, my very dear Mother, take pity on your little house of Opelousas; be its joy and its happiness—you can do so—by consenting to direct it yourself, even if it is so far away. I will not leave you in ignorance of the least thing, and a word, just one little word from you, will be the magnet which I shall use to draw all hearts to Jesus and to bind them to Him.

Philippine was quite aware of Eugénie's independent-minded personality, but she was not conscious of this correspondence between the Mother General and Eugénie. It is significant that Sophie Barat did not choose to let Philippine know anything about Eugénie's private representations to her, especially in light of the fact that Mother Barat subsequently sided with Eugénie on several important matters. Philippine's and Eugénie's disagreements regarding government grew steadily after the foundation of Opelousas. As the next chapter will show, their differences led not only to significant internal divisions within the Society in America: they throw into question the "full powers" which Sophie Barat maintained she had granted to Philippine.

On the return river trip from Opelousas to St. Louis, Philippine contracted yellow fever. Terrible epidemics were frequent in nineteenth-century America. This one had broken out in New Orleans just before Philippine boarded the steamboat. Other travelers too had boarded with the contagion. Philippine described a scene in which men died "like animals." She and several other passengers deboarded at Natchez in order to recuperate, but were denied permission to enter that city on account of the epidemic. Finally, she found lodging in a home outside the town and there she was able to regain her health.

The real trial during this trip for Philippine, however, was not her physical illness at all. She suffered most from the lack of spiritual help available on the journey. Indicative of her own spirituality, typical of many nineteenth-century religious, is the fact that she scrupulously counted all the masses she missed. She even attributed a relapse into fever to her having missed mass and the sacraments. This time was, in her own words, the "most rigorous fast" she had ever made:

> On my trip I missed 120 masses, counting just one a day [she often attended more than one], eighty communions, about twenty confessions, and practically all the Benedictions of the blessed sacrament for four months. But I believe all these sacrifices are not without value; perhaps several foundations may come from them.

The striking success of the school in Opelousas contrasted so sharply with the financial affairs of Philippine's own Florissant foundation, that she had to consider more seriously opening a third foundation in New Orleans. She wrote to Sophie Barat in January of 1823:

> We do not owe the bishop any money now, but we do owe 2500 francs to a gentleman who cleared us of debt. Such is our financial standing at the close of five years, whereas Mother Eugénie at the close of one year gave us more than four thousand francs. From this you may judge of the real necessity there is for our having a convent in New Orleans to help support our work. Here, far from receiving help from anyone, our first duty is to aid the priests, and perhaps Bishop [Dubourg] himself.

Eugénie was quite keen on the idea of opening a school in the prominent city of New Orleans. In fact, Philippine felt compelled to remind her not to make promises to anyone without first consulting with her.

A certain exasperation, perhaps even jealousy, is apparent in a letter Philippine wrote to Mother Barat in early 1823. This is the same frank letter in which she referred to Dubourg as "our Seer." She writes regarding shipments from France which passed through New Orleans, but never reached their destination in Florissant:

> The people in New Orleans always prefer to send things [arriving from France] to Eugénie rather than to me, so completely has she won the esteem and affection of all who have the good of the Society at heart. That is what happened to the box Mr. Jouve [Philippine's brother-in-law] sent me, and I was so eager to get it, for it contained galloon for a pretty vestment I am making. . . . I wrote so often to Grand Coteau [Opelousas] about it, I finally got my galloon, but not the other things that were in the box. I beg you, my very dear Mother, not to pack in the same box things that are for them and for us. It costs almost as much to send a box from New Orleans to Opelousas as to St. Louis because of the difficulty of transportation, and the return and forwarding charges are an enormous expense. Mother Eugénie is quite as well off as we are —if not better, and she has not our obligations and our debts. She receives many presents, and just recently a beautiful clock. There is great inconvenience in not having a house in New Orleans to receive the mail.

A combination of factors such as the financial crisis in the United States and the lack of religious to found a new house, led Philippine, Dubourg and Sophie Barat all to concur that, for the time being, there would be no foundation in New Orleans. As for Eugénie, her enterprise in Opelousas continued to flourish. She even wanted to expand the school by building, but Philippine opposed her arguing that boarding school education was too unstable in the country at that time. The differences between the two continued to mount.

3. THE ARRIVAL OF THE JESUITS: HER RELATIONS WITH VAN QUICKENBORNE AND OTHER ECCLESIASTICS

Although the circumstances of the school in Florissant did not improve, there was a significant turn for the better in Philippine's eyes with the arrival of the Jesuits in 1823. Dubourg had promised to give the Jesuits his large tract of land in Florissant, with its house and cattle, if they would come to work in his diocese. Other than the spiritual direction Philippine had received from Sophie Barat and a few other Religious of the Sacred Heart, most of her significant guidance had been with Jesuits such as Louis Barat and Joseph Varin. In America in 1824 she still claimed, "I much prefer poverty in the shadow of the Jesuits to the comforts of life under any other influence." For years she had longed for them to come to Missouri. She was persuaded that their presence was imperative to any successful work with the Indians. And in terms of their spiritual acumen, they were without rival.

The Jesuits—two priests, three brothers and seven novices—all Belgians, finally arrived, along with their three couples of black slaves, in June of 1823.[8] At the head of their party as novice master and superior was Father Charles Felix Van Quickenborne. In 1820, one of his Jesuit superiors described him:

> He is pious and not unacquainted with our Institute; still, having been admitted to the Society [of Jesus] but recently, he scarcely commands authority, a thing necessary for his office. He is of too vehement a temper and with little experience in governing others. He is an excellent religious, withal, and with time will become a spiritual father of great repute.[9]

Philippine's own experience confirmed the truth of this judgement.

She received the Jesuit band with unabashed enthusiasm and immediately appealed to them for spiritual guidance. But less than a month after their arrival, Philippine wrote pathetically to Sophie Barat:

> My last letter of June 19 must have given you real consolation, for in it I told you of the arrival we had so longed for— the arrival of our Fathers. But you must not think things are

---

[8]The Jesuits included the priests Charles Felix Van Quickenborne and Peter Joseph Timmermans; the brothers Peter De Meyer, Henry Reisselman and James Strahan; the novices Jodocus Van Assche, Peter John De Smet, De Maillet, John Elet, John Baptist Smedts, Peter John Verhaegen and John Felix Verreidt. The slaves included three black couples, Toni and Polly, Moses and Nancy, and Isaac and Suecy; see Rothensteiner, *History of the Archdiocese of St. Louis*, vol. I, pp. 331–32

[9]Gilbert J. Garraghan, *The Jesuits of the Middle United States*, 3 vols. (New York: America Press, 1938), vol. I, p. 27.

the same here as in France. Their interest in us is not the
same at all, and already—four times within this present
month—they have told me they would have nothing to do
with us if the highest authority did not impose it on them.
[several words illegible] This condition still exists, and I depend on Divine Providence not to leave us without spiritual
food.

Van Quickenborne, in short, wanted nothing to do with the nuns. He
reluctantly agreed to be their spiritual director, but only until the
matter could be placed before the Father General of the Jesuits in
Rome. Van Quickenborne and his fellow Jesuits also wanted their
lodging to be well distant from the nuns. Philippine wrote:

They are putting up a building on the Bishop's farm. I did
my best to induce them to build nearer the church, but there
was no getting them to do so. They do not want to be near
us. I was deeply grieved at this, realizing fully that in spite of
their courage we should often be without mass in winter.
They have their own chapel on the farm and our church is
terribly deserted.

In light of the Jesuits' own choice in this matter, one is really incredu-
lous to read Philippine's comment to Sophie Barat about a year later in
which she laments the difficulties the distance has imposed on the
men. She even felt guilty that she could not give them her own house:

One of my anxieties is the fact that it is so inconvenient for
the Jesuits to care for our spiritual needs. The distance of
their farm from the church causes them much trouble. The
Father [Van Quickenborne] says mass on alternate weekdays
here, the other days at the farm, but on Sundays he is obliged
to come at an early hour to hear confessions, and all his
community have to come also—in the heat of the summer, in
the downpouring rain, in the most severe winter weather.
The creeks in flood time are difficult and dangerous to cross
and frequently quite impassable. They really ought to own
our house, which is contiguous to the church. But if we gave
it to them, we should lose all the fruit of our struggle to get
established, and we should have to begin all over again some-
where —and I am too lazy for such an effort.

Good news for Philippine came when the Jesuit Father General in Rome granted permission to Van Quickenborne to be the nuns' spiritual director. Philippine's first assessments of his spiritual insight were glowing:

> The more we see of the Father Rector, the more we appreciate his direction and recognize in him the spirit of his Father, St. Ignatius. I have found a Father Master. I no longer do as I please, but he is not yet satisfied with my efforts. He insists on deeper interior life, greater detail in the account one gives of one's soul—and you know I never have much to say! . . . He has the power to persuade and move hearts. Seeing your daughters in such good hands, I am now quite tranquil as to their spiritual direction.

In spite of the nuns' own poverty, they went to considerable sacrifice for their Jesuit neighbors, whom they deemed in worse straits than themselves. Philippine's admiration, even adulation, for their pastoral efforts was practically boundless. The nuns shared their furniture, food, money and, not surprisingly, did all the Jesuits' sewing. On this point, Philippine's biographer Louise Callan tersely remarked:

> When Father Van Quickenborne wrote to his Maryland superior [in July, 1823], "We *all* go in full Jesuitical dress at all times and in all places," he might have added, "thanks to the *Dames du Sacré Coeur*" who were such a thorn in his side.[10]

Van Quickenborne was an exceptionally dedicated and self-abnegating man in many respects. As Philippine pointed out, he made his way to the church to say mass for the nuns in the most inclement weather and, according to Philippine, was shrewdly insightful regarding her own spiritual life. His severity with her, at least at first, led Philippine to value his guidance all the more. For his part, Van Quickenborne eventually came to respect Philippine and her companions, although his praise was spare. In one of his more even-tempered moments, he wrote to Dubourg's successor, Joseph Rosati, in 1823:

---

[10]Callan, *Philippine Duchesne*, p. 389.

We have the consolation of having the Ladies of the Sacred Heart who work with tireless zeal and are excellently equipped for giving a finished education to persons of their sex. In fine, the example of piety and holiness which they give and the Sunday School which they conduct give reason to hope that the cause of religion will win and piety take root.[11]

Nevertheless, Van Quickenborne's inconstant treatment of Philippine and the measure of abuse which she humbly sustained in her relations with him are vivid reminders of the place of women in the nineteenth-century Church and society. But as we have already seen, as acquiescent as Philippine tended to be with ecclesiastical authority, on occasion she disagreed forcefully.

Especially enlightening are two incidents in which Van Quickenborne used his authority as a priest to withhold, unjustly, the sacraments from Philippine. Since the eleventh century, in fact, when the sacraments became increasingly emphasized both as central to spiritual growth and as the sole domain of ordained ministers, there have been many provocative cases similar to Philippine's and Van Quickenborne's. Priestly withholding of the sacraments, justly or unjustly, was an effective means of punishing, controlling and changing the behavior of those desirous of receiving them. For women, who were traditionally more devoted to the eucharist than men, and who were excluded from entering the clergy themselves, such withholding could be particularly painful. Philippine's niece, a Religious of the Sacred Heart, recorded the following altercation between Van Quickenborne and Philippine. It concerns a rather petty argument which the two fiery-tempered individuals had in 1825 concerning a carpet in the sanctuary:

Both held to their views on the subject with that tenacity which is sometimes to be observed in the saints when there is question of what is for the greater glory of God, Father Van Quickenborne went so far as to threaten to have the altar removed, as he said he had given it to the church. "In that case," replied Mother Duchesne, "I shall take the tabernacle, which belongs to me." An altar without a tabernacle, or a tabernacle without an altar—either condition would

---

[11]Quoted in Garraghan, *Saint Ferdinand de Florissant*, p. 194.

have been embarrassing—so very embarrassing that the matter rested there. But the feast of the Sacred Heart was at hand. On the eve Mother Duchesne presented herself for confession, but instead of absolution which she had come seeking, she heard this terrifying sentence: "Tomorrow you will not renew your vows," and the shutter closed, putting an end to her pleading. Next day the poor superior, in order to avoid comments [for all the religious renewed vows together on that day], could only feign illness and remain in bed instead of leading the community to the altar rail for the renovation of vows. When she was sure they were all in the chapel and no one would see her, she crept noiselessly across the hall and prostrated herself behind the chapel door, weeping silently. When mass was ended, she went back to her cubbyhole, to spend a day of agony and shame. And only after a week of suffering was she accorded the absolution she had sought.[12]

The second incident took place in 1827. Philippine had just founded a new convent in St. Louis and she had offered a job to Martin Lepere, the hired hand in Florissant. Although Van Quickenborne considered Lepere lazy, he did not want him to go with the nuns, but to remain with the Jesuits in Florissant. Philippine offered Lepere the job anyway and the man accepted. Van Quickenborne was furious. He informed the nuns that he would no longer say mass for them nor would he send anyone in his place since the others, he said, would be engaged in their tertianship, a prolonged time of spiritual reflection for Jesuits. Philippine wrote during this period:

Meanwhile we must live on privations. We have no exposition of the blessed sacrament either in the Octave of Corpus Christi or in that of the Sacred Heart; often we lose four communions a week. These are my fast days, for I just cannot take any breakfast while I am hoping that some stroke of Divine Providence may bring a priest to give us communion. . . .

---

[12]Amélie Jouve, *Notes de la Révérende Mère Jouve concernant la vie de Notre Vénérable Mère Duchesne*, Religious of the Sacred Heart Archives, St. Louis, Missouri.

It is important to bear in mind that Van Quickenborne's withholding of the sacraments in these cases was not owing to some egregious sin he, as confessor, had discovered in Philippine's spiritual life, but rather to her opposition to him in matters of opinion, rather insignificant opinions at that. In the nineteenth century, depriving Philippine and her companions access to the eucharist signified genuine soul-suffering for all of them.

Philippine eventually developed strategies to protect herself. In this, she also followed the lead of numerous holy women since the Middle Ages, such as Saint Angela Merici, who found solace in "spiritual communions" when they were denied the eucharist or sacraments. In a "spiritual communion," Philippine encountered God in her heart. She by no means lost her devotion to the mass and eucharist, but she learned to appreciate more the many other ways in which she could encounter God. She suggested to Bishop Rosati, for example, that she and her sisters could remain in prayer before the exposed blessed sacrament on those days when there was no priest to give them communion. This was a practice already common in Sacred Heart convents in France. Rosati approved of the nuns' replacing "real" communion with this "spiritual" communion, but he said he could never approve of their leaving the tabernacle open to pray before the eucharist. "It would be a great irregularity," he said, "to allow religious women to do what the Church allows only to priests and deacons" [that is, to open the tabernacle]. Philippine also pointed out to Van Quickenborne that "there have been saints who became holy without mass," although she still regretted the sufferings its absence supposed for her religious sisters.

Philippine expressed her anger about such matters to Bishop Rosati. When he agreed to remove Van Quickenborne as the nuns' ecclesiastical superior, she wrote to him:

> I can never sufficiently express our joy over this. It is a great grace from God for which we shall never cease thanking Him. . . .

When Van Quickenborne chastised her in 1827 for giving certain jobs to novices during their period of spiritual formation, something he himself had done with his novices in 1823, Philippine complained openly to the bishop:

I avoid going to confession to the Father [Van Quickenborne],
for if he should say the same things to me in the confessional,
I should be in much greater difficulty. . . .

In the confessional, she would be compelled to obey his priestly authority, so Philippine simply chose not to put herself in such a vulnerable
position! Van Quickenborne, of course, is an extreme example of someone who, on occasion, used his religious authority abusively. And Philippine's generous regard for him continued despite their differences.

Her life, however, is replete with other examples of thorny relations with ecclesiastical authorities, authorities it should be added,
whom she respected enormously. Nineteenth-century religious, particularly cloistered nuns in isolated frontier situations, were especially
dependent upon the spiritual care of priestly confessors. Both Bishops
Dubourg and Rosati did what they could to provide the nuns with a
chaplain, but on the frontier, Philippine and her companions were
hard-put to find adequate spiritual assistance. On several occasions,
Philippine found herself faced with a confessor who used his privileged
position as confessor and confidant of each of the nuns to undermine
her own authority as superior of the community and promote his own
views. This was the case with Father Borgna whom Philippine finally
persuaded the bishop to remove in 1833. Another priest, Father
Saulnier, would rarely give her absolution after confession, causing her
genuine anguish. He also denied the other religious holy communion
on the days when their care of the sick children kept them from attending mass. One of Philippine's only outlets for her deepest feelings,
letter-writing, was forbidden to her on Sundays by a man who was her
friend, Father De La Croix. Perplexed but obedient, she set this matter
before the bishop too.

Of course these men, some as astute observers and confessors,
were presumably guided by their desire to give greater glory to God.
In some cases, they probably intended to put to rights a community or
individual situation in which they saw Philippine's judgement as mis-
guided, as it no doubt was on occasion. The point is not that Philippine
was always right in these moments of conflict with ecclesiastical authorities, but that she was always dependent. By nineteenth-century
norms, there is nothing that is surprising in these accounts. One of
Philippine's religious sisters captured the spirit of the age when she
recorded another incident between Van Quickenborne and Philippine.
On this occasion, he had gruffly refused to give her communion when
she drew near the altar to receive. The religious noted that he "greatly

appreciated Mother Duchesne and lost no opportunity of trying her by the sharpest mortifications," that Philippine and the other nuns "were used to his oddities and did not mind them," and, perhaps most revelatory, that "he was a real father to us." Eugénie Audé made the significant remark to Sophie Barat in 1830 that she was not so fond of the Jesuits in Florissant.[13]

Philippine was consistently deferent and sincere in her allusions to the priests with whom she disagreed. Shortly after her hot disagreement with Van Quickenborne concerning the carpet, after which he denied her absolution, and the opportunity to renew her vows and receive communion on the feast of the Sacred Heart, she praised his dedication to attending four parishes, sometimes risking his life to reach his isolated parishioners. Then she added discreetly:

> The firmness of this holy minister displeases many. . . . I see perfectly that a second [Father] would put hearts at ease. One cannot find greater merit, but sometimes [human] weaknesses need to be indulged.[14]

4. THE INDIAN SCHOOL

The failure of the Florissant schools to prosper did not dampen Philippine's dedication in the New World. Rather, it convinced her even more that the Society's true work was among the Indians. She wrote to Sophie Barat in July of 1824:

> In this section of the country there are so many reverses of fortune, so much instability in enterprises, so little support to rely on, one would almost need the visible finger of Divine Providence pointing the way before one would change one's residence. Here at Florissant we are no longer afraid of starving to death, and that is something. If God takes from us the means of doing good, we must accept His will. Sometimes I think God upset all our original plans and our first school in order to build up gradually the important work of training the savages. One really must merit a share in that work by humiliations and other sufferings. Do not worry about us.

---

[13]Cunningham, *Eugénie Audé*, p. 42, n. 9.
[14]Quoted in Garraghan, *The Jesuits of the Middle United States*, vol. I, p. 114.

Not a single one of us is discouraged. I am the most dissatisfied because I have reason to think I have turned God's blessing from our labors.

Philippine finally got her chance to educate Indian girls in April, 1825. Van Quickenborne brought her two little girls to be boarders with the nuns. He had begun a boarding school, called a Seminary, for Indian and mestizo boys the previous year and felt that a school for girls was necessary so that the boys would one day be able to marry Christian wives![15] Van Quickenborne's own account of the opening of the boarding school for boys captures the sense of uprooting it signified for the Indians:

The Indian youths [of the Iowa Indian nation] did not submit without a protest to what must have seemed to them, accustomed as they were to the freedom of the forest, as nothing short of imprisonment. They began to cry piteously as their parents prepared to depart, whereupon one of the scholastics took up a flute and began to play. The music had the effect of quieting the lads and making them resigned, as far as outward indications went, to their new environment. But Vasquez, the [United States Government] agent, warned Father Van Quickenborne that a sharp eye would have to be kept on the boys, as flight was an easy trick for them. Accordingly, Mr. Smedts, the Prefect, rose at intervals during the first night of the Iowa's stay at the Seminary to see that his young charges were all within bounds, while another scholastic was also assigned to sentry duty. But somehow or other the watchers were outwitted. About one o'clock in the morning the Iowa made a clever escape. Their flight was soon detected, and immediately a party of two were on the track of the fugitives. They were nimble runners, for they were five miles from the Seminary, when their pursuers came up to them. They made no resistance to capture and returned, apparently quite content, though determined, no doubt to repeat the adventure when opportunity offered.[16]

---

[15]Garraghan, *The Jesuits of the Middle United States*, vol. I, pp. 158–60; and Rothensteiner, *History of the Archdiocese of St. Louis*, vol. I, pp. 348, and 343–44.

[16]Van Quickenborne to Dziorizynski, June 12, 1824; quoted in Rothensteiner, *History of the Archdiocese of St. Louis*, vol. I, p. 341.

The Indian girls were, of course, educated apart from the other girls boarding with the nuns. Philippine begged both her relatives and Mother Barat for money to support the Indian children. She was at last involved in the work of her dreams, but it was doomed to an early failure. Although more Indian girls came, bringing their number to about a dozen in 1827, they never reached the expected numbers of forty to sixty pupils.[17] A little over a year after the school's opening, Philippine had already identified a central problem:

> God seems to raise great obstacles to the work of teaching the savages. The government is buying their land and pushing them out of the states of the Union, forcing them to live within the narrow limits of restricted territory that has not nearly enough space for hunting, and that is their only mode of subsistence. The various tribes thus herded together make war on each other and so destroy themselves, or at least the weaker nations are wiped out. Beginning this year the Indians are no longer allowed to hunt in the state of Missouri, so the parents of several of our Indian children have come to take their boys from the Jesuits and their girls from us, and we have no means of keeping the children here. Their parents simply said they could no longer come to see them, and as they are pagans they could not bring themselves to make this sacrifice. . . .

By July, 1831, there were no Indian children at all in either the boys' or the girls' school. In the case of the boys' school, contemporaries attributed the failure to the distance separating the school from the Indian villages, the brevity of school hours, the excessive physical labor imposed on the boys, lack of financial support, and the severity of Van Quickenborne's discipline.[18]

The efforts of Van Quickenborne and Philippine among the Indian children were, as are all missionary efforts, a two-edged sword. They both brought something to these children and took something away. Both recognized the intelligence of the Indian children and compared them favorably to children of European descent, so there was no overt prejudice in this regard. But Philippine was in complete accord with the Jesuit philosophy that successful conversion of the Indians

---

[17]Garraghan, *The Jesuits of the Middle United States*, vol. I, pp. 160 and 165.
[18]Garraghan, *The Jesuits of the Middle United States*, vol. I, pp. 165–69.

involved changing most aspects of their own culture.[19] Christian missionaries brought to native Americans not only Christian belief; they took away from them many of their customs and tribal traditions, even those not contrary to Christian dogma. This explains the importance for Philippine of removing the children from their own environments, the Indian villages.

Philippine also believed with the Jesuits that if parents would not give up their children, the only alternative was to go and live among them. Philippine's and Van Quickenborne's dedication to this notion reflects their radical commitment to the Christian missionary ideal as it was construed in the nineteenth century. They were both willing to live out their lives in far-removed Indian villages for the sake of "saving" these people. Many early Jesuit missionaries also made efforts to "redeem" certain Indian customs by underlining their similarity to Christian belief.[20] There was, of course, a certain cultural imperialism involved in even these altruistic ideals of nineteenth-century missionaries among the Indians. After all, the only Indian customs which to them were worthy of redemption were those which were similar to Christian beliefs.

A tendency to idealize missionaries and saints leads some biographers to omit the negative side of evangelization in the Americas. The depth and integrity of native American faith was rarely appreciated. "Christianizing" the Indians was usually tantamount to destroying their culture. Philippine herself frequently made remarks about Indians, typical of European missionaries, which betray her own bias about their culture. A more extreme example is the following reflection which she shared in 1827 with her cousin Josephine regarding the Indian school:

> The work for the Indians is of very doubtful value. To carry it on successfully, the miracle of miracles is needed—that is, to change their very nature, which is corrupted from their earliest years. One would need to live in their midst.

The official charged with "care" of the Indians in the United States at this time was, ironically, the Secretary of War. Van

---

[19]See Rothensteiner, *History of the Archdiocese of St. Louis*, vol. I, p. 348.

[20]For a good discussion of these points, see Henry Warner Bowden, *American Indians and Christian Missions: Studies in Cultural Conflict* (Chicago: The University of Chicago Press, 1981), especially "Jesuit Missions," pp. 75–95.

Quickenborne wrote to him about the schools he and the Religious of the Sacred Heart were managing. It is patent that he associated, or even identified, the question of the Indians' religious belief with such non-religious issues as their work habits and their obedience to the United States government, a government still engaged in decimating their ranks. The "spirit" which the Jesuits and the Religious of the Sacred Heart were trying to inculcate in the children, according to Van Quickenborne, was

> a spirit of the fear of the Lord, a spirit of regularity, industry and subordination, [and] a sincere attachment from principle and Religion to our most beneficent Government in their behalf. . . . [21]

The cultural conflict which took place in the Americas with the arrival of Europeans was not a simple matter of greedy and insensitive Christian Europeans versus innocent and victimized native Americans. In many cases, Christian missionaries forthrightly defended the human rights of the Indians against unjust incursions of white traders and the United States government. Philippine recognized and complained of many such abuses. But the above account also shows that even Christians sympathetic to native Americans betrayed their sense of cultural and religious superiority.

---

[21]Quoted in Garraghan, *The Jesuits of the Middle United States*, vol. I, p. 160; and Rothensteiner, *The History of the Archdiocese of St. Louis*, vol. I, p. 344.

VIII.

Leadership for the Poor and Marginalized

The subject of Philippine's leadership as superior in the United States has generated conflict among her biographers. During the years of the Society's expansion in the United States, Philippine strongly disagreed with some of the other religious on issues key to the Society's success. These included decisions to open and to close schools, the style of schools to be established and the upkeep of the convents. They also disagreed about the degree of religious uniformity necessary between the United States convents and the convents of France. On a number of occasions, the other religious simply ignored Philippine's authority. Significantly, they sometimes had the support of Mother Barat or Bishop Rosati, Dubourg's successor. The temptation in writing a saint's life is to portray her as always in the right in such cases, and the other religious as unenlightened or even self-serving.

Errors in judgement were no doubt made by all involved, but the central question is not who was right or wrong in each particular case, but rather, how did Philippine choose to lead the Society of the Sacred Heart in America. Two points are significant in this regard. First, Philippine's vision of the Society of the Sacred Heart in the United States obviously affected the choices she made as superior. Another vision, held by another religious and perhaps equally valid, would have led to an entirely different style of leadership and a "different" Society of the Sacred Heart. Philippine's commitment to support poorer foundations, as discussed in the previous chapter, tended to soften her commitment to financial realism. In several instances, it hampered the Society's outward success in the United States. Some of her religious sisters disagreed with the choices she made in this regard. Philippine's commitment to the poor, however, grew stronger in the face of this criticism. With the mature conviction of a wise, old

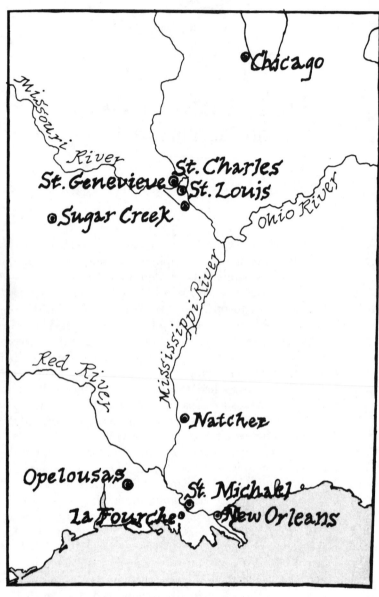

The Mississippi Valley and first foundations associated with Mother Philippine
Duchesne and the Society of the Sacred Heart.

woman, she became more outspoken in her later years. Always humble, still self-denigrating at times, Philippine found her voice regarding the Society's work among the poor.

Second, Philippine was superior in the United States for twenty-two years and for twenty-two years she protested that she was not fit to be superior. She continually pleaded with Sophie Barat to remove her from this office. On several occasions, her confessor Father Van Quickenborne ordered her under obedience to write to Mother Barat requesting that someone more suitable be appointed to replace Philippine. How Philippine felt about her ability to be superior influenced how she chose to lead—and who chose to follow her.

Several factors influenced Sophie Barat to deny Philippine's request to be relieved as superior. She knew that Philippine consistently underrated her own talents. The foundation of the Society in the Americas needed someone strong like Philippine, strong enough to endure the hard physical test of the frontier and strong enough to remain steadfast despite loneliness, conflicts and failures. It is especially significant that Sophie Barat named her superior of the little missionary group in 1818. She was well aware of Philippine's failings as an administrator. Her correspondence with Philippine and Eugénie Audé indicates that she generally favored Eugénie's style of government and administration. But she recognized another value in Philippine: her staunch dedication to the poor. It would keep the Society in the United States faithful to the congregation's original spirit. There was a tendency already evident among some Religious of the Sacred Heart in France to favor works among the well-to-do at the expense of works among the poor. It was a tendency which risked leading the Society into a sort of spiritual bankruptcy. This insight into Mother Barat's motives for maintaining Philippine as superior in the United States helps explain the fact that she sometimes disregarded Philippine's authority in administrative matters, favoring instead the advice of other religious on the frontier. But in matters touching upon the spirit of the congregation, or the Society's works among the poor, Mother Barat counted on the advice of Philippine over that of the other religious, even when she chose not to follow it.

Ultimately, these two characteristics, Philippine's own insecurity about herself as superior combined with her personal desire to serve the poor, explain most of her disagreements with other religious. These traits colored her judgement about opening and closing various convents and schools. Visible success mattered little to Philippine, a quality easy to admire from afar, but more difficult for some of her religious sisters who preferred a different approach to evangelization on the frontier.

1. NEW FOUNDATIONS

Between 1825 and 1828, four new foundations were made in addition to the two already existing in Florissant, Missouri and Opelousas, Louisiana: St. Michael's, Louisiana (1825), St. Louis, Missouri (1827), La Fourche, Louisiana (1828), and St. Charles, Missouri, where the religious returned for a second time in 1828. Twelve women had already entered the Society in the United States and been trained as Religious of the Sacred Heart before these foundations were made. Other nuns had joined them from Europe. By 1830, just twelve years after the Society's foundation in America, there were sixty-four Religious of the Sacred Heart in America, fifty of whom had entered the Society in the United States.

St. Michael's: The foundation in St. Michael's, Louisiana provides an interesting case of the complex relations among Philippine, Sophie Barat, Eugénie Audé and the new bishop, Joseph Rosati. Since a house in New Orleans still could not be opened, the nuns began to consider an offer they received to found a convent and school in St. Michael's, a town on the Mississippi near New Orleans. Both Eugénie and Philippine agreed that a second house in Lower Louisiana was essential to support the languishing foundation in Florissant and its Indian school.

Philippine, in her capacity as superior in the United States, wrote to Mother Barat in 1824 to apprise her of the situation. She mentioned too that she had invited Eugénie to Florissant to confer on the matter. But shortly thereafter she received a letter from Eugénie. This letter informed Philippine that Mother Barat had already granted her approval of the new foundation. She gave her approval through her correspondence with Eugénie, not Philippine. The foundation was a *fait accompli.* In fact, four thousand dollars, a formidable sum in those days, had already been raised to finance the construction of a convent. Within two months, the voluntary contributions for the new foundation had risen to almost seven thousand dollars. Surely Philippine had feelings about how the foundation had been decided without her, but she guarded silence.

It was also indirectly that she learned that Mother Barat wanted her to go as superior of the new foundation. Philippine wrote to the Mother General in March, 1825, to protest such a move. She claimed that the reputation, talent and zeal of Eugénie were much more suited to the task. Now fifty-six, Philippine added these comments about herself to clinch the argument:

> Here, more than in France, the old and the ugly are held in low repute. I grow more unsightly every day. Gray hair, no teeth, horribly roughened hands, all make me in no way suitable to cut a figure in that fastidious section of the country. They are all right here in the village where, indeed, they call me quite affectionately "poor devil."

She feared too that without her, Florissant would close:

> True, it is miserably poor, but for that very reason it is dear to me. . . .

There is a sense in which Philippine identified the poverty she felt regarding her own talent, looks and leadership capacity with the poverty of the places she chose to live and work. Her personal poverty in these regards was less real than it was imaginary, but it had an enormous impact on her choices. A cliché has it that the greatest saints think themselves the greatest sinners, and that the greatest sinners think themselves the greatest saints. Philippine's low opinion of herself should be weighed against the judgement of another religious who was with her at that time:

> [Mother Duchesne] used to give the General Instruction [to the children] herself, and her exhortations, supplemented by her holy example, sank deep into their hearts. . . .
>
> Mother Duchesne made the recreations very pleasant. The dignity of her manner did not detract from her amiability, while her extensive and varied information, her ready command of French, and above all the love of God which seemed the very breath of her life, made her conversation not only entertaining and instructive, but also calculated to keep alive the fervor of us all. There was a singular earnestness and unction in everything she said that gave her a kind of power for drawing souls to God. . . .
>
> Mother Duchesne slept very little, for besides her prolonged vigils before the blessed sacrament, she used also to sit up with the sick whenever this was necessary; and when dressing in the morning, the religious often found their shoes

and clothing mended and knew whose charitable hands had
done the work. . . . She also reserved for herself the night
visit of the house and the morning call. . . . [1]

There were now practically no paying boarders at all in Florissant, while there were twenty-seven in Eugénie Audé's school in
Opelousas. As early as 1824, Eugénie was suggesting to Mother Barat
that Florissant, which she felt "for six years has only vegetated," be
closed in favor of a foundation in a more promising place. Sophie
Barat, who had originally opposed the Society's foundation in that
village, agreed with Eugénie and recommended that at least the boarding school be moved to a more promising location.[2] Eugénie had a
temporary change of heart about Florissant after visiting the foundation in 1825, and joined with Philippine in convincing Sophie Barat to
leave Philippine there for the time being.

Closing Florissant because of its minimal success never even occurred to Philippine. She measured success with a different ruler. She
reminded Sophie Barat in March, 1825:

And if, as our Rule says, the poor should be preferred to the
rich, we have no reason to envy Opelousas. We care for as
many souls as they, and we shall always have more novices.
You know Mother Eugénie has trained only one novice so far,
and here ten have persevered.

In late 1824 she had also written to the Mother General:

I cannot conceive how Mother Eugénie could advise our abandoning this house. Though it is poorer, I find it much happier than hers. The *essential spirit* can be preserved here always under influence of this good spiritual direction. . . .

It is difficult to judge at this distance the "spirit" of the houses in
Florissant and Opelousas. In 1823, although Opelousas was flourishing, Philippine prevented Eugénie from undertaking any new construction. She wrote to Sophie Barat criticizing Eugénie's government of

---

[1]Mother Anna Shannon, *Notes on Reverend Mother Duchesne*, Religious of the Sacred Heart
Archives, St. Louis, Missouri.

[2]See, for example, her letters to Eugénie Audé, April 8, July 16, July 28, August 20, and
October 15, 1824.

the convent and school there. Philippine cited the sudden misfortunes of institutions in the United States and argued that Eugénie's rapid build-up of the Opelousas venture would spell disaster. Given the financial situation on the frontier at this time, Philippine's points were well-taken. But also to the point is that Opelousas not only survived the crisis: it was an impressive success.

St. Michael's finally opened in November, 1825, and Eugénie Audé went as its superior,[3] leaving Mother Xavier Murphy in charge of Opelousas. Within just sixteen months the St. Michael's boarding school alone had ninety students enrolled, compared to about twenty in Florissant. Its novices also outnumbered those of the Florissant foundation. St. Michael's was, of course, placed in a more affluent and Catholic area of the United States, but there is no doubting the excellent administrative and educational talents of Eugénie Audé.

Her leadership differed from Philippine's not only in style, but in direction as well. She sought to build strong, successful schools following the French model she had known in Europe. Although Sophie Barat, plagued by debts of her own in France, occasionally warned her about the dangers of over-spending and the temptations of success,[4] she was generally supportive of Eugénie's ventures. Unlike Philippine, whose nuns at one of her convents complained of the cramped conditions and Philippine's refusal to build, Sophie Barat encouraged construction projects which would enhance a foundation's reputation and make possible a more regulated religious life.[5] Sophie Barat congratulated Eugénie for the good government of her houses.[6] On August 5, 1826 she wrote thanking her for a letter describing the foundation's beginnings. She said regarding the ordering of the house à l'Européenne, "all of that charms me."

The City House in St. Louis—The Orphans: In 1827, a foundation was finally made in St. Louis. It was called the "City House" to distinguish it from the "Country House" in Florissant. Sophie Barat favored foundations in cities where a large population ensured many boarders and a large free school. But the numerous Protestant schools in St. Louis, a

---

[3]On Eugénie Audé's administration of St. Michael's, see Cunningham, *Eugénie Audé*, pp. 43–63.

[4]See her letters to Eugénie Audé, September 14, October 23 and November 8, 1828; March 5, 1829; and May 5, 1832.

[5]See her letters to Eugénie Audé, April 15, 1828; August 7, 1830; May 8, October 22, November 8 and December 13, 1831.

[6]See her letters of July 30, 1822; February 1, May 28 and August 5, 1826; and October 22, 1831.

lack of sufficient interest on the part of Catholic St. Louisans, Dubourg's opposition to the venture, Philippine's commitment to maintaining the Florissant establishment, and a lack of funds made this foundation difficult. Mother Barat continued to urge Philippine to try to overcome these problems.

From her perspective, Philippine recognized that the new school could be a fresh source of aid for the poor school in Florissant. Since her St. Louis acquaintances offered little help, her only recourse was to go to John Mullanphy. She had calculated that a good house in St. Louis would cost her at least thirty thousand francs, money she did not have. In March, 1827, she explained her predicament to Sophie Barat:

> So I wrote to Mr. Mullanphy, asking him if he would not give us a house, as he owns a great many, and that on favorable conditions in view of our intention of opening a free school for the children of the poor. He answered by asking in turn how many orphans we would house on the following conditions: 1. that he would give us a brick house built about seven years ago, situated at a distance of a fifteen-minute walk from the Catholic church, with twenty-four arpents [about twenty acres] of land around it, not cultivated except for a vegetable garden, the house having twelve fairly large rooms, but not being as large as our convent here; 2. that he or his heirs would give each orphan at her entrance the sum of fifty francs for her bed, etc., and twenty-five francs yearly for clothing; and 3. that he would give five thousand francs cash for the initial expenses of the foundation. I replied that we would accept fifteen or twenty orphans; he wanted twenty, and they were to be presented by himself or his oldest daughters.

Mullanphy's generous offer was only dampened by the financial burden the orphans would be for the institution. The money he proposed for their support would not begin to cover the real costs, costs which would be a constant drain on the foundation's finances. Philippine needed the income from the paying students to subsidize the poor schools of both Florissant and St. Louis. But she still recognized the overall benefits of Mullanphy's offer and defended it to Mother Barat:

> True, we are taking on a burden for which we shall be responsible, but think of a debt of twenty or thirty thousand francs [for building], or the necessity of being confined to a village

[Florissant] where we are shut in by six feet of water up to our door five or six times a year, and that quite suddenly and with such force as to wash away the bridge leading to our house, to flatten all our fences, to destroy our entire garden, which has produced nothing these last two years, as the vegetables have rotted in the water. Besides that, there is the probability that if we do not take the lead [in opening a school in St. Louis], someone else may do so, and we shall be without any means of supporting ourselves. . . .

The initial reaction of Van Quickenborne, Bishop Rosati and Sophie Barat was that the contract Philippine had made with Mullanphy to support twenty orphans was too burdensome. Given Philippine's financial straits, however, it was the best bargain to be made.

The feeling that these orphan children were a burden is somewhat puzzling in light of the fact that the institution to be opened was, after all, dedicated to the education of all children, rich and poor. But Philippine implied that they were an obstacle when she wrote to Sophie Barat:

In a country so destitute of opportunities for the education of youth, should I have held back because of the orphans?

Of course, it was not the orphans *per se* who were the burden, but the financial agreement about their care. This contract was to be binding for the entire 999-year lease of the house and land. Even so, orphans in this period routinely helped defray some of the costs of their upkeep by doing a share of the housework in the institutions which accepted them. For example, Eugénie Audé said of those in St. Michael's:

They wait on themselves, are poorly clothed, have plain food, are trained to do all kinds of work and prepared to support themselves by manual work.

Philippine pointed out in a letter of 1834, moreover, that the government contributed ten thousand francs toward the support of the orphans at St. Michael's.

The homes the orphans found in the many Convents of the Sacred Heart provided them with a warmth, security and future they would not otherwise have had. The cruel treatment orphans commonly received in many institutions inspired novels such as Charles Dickens' *Oliver Twist* which is, in part, a social protest against such mistreatment. But most people in the nineteenth century, including the Religious of the Sacred Heart, treated orphans quite differently than other children. They were "kept" by the institution, and thus were separated in the nuns' minds even from the children attending their free day school. The orphans were educated apart and "trained" particularly in manual labor. This often meant doing many of the household chores. Their plight was even spiritualized. On several occasions the orphans' very misfortune was subtly highlighted as a way of invoking God's attention in times of distress.

Two incidents concerning the orphans of the St. Louis foundation are especially revelatory of nineteenth-century attitudes toward them, even among charitable Catholics concerned for their care. First, the orphans were especially valued as members of funeral corteges, a practice dating back centuries in Western Europe. In 1833, for example, the girls of the orphanage were made to walk in John Mullanphy's funeral cortege dressed in black and white. Just a few weeks later, when Octavie Berthold died, the orphans led her funeral procession. On first consideration, it was natural that these children march before the coffins of those who had helped them during their lives. Nevertheless, particularly in the case of John Mullanphy, the parallel with a charitable practice in seventeenth-century France and elsewhere is certainly significant. Paupers who had received charity from the largess of wealthy donors were expected to march in the funeral corteges of their benefactors. This was not only considered payment for what they had been given;[7] in the case of Mullanphy, it also reflected a spiritualized notion attached to the poor, orphaned children. A singular poignancy was attached to the prayers and laments of these children.

A second, less subtle incident, confirms this point. In 1834, St. Louis was struck by a terrible cholera plague. Philippine, now in her mid-sixties, had already entered a period of her life of increased spiritual anxiety. For her the plague was evidence of divine displeasure and she gave herself to prolonged prayer and penance to assuage God's wrath. A number of the St. Louis religious were so sick that they were sent to Florissant to recuperate. That left only Philippine and Catherine Lamarre, one of the religious who came with Philippine in 1818, to implore God's mercy before the eucharist. They had the orphans substitute for the missing religious in the nuns' all-day adoration. But that is not all. Philippine wrote in her *Journal:*

---

[7]Norberg, *Rich and Poor in Grenoble*, pp. 150–51.

On the eve of the feast of the Holy Heart of Mary, nine of the orphans fasted on bread and water to obtain the cessation of our trials, if such be the will of God. These young penitents made a procession in honor of our Lady, walking barefoot and with ropes around their necks. A few days later our religious returned from Florissant quite recuperated, and several of the pupils came back.

Although jarring to modern sensibilities, this peculiar penitential practice was not so peculiar in the nineteenth century. It was not mistreatment of the orphans. Saints and Christians since the Middle Ages, including Francis of Assisi, had performed exactly this same penance to express human contrition and invoke God's mercy. Moreover, since religious practice derives its meaning from the inner attitude of the believer rather than from the external act itself, it is even possible that the orphans derived some spiritual satisfaction from their penance. Philippine's concern for them, as for all the children, was always principally their spiritual growth.

But the above incident affords us a window into other less appealing aspects of nineteenth-century attitudes toward orphans. If God hears the prayers of the poor in a privileged manner, it is owing to the urgency of their needs. To use their prayers and supplications for the benefit of others, whether to obtain reward for the largess of their benefactors, to appease God's anger or calm the fears of those who imagine it, is to miss the point. The sight of forlorn orphans processing at the head of a funeral cortege certainly enhanced the sadness of the occasion. The spectacle of poor children processing with ropes around their necks in penitence seemed to some people in the nineteenth century an effective way of drawing God's pity. But to make poverty poignant, even poetic, by such displays also trivialized its effect in the lives of its victims. This insensitivity was, of course, entirely unconscious, and it existed simultaneously with genuine care and concern for the orphans in other respects. The paternalistic attitudes toward orphans at the City House, attitudes which unfortunately persisted well into the twentieth century, were typical of a time in which any aid to them was considered extraordinary.

The City House—The Convent and Schools: When the City House opened in 1827, it was Philippine herself who went to found it. She was fifty-seven years old. In the nine years since her arrival from France, English had overtaken St. Louis as the dominant language, a language she had since learned how to write, but felt too insecure to try to speak. She wrote about the new foundation to the nuns in Paris:

I was acting without the least promise of success. Mother Octavie [in Florissant] was ill; Mother Eugénie refused to send anyone to help me; I had one leg so crippled with rheumatism, it threatened to incapacitate me. . . . I had to come to St. Louis with just one Irish aspirant. The house was not ready; there were no teachers for the classes; and we could have had a crowd of children at the moment, but now that we can take them they are going elsewhere. Our greatest trial is the uncertainty with regard to spiritual help. Beg our Lord to remove this privation by one of those strokes of His Providence that cost Him nothing at all.

Our chapel is most unworthy of the Divine Majesty. It is located in what was formerly the kitchen, partly underground—what they call here a *cellar*. You can touch the ceiling with your hand. The fireplace serves as an altar. I have killed several toads down there and some other horrible creatures, and huge spiders that chirp a little like birds. They kept up their music at night when I was there alone in the chapel. There was also a fierce big cat that had gone wild and made a home under the roof. These were the only ghosts we discovered in the house. I must admit that I was less afraid of them when we first came here than I was of living human beings, for the place is so isolated. . . .

Work on the house, in addition to a new building project, and new loans, were necessary before the schools could be opened. Several new religious arrived from France to help with the foundation. By March, 1828, the St. Louis school had twelve boarders, ten day pupils, ten orphans, thirty free school students and a Sunday school for mulatto girls. The direction of the schools betrays the stamp of Philippine's personality for by May, 1829, there were sixty free school students, eighteen day pupils (on whose tuition the nuns depended) and just eight boarders. The St. Louis girls choosing to enter the Society, moreover, were all from the poor school.

Philippine frequently commented on the "worldliness" of the boarding school alumnae, both in Florissant and in St. Louis. Despite her own well-to-do background, she was uncomfortable with shows of wealth. There are two reasons for this. First, the series of choices she had made as an adult regarding her own wealth removed her from the world of pleasure and ease. By temperament and spirituality, she was not attracted to the comforts and amenities which wealth afforded. She had chosen to put her gifts, both personal and material, at the service of others. Second, Philippine found both self-indulgence and the desire for wealth to be more pronounced on the frontier than in her native Dauphiny. She was shocked by the luxury she found upon her arrival in the New World. Many years later, she continued to be perplexed by traits she identified as peculiarly American. She wrote to her friend and cousin Josephine in 1837:

> The people of the United States are quite remarkable for their care about external forms, their keenness of intellect, and their genius for science and art. It may be that from the Christian point of view they go much too far in their passion for knowledge, their personal ambition, and their desire for worldly success. Being so old-fashioned, I love simplicity all the more in contrast to the affectation of wealth and knowledge that I see at times.

And again in 1838:

> In this country, where everything is new and where luxury and soft living are indulged in to a disgusting excess, I find delight in recalling the simple pleasures of our childhood. . . . Those happy days in the big family were surely preferable to the proud disdain, the indifference, the affected languor, by which people think they make themselves important and attractive.

It is hardly surprising then to discover that disappointment and scandal at the behavior of the boarding school alumnae pepper Philippine's letters from both Florissant and St. Louis. The following remarks from Florissant in 1823 and 1824 are typical:

> Can they [the parents] love us when they expose to danger the young girls who leave our school? It is hard for these girls to struggle when their own parents thrust them into temptation. The most outstanding pupil we had last year gave herself up immediately to balls, comedies, expensive clothes, hence to loss of time and neglect of prayer. And these are the fruits of our labor.

> One does not find friends and protectors easily out here. Each one thinks of himself, and no one will sacrifice his ease and pleasure for the sake of good works. There is not *faith*

enough for that. Our greatest suffering does not come from being mocked and calumniated in social circles by our former pupils, but rather from seeing them rushing headlong on the road of pleasure and indolence.

The hardest of all has been the fact that practically all the pupils who have left us and who seemed so fervent and thoroughly good, have fallen back into their former neglect of religion, as a result of their natural levity and the influence of pleasure and bad example. I still hope that their faith is not dead and that age, reverses, and other trials from the hand of God will someday bring them to repentance—that is my only hope for them.

Philippine often encountered parental resistance to the choices she made as superior in St. Louis from 1827 to 1834. For example, the parents objected to the school's strictness. In 1829, Philippine made the following report to Sophie Barat:

The parents of our children have been acting in a most unreasonable manner, demanding two months of vacation, two outings a week, etc. Then they held a meeting at the home of one family and gave out the report that I was leaving the city because the institution was going to pieces. I ignored all this. . . .

In 1831, she wrote again to Mother Barat:

I can never deal easily with the parents of our children. The Americans do not understand me. The Creoles want good looks and attractive manners. The best thing for me to do is to disappear, either teaching a class or caring for the sick. I tell you this in all sincerity. . . .

It is difficult to assess the situation from this distance. Was Philippine too harsh a disciplinarian? Did wealthy parents desire only a frivolous life for their daughters? Even some of the religious themselves, while recognizing Philippine's spiritual stature, occasionally complained that she could be severe as superior. On the other hand, there were some parents interested primarily in providing their daughters with a solid—and stylish—French education, who were indifferent to its religious content.

In an article in 1832 in the diocesan journal, *The Shepherd of the Valley*, Mr. Francis Taylor, a journalist and convert to Catholicism, wrote an article about the City House. He was the only male teacher in the establishment and had been hired by the nuns to teach English, a subject they were not able to teach. In his article, Taylor painted a picture of the kind and genteel education which would attract many parents then:

> The Female Academy under the direction of the Ladies of the Sacred Heart (St. Louis) is already well known by the accomplished young ladies who have received a finished education in it and who have brought from it to the bosom of their families, and to the world a greatful [*sic*] affection for their teachers who, with tender and maternal care, guided them in their advance to virtue and useful knowledge.[8]

Taylor also admired the elegance of the embroidery, needlework and samples from the other "branches of female education" on display at the school's annual "Literary Exhibition." He praised their melodious singing, their artful mastery of the piano and their elegant recitations of poetry in both French and English.

There is no doubt that the City House boarding school was offering one of the best educations available to young women in nineteenth-century America. This is something Philippine, ever self-effacing and perhaps too absorbed with difficulties, failed to mention. Mr. Taylor was impressed that the school provided young women with skills "suitable to their sex," but it was also giving them foundations in history, literature, mathematics and other subjects common in young men's education. Even given its bias toward the feminine arts, the curriculum at City House was virtually as advanced an education as a young woman could receive on the frontier.[9] At the time of Philippine's death years later in 1852, there were still very few schools of higher education which would even consider admitting women. Elizabeth Cady Stanton, Lucretia Mott and hundreds of other women in the United

---

[8]Mr. Francis H. Taylor, "Education," *The Shepherd of the Valley*, October 13, 1832; quoted in Callan, *Philippine Duchesne*, p. 537.

[9]For an account of the primitive schooling available to most children on the frontier in nineteenth-century America, see Stratton, *Pioneer Women: Voices from the Kansas Frontier*, pp. 157–70.

States had already voiced their outrage at women's exclusion from higher education, but to little avail.[10]

Furthermore, the years a young woman spent at a Sacred Heart boarding school, albeit under the tutelage of the nuns, were probably among the most independent years of her life. They were probably the only time during which men would not be the dominant individuals in her social and domestic life. As the Massachusetts journalist Judith Sargent Murray remarked in the late eighteenth century, such education instilled a new self-confidence, self-respect and aspiration in American women. In 1798 she predicted, "I expect to see our young women forming a new era in female history."[11] The first issue of the *Ladies Magazine* appeared in 1828, just a few months after the City House was founded. In it, Sarah Hale applauded the new rise of female academies in the States. She wrote:

> Perhaps no experiment will have an influence more important on the character and happiness of our society than granting to females the advantages of a systematic and thorough education.[12]

Not surprisingly, many parents were eager that their daughters receive such an education, regardless of their own religious convictions or humanitarian concerns. For Philippine and the other Religious of the Sacred Heart, religious formation and humanitarian concern were the cornerstone of any good education. When she complained of alumnae who simply wasted their education, she was referring to their lack of religious commitment, which would guide them in their use of all other knowledge. As Mary Ann Rourke Cartan, a student of that time, recalled years later: "The strongest point of the education was religious instruction. Those nuns spoke like priests."[13]

In spite of its solid curriculum, the City House boarding school survived, but never really flourished under Philippine's supervision. In 1832, five years after her arrival, there were few boarders, but ninety-

---

[10]See for example, the "Seneca Falls Declaration" drawn up by about three hundred women in Seneca Falls, New York in 1848; in *Feminism: The Essential Historical Writings*, ed. Miriam Schneir (New York: Vintage Books, 1972), pp. 77–82.

[11]Quoted in Nancy Woloch, *Women and the American Experience* (New York: Alfred A. Knopf, 1984), pp. 92–93.

[12]Quoted in Woloch, *Women and the American Experience*, p. 126.

[13]"Recollections of Venerated Mother Duchesne" (St. Louis, 1910), Religious of the Sacred Heart Archives, St. Louis, Missouri.

three students in the free school. The financial situation of St. Louis could account for some of these numbers. The majority of students in the Jesuit school were also non-paying. But Philippine's own partiality toward the free school and her discomfort with wealth must also have contributed to the boarding school's struggle and her difficult relations with some of the parents of these children. Sophie Barat received letters of complaint from some of the religious in Philippine's convent that Philippine did not know how to cultivate relations with influential people in St. Louis.

La Fourche: Shortly after Philippine's arrival in St. Louis in 1827, Bishop Rosati proposed to her yet another foundation in Lower Louisiana. The Sisters of Loretto at La Fourche, not too far from St. Michael's, wanted to transfer into the Society of the Sacred Heart. They were all English-speaking Americans and were unable to work in La Fourche, a French settlement.

This short-lived foundation is interesting primarily for the light it sheds on the relationships among Philippine, Rosati and the other religious who were superiors of houses in the Society. Despite the fact that all of these superiors were technically under the authority of Philippine, who acted as a sort of provincial, it is clear from this episode that she held little or no effective authority. Bishop Rosati himself chose to discuss the possibility of a foundation at La Fourche first with Eugénie Audé rather than Philippine. Eugénie opposed the foundation since she feared it would be in competition with her own school of St. Michael's. Xavier Murphy, the superior of Opelousas, agreed.

Philippine, on the other hand, favored the foundation when she learned of the possibility. She and Eugénie each launched campaigns to persuade Mother Barat and Rosati to her own point of view. Philippine wrote to Rosati in January, 1828, a strong point by point refutation of Eugénie's arguments. Her frustration with her own lack of authority is clear from what followed in the same letter:

Finally, our Mother [Barat] did indeed advise us not to make any more foundations for a time. She was afraid we would ask her for money and subjects which she wanted to save for the foundation in the East [of the United States], but which she is now postponing. I am surprised at Mother Eugénie's displeasure—of which she says I am partly the cause. Our Mother General, in spite of my representations, has given me charge of all the houses in this country. Mother Eugénie refused to give any religious for this foundation [in St. Louis] and she has kept a Sister from here whom I need—but I left her there. Now her community numbers seventeen, and she wants to take a very necessary member from the Opelousas community, which numbers only five. Do you think this is fair? Because I told Mother Eugénie she was going beyond her power, she has taken offense. I cannot say that something wrong is right. And I have been telling her for a long while that, instead of getting herself into even greater debt by expansion, it would be wiser to limit her enrollment to the number of children that can be actually cared for.

Philippine was unaware when she wrote this letter that Eugénie had changed her mind, at least for the time being. In fact, in December, 1827, she and Rosati had decided together to go ahead with the La Fourche project.[14] They did not consult Philippine; they did not even consult Mother Barat, who they simply assumed would agree to the foundation. The assumption may appear cavalier,[15] but it proved to be absolutely correct. Eugénie understood better than Philippine Mother Barat's concern that the Society in the United States flourish through the establishment of promising foundations. Only in mid-March did Philippine learn that the novices of the Sisters of Loretto at La Fourche had been transferred to St. Michael's to be under Eugénie's care. The final blow came in April, 1828. She received a letter from Rosati telling her that Eugénie had proposed which Religious of the Sacred Heart would be superior of the La Fourche foundation. Philippine's forbearance was exhausted. She wrote unequivocally to Rosati that, "Mother Eugénie has said nothing to me about who is to be superior at La Fourche, and she cannot supply one."

Although Eugénie did not get her way about who was to be superior at La Fourche, neither did Philippine. Rosati preferred Mother Hélène Dutour for the post. Philippine opposed the choice of Dutour, a woman who had been a thorn in her side since her arrival from France less than a year before. Dutour, a woman Sophie Barat respected, had already written letters of complaint to the Mother General about Philippine's management of the St. Louis convent. Philippine realized that Dutour might be happier at La Fourche and allowed herself to be persuaded.

---

[14]Callan, *Philippine Duchesne*, pp.468–70; but see also Cunningham, *Eugénie Audé*, pp. 48–53.

[15]Louise Callan finds their assumption "astonishing"; see *Philippine Duchesne*, p. 469.

Both the appointment of Dutour and the foundation at La Fourche proved to be disastrous decisions for the Society. Eugénie continued to feel threatened by the new institution despite her own school's success and the distance of the new foundation. Sophie Barat, initially at least, found Eugenie's "pure panic" about this amusing.[16] The new foundation lay on the other side of the Mississippi and a good thirty miles down the Bayou La Fourche.

Dutour lost no time in establishing her independence from Philippine and the two other superiors, Eugénie Audé and Xavier Murphy. Mother Barat had written to both Philippine and Eugénie that the La Fourche boarding school was to be geared for a less wealthy population and have a more limited curriculum than the other southern schools.[17] But Dutour published her own description of the school in a local newspaper shortly after her arrival there in July, 1828. Philippine wrote to Rosati in November about the matter:

> Mother Eugénie complains that all the subjects we teach are offered there at a lower tuition, which will, she thinks, take pupils away from her house and perhaps prevent her from paying her debts. She adds that a group of people at La Fourche have sworn to make St. Michael's close in favor of La Fourche. I find, too, that Mother Dutour has completely disregarded the conditions laid down for her foundation. She has done things that only the Mother General may do. . . . I warned her about all this, but my warning had no effect.

In another letter, she informed Rosati that Dutour refused to change any of her plans. Nor would she answer any of Philippine's letters. Like Eugénie, she was hoping instead to receive all her orders directly from Mother Barat in France.

Rosati, in any case, was delighted with the new establishment and rather disenchanted with the nuns' quarrel. He wrote to Philippine in April, 1829:

> I am of the opinion that you should see things for yourself, for it is just possible that seculars may perceive a kind of jealousy in the fears for the welfare of St. Michael's which are

---

[16]See her letter to Eugénie Audé, October 23, 1828.
[17]See, for example, her letters to Eugénie Audé, November 8 and December 20, 1828.

utterly unfounded, fears that these people should never have been allowed to hear expressed.

Although Sophie Barat was not pleased with Dutour's behavior, she also realized that, in fact, the new foundation did not hurt St. Michael's. Rosati used his influence with the Mother General to keep La Fourche on a higher footing.[18] Parents were likewise pleased with the school.

It was above all the "spirit of isolation" that most bothered Philippine. Dutour refused to regard the opinions of any of the other superiors, including Philippine. She insisted on training her own novices to staff her school, was rather authoritarian and eccentric in her assignment of duties within the convent and, most disastrous to the foundation, planned building projects far beyond her means. Her misjudgements in these matters, which would have been avoided had she been willing to listen to others, eventually led to the foundation's rather extraordinary end.

We are left to guess at many of the details of the calamity which Dutour engineered. By November, 1830, nuns within the La Fourche convent and a priest familiar with the situation were writing strong letters of complaint. As Philippine obliquely remarked to Rosati in November, 1830, there were indications that "the spiritual needs of the convent [were] as great as the temporal ones." The convent's debts, moreover, were phenomenal. In December, she wrote to Rosati again:

> I have the honor of sending you a letter from the Bishop of New Orleans [De Neckere] concerning La Fourche. I beg you not to let anyone know the contents, but to be good enough to suggest some way of supporting this work. I have already written to our Superior General, asking her to send someone to La Fourche, since the two oldest religious can no longer endure to live there.

In April, 1831, Sophie Barat removed Dutour from La Fourche and sent her to Opelousas. She appointed Julie Bazire to replace her and put the burdensome financial affairs of the foundation in the expert hands of Eugénie Audé. Philippine wrote to Rosati less than a month later:

---

[18]See letters of Sophie Barat to Eugénie Audé, February 1 and June 12, 1829.

When Mother Eugénie realized that the contractors would come to no agreement with her and that they are planning to sue Mother Dutour, she advised her to go further away, and I do not know what tells me that she may be on her way to St. Louis on the *North America*. Though I resolutely disapproved of her actions, I do hope she will not be afraid of her Sisters.

The conclusion of the La Fourche foundation is shrouded in as much darkness as the details of Dutour's objectionable management of the convent. Bishops De Neckere of New Orleans, Rosati of St. Louis, Mother Barat and Philippine had all wanted the foundation to continue, but under a new superior. Nevertheless, Philippine's *Journal* entry for March 15, 1832, rather dryly notes the closure, apparently for financial reasons:

> News from Mother Eugénie Audé, who informs us that she has been authorized by our Mother General to close the convent at La Fourche, with the approval, of course, of the Bishop of New Orleans. He gave his consent very reluctantly. The two superiors of St. Michael's and Opelousas carried out the instructions. On March 26 the five religious who remained at La Fourche will go to Opelousas; the others went to St. Michael's. The house has been closed and given back to the bishop, to whom the property belongs. The religious of this convent, the pupils, and their parents were greatly grieved by this action.

But it should be kept in mind that the superiors of both St. Michael's and Opelousas, Eugénie Audé and Xavier Murphy, had opposed having the La Fourche foundation on an academic footing with their own. Eugénie, who was overseeing the financial negotiations necessary to save the foundation, was singularly adamant in this regard. Did her personal desires color her handling of the matter? Philippine cannot be sure, but she implied as much in a letter to Rosati just two days after the above journal entry:

> Letters from Louisiana give me very different versions of the closing of the convent at La Fourche. According to Mother Eugénie, she was about to have another lawsuit on her hands. According to those who were obliged to forsake that convent: 1. she would have had, on the contrary, a house that would

have cost her nothing; 2. Bishop De Neckere was misin-
formed; they told him the house at Opelousas would be
closed unless it received the help of the religious from La
Fourche. 3. The parents were distressed and offered to increase the tuition of their children, only five of whom went to
St. Michael's. 4. They say Mother Thiéfry will soon be in
charge here in St. Louis. . . .

The last remark in Philippine's letter betrays her fears that plans
were afoot to change the status of the Florissant or St. Louis convents
too. She was in charge of the St. Louis foundation and rumors of a
change were bound to awaken her suspicions. Eugénie had frequently
argued, both with Philippine and with Sophie Barat, that the two
Missouri foundations should be combined. Philippine knew her authority could be circumvented again. She continued in the same letter to
Rosati:

These reports urge me, Bishop, to beg this favor of you: if
they try to precipitate matters here in the same manner [as La
Fourche], please oppose them firmly, requiring that the article of the Constitutions which forbids the closing of a house
of the Society without the approval of the Cardinal Protector
be held to rigidly. It took just three days to destroy a convent
that had cost so much painful effort. . . .

The fall of La Fourche just four years after its establishment provides a
microcosmic study of the rise of disunity among the United States
superiors during this period.

The Return to St. Charles: Ever since the Religious of the Sacred
Heart had been compelled by Dubourg to leave their foundation
among the poorer people of St. Charles in 1819, Philippine had wanted
to return. In 1825, hearing that the Jesuits might found there, she
began to speak of it in letters to Sophie Barat. On October 10, 1828,
just a few months after the foundation of La Fourche, Mothers Mary
Ann O'Connor and Lucille Mathevon finally returned to the village
where the Religious of the Sacred Heart had first lived in 1818. Philippine must have considered this a miraculous victory. She wrote a
colorful account of their return to the old Duquette house. The account inadvertently provides a fascinating description of the distinctive
social roles played by townspeople, priests and religious women in a
nineteenth-century frontier village celebration:

Inner doors, as well as window frames and glass, were gone. In places the floor had rotted and fallen into the low basement, where pigs and sheep of the neighborhood had found shelter for the past years. The atmosphere was foul with musty dampness and decay. With the aid of an Indian woman who had come with the nuns from Florissant, they soon had the rooms in a presentable condition. Village carpenters closed the gaping holes in the floor and roof and laid in place the stones of the foundation which had been rooted out by animal intruders. The work accomplished was phenomenal, for by the afternoon of the second day the central room had been transformed into a temporary chapel. An altar was set up, and roughly constructed benches ran the length of the room on two sides. At six o'clock in the evening a small bell tinkled. Bishop Rosati and twelve priests filed in processionally, took their places, and chanted the Office for the Dedication of the Church "with all the dignity and piety that befit the liturgical service."

At dawn the following morning a series of nine masses began in the little chapel on the altar stone prepared for the new church. The priests, long accustomed to pioneer life, accepted good-humoredly the breakfast served them in turn on top of an empty barrel. There was food in plenty, for the village folk had supplied roasted meats, corn bread, and many other provisions. Their generosity won the heart of Mother Mathevon before she had been a day in their midst. At ten o'clock the dedication ceremony began. . . . The Religious of the Sacred Heart assisted at it and shared the enthusiasm of the people, who flocked to the church the following day when the Bishop confirmed sixty-six persons and preached in his simple and captivating style.

It must have given Philippine great joy to see the "next generation" of Religious of the Sacred Heart established in the place where the Society had been founded in America just ten years earlier.

Lucille Mathevon described the nuns' work and their hardship and happiness in the new St. Charles foundation in a letter written to Sophie Barat in November, 1828:

> I am among good people who love us very much, but who are poor. There are three towns not too far away which are larger and can send us their children. It is astonishing how this part

of Missouri is growing: last year fourteen thousand people
settled here and we are growing by more than twenty families each day, who settle here and there throughout the State.
The lead mines are attracting so many people.

I moved into our house here, where there were neither
frames nor glass in the windows. I didn't even have a bed in
which to sleep, having given my own to Mother Duchesne. I
found an old carpet from the church, took it and sleep very
well on it, together with an Indian woman whom I brought
from Florissant to be the cook. Everything goes the same way
in this place of poverty; our linen consists of four pairs of
sheets, six towels and eight chemises that you wouldn't even
pick up off the ground in France. There was still no closet in
which to store them. I spotted one in the middle of the yard
and I had it fixed up. Now it serves as bookshelf, linen closet
and medicine cabinet. And there we were as happy as
queens, but the rats made havoc everywhere. I asked myself
where we might find a cat. The next day a fine, beautiful cat
appeared and took over all the rat holes. We had only to open
all the doors for him and in no time he destroyed the rats.
Now we don't see any more. In order to spare our savings,
we have worked as mason, carpenter and woodworker in the
house. We have whitewashed and painted the walls, made
twelve benches, a table and a hen-house. One does not recognize the house anymore, it has so changed. Indeed, Providence has been so great in our regard that my admiration for
God's goodness toward his little servants has no end. The
good Fathers [Jesuits] who attend the parish send us everything that occurs to them. Our food is always adequate; we
lack nothing, not even a good appetite which we did not have
before. You must excuse us, my reverend Mother; in the
beginning here we could only laugh. We wanted to keep
silence and religious decorum, but just the sight of one room
with eight doors and two windows was enough to start us
laughing. In a word, I cannot tell you of the joy which our
poverty gives us. We are happy, because we feel united to all
our dear Mothers in spreading the glory of the divine
Heart.[19]

---

[19]Quoted in Adèle Cahier, *Vie de la Vénérable Mère Barat*, 2 vols. (Paris: de Soyes, 1884),
vol. I, p. 493; translation mine.

Sophie Barat soon sent the two nuns three more religious from France and a number of items which would lessen the hardships of their life on the frontier. By the end of 1829, the religious were happily established in their new mission. There were excellent relations with the people of St. Charles and the nuns had forty-five students in the day school, a school which continues to this very day.

2. THE SUPERIORS' MEETING

From the above accounts, Philippine emerges as a woman somewhat embattled as leader of her religious society in the United States. From her entrance into religious life, she had dreaded being named superior, a somewhat paradoxical fact given her strong temperament and definite ideas. But Sophie Barat had sensed Philippine's leadership qualities when she named her superior of the American mission in 1818. Philippine's tenacious faith helped her through repeated hardships on the frontier. Her grasp of the Society's spirit helped her act with compassion toward other religious even when they circumvented her authority or criticized her severely to the bishop or to Mother Barat. Her educational vision kept the religious and value-oriented aspects of Sacred Heart education always in the forefront at the schools she managed. Finally, and most significantly, Philippine gave tangible expression to her devotion to the Sacred Heart through her preferential love for the poor and marginalized.

But she also had certain drawbacks as superior. Though generally a force for communion and compassion, her extraordinarily high expectations for herself made her seem severe to some religious. Though she was a hard-headed realist in staying out of debt, her own commitment to education for the less fortunate meant that she gave less attention than other superiors to the visible success of her schools. She was mystified by the American "care about external forms," but it was a quality some of her French sisters surely shared. Her inability to learn English kept her from forming some of the warm ties with English-speaking parents which, for example, Eugénie Audé had formed. Finally, her very humility, or rather, her exaggerated self-effacement, proved a drawback in her leadership. Philippine did not feel fit to be superior.

In fact, she repeatedly asked Mother Barat to relieve her of this office. Her pleas in 1826, when there were just three Society houses in the United States, Florissant, Opelousas and St. Michael's, are typical:

The first [point which troubles me greatly] regards myself
and is the responsibility to watch over three houses when I
manage just one so wretchedly. My heart yearns more than
ever for solitude, and I have neither silence nor solitude. I am
growing old; my health is declining. I should weep in reparation for many years of my life, especially those of my religious life. I accept the work as penance, but it robs me of the
spirit of prayer. If you only give heed to my request, I shall
gladly obey anyone whom you may give us as superior.

Although Philippine was just fifty-six years old, allusions to old age
and death appear regularly in her letters over the next twenty-six
years. Just a few weeks before the above letter, Mother Barat had
refused a similar request:

Now a word regarding your request to be relieved of the
office of superior. If you will just reflect a little, you will
realize that this is impossible, for I have no one to put in your
place. . . . How can you hope to be relieved of superiority?
Besides, my dear daughter, would someone else do better
than you? I think not. She might, perhaps, have more virtue,
but certainly less experience and less self-diffidence.

In late 1827, Sophie Barat directed Philippine to go south to meet
with Eugénie Audé and Xavier Murphy. The three superiors held
significantly different opinions regarding the possible foundation at La
Fourche, the regulation of their schools, the adaptations necessary for
religious life on the frontier and the advisability of closing the Florissant house. But Philippine expressed her reluctance to travel south in a
letter to Mother Barat, pointing out the time such a trip would rob
from her already busy work schedule. By early 1829, however, Sophie
Barat had received troublesome reports about La Fourche, about Philippine's management of the St. Louis house and other matters. For the
third and not the last time, she advised Philippine to meet with the
now three southern superiors, Audé, Murphy and Dutour. Philippine
preferred that they meet without her and urged the Mother General
"to consent to whatever they will regulate among themselves." On July
17, 1829, Sophie Barat wrote to Eugénie Audé that she was irritated
that Philippine had not yet made the trip. Philippine's reluctance was
clearly related to her own ambivalence about being superior.

It was also owing to some doubt in her own mind about the extent
of her authority in the United States. When she left France in 1818,

Sophie Barat had given her many of the powers held normally only by the Mother General. In 1821 she wrote to Philippine and Eugénie that Philippine was to be provincial over the new house in Opelousas. She wrote unequivocally to Eugénie in 1822 that she was to refer all urgent questions to Philippine. All the superiors in the United States knew that Sophie Barat had designated Philippine as "provincial" in the United States and that they were to consult her on matters which could not wait for a response from France.[20]

But how real was her authority? An examination of one of the powers she had been granted, the authority to found and to close houses in the United States, a power held usually only by the Mother General, illustrates Philippine's dilemma as superior. First, for example, when both St. Michael's and La Fourche were founded, it was Mother Barat who gave the final approval and she communicated her decision not to Philippine, but to Eugénie. Philippine was informed only after everything had been decided. In both instances, she received the news gracefully, but with surprise.

A second example concerns the opening of the City House in 1827. One of the principal reasons Philippine accepted the difficult terms of John Mullanphy is that Mother Barat had forcefully urged Philippine to make a foundation in St. Louis as soon as possible. Mother Barat was following bad advice she had received from a St. Louis priest in Paris. Philippine, rightly or wrongly, read such advice as an order.

Third, only by dint of Philippine's tenacious defense did the foundation at Florissant survive for so many years. As early as 1824, Sophie Barat had begun to hear from several religious, among them Eugénie Audé, that it should be closed. Mother Barat was deeply influenced by their arguments and periodically made remarks to Philippine such as "it really ought to be closed. The works are so small."[21] She wrote in frustration to Eugénie Audé on October 17, 1835, that she continued to insist on the closure of the Florissant house, "which really accomplishes nothing or very little." Mother Barat ultimately upheld Philippine's spirited and steadfast support of this "little work" on behalf of those who had less, but it demanded constant prodding on Philippine's part. It is significant that Mother Barat followed Philippine's advice precisely in this last case, a situation which involved the Society's work

---

[20]See, for example, letters of Sophie Barat to Eugénie Audé, January 28, 1824, and to Philippine, July 30, 1822.

[21]September 2, 1835.

among the poor. Against her own better judgement as an administrator, Sophie Barat allowed the little foundation to continue out of delicacy for Philippine.[22] After Philippine ceased to be superior in the United States in 1840, the Florissant foundation was closed.

The above cases illustrate how dependent Philippine and the other superiors in the United States remained on Sophie Barat's direction of the Society in the New World. They were eager to remain of "one heart and one mind," the Society's motto, with their European sisters. They had each known personally the charismatic leadership of Sophie Barat and were reluctant to let anyone else assume that role. In addition, Sophie Barat's "little Society," as it was first known, was fast becoming an enormous religious order reaching into many countries. As an astute administrator, she intended to remain as involved as possible in the new foundations being made in the United States.

There were decisions regarding the American foundations, however, she simply could not make from her position in France. She realized this to a certain extent and said so in letters. The conflicting reports she received from her nuns, their bishops and various priests in the United States must have exasperated her. While the variety of viewpoints helped her construct a fuller picture of the situation, it was inadequate to determine issues such as the amount of adaptation the religious Rule required on the frontier and the extent to which the French curriculum had to be modified in American schools. She recommended that Philippine go south to meet with the other superiors not only to resolve such issues themselves, but so that the four superiors might listen to each other, a necessity if the Society was to preserve its spirit of "one heart and one mind" in America. Be that as it may, on the eve of this meeting, Eugénie Audé was still imploring Sophie Barat to remove her convent of St. Michael's from Philippine's jurisdiction:

> You want to know, Reverend Mother, whether I ask advice of Mother Duchesne. I consult her, as I consult you, on all that concerns religious virtue, which she possesses after the manner of the saints. But in all other matters, I prefer to have recourse to you. Your answers come as quickly as hers but with this difference—yours give me the assurance of acting in the Society's way and hers do not offer the same assurance. I am no further from you than from Mother Duchesne. . . .

[22]See letter of Sophie Barat to Eugénie Audé, April 30, 1837.

Then, dear Reverend Mother, let me have direct recourse to
you. Do not refuse this favor to your Eugénie. . . .

In fact, Paris is actually over six times farther from St. Michael's than
is St. Louis and correspondence, though undependable, arrived with
greater speed and security from St. Louis than from France.

But it is significant that Sophie Barat's response to this letter is far
from forceful. She did recognize that she was incapable of evaluating
the conflicting viewpoints regarding La Fourche, one of the subjects
Eugénie had touched on in her letter. And she also intimated that
Eugénie was over-concerned for the welfare of her own enterprise. But
Mother Barat, who had reason to trust Eugénie's experience in government, did not reprove Eugénie for seeking to circumvent Philippine's
proper authority over her. She wrote on October 23, 1828:

> I am sending you, my daughter, a letter for Madame Dutour.
> Read it and then send it to her, but take care lest she discover
> that I am taking you into my confidence. . . . Truly, I was
> amused at your pure panic. . . .
>
> Write me all the details about La Fourche and tell me if
> my response on the subject made sense. Indeed, I don't know
> what to say at such a distance or if what I say is right. . . .
>
> It seems to me that your house is flourishing grandly.
> Your prosperity would almost frighten me, my daughter, if
> you did not attribute all this success to the Heart of Jesus and
> ground yourself in profound humility.[23]

When complaints reached Mother Barat about Eugénie's management
of the closing of La Fourche, she wrote her a rather strong letter
demanding responses to the criticisms. Eugénie's detailed explanation
of her actions more than satisfied the Mother General.[24]

Some questionable behavior on the part of Eugénie, especially
toward Philippine, also made a meeting of the superiors imperative for
Sophie Barat. About this time, Sophie roundly chastised Eugénie for
"helping" other convents by sending them religious who were more
trouble than they were worth: Eugénie rid herself of a puny, deaf and
unintelligent novice by sending her to La Fourche,[25] and to Philippine,

---

[23]Translation mine.
[24]Cunningham, *Eugénie Audé*, pp. 55–56.
[25]See letters of Sophie Barat to Eugénie Audé, December 20, 1828; and April 6, 1829.

she sent two subjects who were "little more than nothing, and another who was dying of consumption" and needed to be nursed. Sophie was irate with Eugénie that the financially struggling Philippine also had to pay for the three nuns' travel expenses.[26] Finally, the Mother General was furious that Eugénie consistently failed to pay Philippine 2,500 francs, money always intended for Philippine, but which Sophie Barat had had to spend in France to cover one of Eugénie's bills.[27] On February 1, 1829, Sophie wrote to Eugénie:

> It is hard for me to conceive how you treat this good Mother Duchesne who has suffered so much to establish the Society in this part of the world. She doesn't complain, but what she has said pains me. I cannot understand the extent to which you abandon her.[28]

Eugénie took these scoldings to heart, paid Philippine her money and repented to Mother Barat.[29]

Philippine finally submitted to Mother Barat's request that she meet with Audé, Murphy and Dutour. She traveled south in November, 1829. The superiors were to reach accords regarding new foundations, the regulation of the schools, convents, and the extent to which the religious Rule had to be adapted to the situation in the United States. Mother Barat named Philippine to preside at the meeting and counseled her regarding the above issues:

> At least let all the American houses do the same thing and let the dispensations or modifications be uniform in all our convents there. This little meeting should heal all breaches of charity and encourage each one to put the general interests of all before the particular interests of her own house.

She wrote in a similar vein to Eugénie in February, 1829 and added:

> It is advisable that you have recourse to one among you who can decide the many details which cannot be left to me given

---

[26]See letters of Sophie Barat to Eugénie Audé, February 1, March 5 and April 6, 1829.

[27]See letters of Sophie Barat to Eugénie Audé, April 30, September 14, October 23 and December 20, 1828; February 1 and March 5, 1829.

[28]Translation mine.

[29]See letters of Sophie Barat to Eugénie Audé, October 22 and 26, 1829.

the great distance. Now, it is appropriate that this be Mother Duchesne who has more experience than anyone, and who could, if need be, get advice from the Jesuit Fathers who are an invaluable resource.[30]

In terms of Philippine's real authority, however, it is also to the point that Sophie Barat said she awaited the results of the meeting so that she could give her own approval of the decisions made.[31]

The meetings took place in St. Michael's and lasted about two weeks. Philippine alone represented all three Missouri houses before the superiors of each of the three southern houses. The Missouri houses compared unfavorably to the southern establishments. Philippine did not affect even the illusion of authority at the council meetings. She wrote to Mother Barat in December, 1829:

> I have been obliged to tell the superiors that I have no real authority, that I come as a Sister, an equal, that you wished us to consult together but reserved to yourself and your advisory council the decisions to be made.

> What influence can I have in a house [St. Michael's] where all is admiration from within and from without, while in St. Louis I am in just the opposite position? I gave my opinion on every point discussed, but I was convinced that I should step aside without pressing my point in any way except in a friendly fashion as a sister would act among her sisters.

Not surprisingly, the outcome of the meeting was largely continued disunity. Biographers such as Louis Baunard and Louise Callan point out that effective authority was still wielded by Mother Barat since individual superiors continued to have recourse to her as the ultimate authority. Baunard writes:

> At this time and until 1839, all the convents of the Sacred Heart, in the New World as well as in the Old, were directly under the Superior General, who still found it possible to fulfill this task of government.[32]

---

[30]Translation mine.

[31]See her letter to Eugénie Audé, June 26, 1829.

[32]See Baunard, *Histoire de Madame Duchesne*, pp. 401–402; quoted in Callan, *Philippine Duchesne*, p. 495; and see Callan's discussion of same, pp. 494–95.

A letter Sophie Barat sent to Philippine after the meeting seems to contradict Philippine's understanding that she had no real authority. Mother Barat chided her:

> Let us come now to the results of your trip to Louisiana. . .
> Without doubt it will do good, but it would have been much
> better had you followed the plan laid out for you, which was
> to hold a council at which you were to preside.[33]

But the task of government was not being adequately fulfilled, either by Philippine or by Sophie Barat. Some accords were reached, but there remained deep divisions among the superiors. The impending La Fourche disaster would all too quickly dispel any notions of either harmony among the superiors or effective leadership by either Philippine or Sophie Barat. The compromised position of Philippine, the "provincial" of the United States, is transparent in the letter she wrote to Sophie Barat regarding the outcome of the meeting:

> I do not know whether God has been pleased with my trip or
> not. Your will alone made it pleasant for me. My heart leans
> always to the side of the less fortunate, and that is Missouri. I
> am not made for a life of leisure, and I have not succeeded in
> bringing about the union which you desired to have re-
> established. Bishop Rosati's letter has made you decide to
> leave La Fourche as it is. Father Richard also told me to tell
> you that he believes that convent is really needed in that
> section of the country; he thinks it would give great offense to
> people if it were reduced to a lower scholastic level. There is
> a kind of rivalry between the parishes on the two sides of the
> Mississippi [La Fourche and St. Michael's], and Mother
> Dutour has already found more sources of outside help than
> the other houses have, for that section is religious-minded
> and offers many influential backers among the rich planters.
> She is, moreover, under a great trial right now: the one priest
> stationed there is ill; she herself has had a hemorrhage and
> has had fever for a month; and her nuns, so few in number,
> are nearly all ill. Mother Xavier Murphy [superior of
> Opelousas] had seemed willing to let Mother Carmelite Lan-

---

[33]Quoted in Cunningham, *Eugénie Audé*, p. 52.

dry go to help her [Dutour]; now she refuses to give up either her or Mother Dorival. I urged Mother Eugénie to send her [Dutour] at least one nun—I think she could have done so— but she does not want to. . . . Will you please send directly to me a copy of the instructions you send Mother Dutour, so I may not suggest anything to the contrary, and if possible word the articles so definitely that we shall have done with objections. . . .

I shall try to combine the two [Missouri] boarding schools in St. Louis, as you desire, and so bring together the religious who are teaching. I shall not repeat myself, as I have already written you the details of this plan, but I beg you to consider it well before it is carried out. . . . Please accept, dear Mother, my apologies for the mistakes you will notice in my letters. Old age, which weighs on me, is my excuse.

Philippine set about transferring the Florissant boarders to St. Louis, a change she regretted, but accepted as the will of Mother Barat. Eugénie Audé's letter to Mother Barat after the meeting underscores Philippine's lack of authority. She stated that she objected to some of the resolutions reached and, therefore, did not intend to follow them in her own institution. She wrote to Mother Barat to secure sanction for her independent action.

In short, neither Philippine nor Sophie Barat was in a position to govern effectively at this time in the United States. Perhaps the most insightful comment in this regard was a comment made by Eugénie Audé to Mother Barat:

If you would only have the goodness to send as visitatrix one of our Mothers who is thoroughly imbued with your spirit, she could judge of the truth of what I am bold enough to state, and her visit would do the greatest amount of good in our little American mission.

Barring granting effective governing authority to Philippine Duchesne, Sophie Barat's only realistic option for achieving union in the United States was to send someone empowered to make binding decisions. The wisdom of Sophie Barat's government through individual correspondence with each superior had clearly played its course.

3. THE AFTERMATH OF THE MEETING

Philippine returned to St. Louis shaken both by the lack of peace she perceived within the Society and by the contrast she saw between the struggling and poor Missouri houses in Florissant, St. Louis and St. Charles and the prosperity of the southern houses. St. Michael's especially was a model of French elegance and regularity. During 1830 and 1831, moreover, Mother Barat continued to receive letters of grievance regarding Philippine's leadership of the St. Louis foundation. Complaints ran the gamut: the house was unkempt; Philippine failed to cultivate friendships with the finest families of the city; she lagged behind the times given St. Louis' expanding urban environment; she was too reluctant to enlarge the building; the furnishing of the boarding school was woefully inadequate to attract pupils; her regulation of the children's outings was too strict; and if that were not enough, Philippine was also accused of being excessively generous in charity. She gave too much away, especially to the Bishop and priests whom she saw in need.

Finally, Sophie Barat took action. Although she still trusted in Philippine's profound grasp of the congregation's spirit and her commitment to maintaining works for the poor and the wealthy alike, Mother Barat felt that the growth of the Society on the frontier had surpassed Philippine's more modest leadership abilities. She even despaired of Philippine's ability to govern her own house in St. Louis well, a house Sophie Barat would have much preferred to be in the image of Eugénie's southern house *à l'Européenne:* a first-rate boarding school, with spacious buildings and a well-regulated convent life.[34] Instead, Sophie had been plagued by complaints that Philippine's house was just the contrary.

In November, 1831, she removed Philippine, now sixty-two, from her post as superior in the St. Louis convent. Philippine was to be superior instead in one of the more modest Missouri establishments of Florissant or St. Charles. Unbeknownst to Philippine, Mother Barat was also planning to remove Philippine from her post as superior in the United States. Although long desired by Philippine, this demotion is indicative of Mother Barat's failing confidence in Philippine's leadership ability:

I sent you a letter quite recently, dear Philippine, answering one from you, but I had not then read all the mail that has

---

[34]See, for example, her letters to Eugénie Audé, August 7, 1830; October 22, November 8 and December 13, 1831.

since come from you, from your companions, and from the newly arrived religious. From the ensemble of details given me I cannot help being worried about the present condition of your house. For a long time I have been saddened by the small success attained in St. Louis and by the anguish this has caused you. I have tried to send you recruits for the community, such as Mother Thiéfry, and I hoped that you would be able to keep at least one of them to help you in St. Louis, and that the convent there might be established on a footing with St. Michael's or Opelousas. Friends had given me reason to hope for this. But after all I have read, it seems to me we shall never obtain this result unless we follow a course of action different from yours, dear Mother.

I must then, for the sake of the general good, submit a plan to you. You will, of course, consult Bishop Rosati, to whose judgement I refer it for final decision, and I beg you to follow his advice. This is what I suggest: let Mother Thiéfry take your place in St. Louis and give her, as Assistant, Mother de Kersaint, and perhaps Mother Regis as Mistress General. Do your utmost to build a separate orphanage first of all, then little by little on a well constructed plan erect the other buildings necessary as the academy grows and additions can be undertaken prudently. You, dear Mother, may go either to Florissant or to St. Charles, whichever you think the better.

I realize, my dear daughter, that at your age and after all you have suffered, the foundation of an American academy, which calls for so much care and perfection along all lines, quite surpasses your strength. For several years all those who have been at the St. Louis convent have complained of the lack of order, the shabbiness, even the uncultivated condition of the property. Alas! God forbid that I should blame you, dear Mother. I know only too well all that you have done and suffered. But times change and we must change, too, and modify our views. I realize from experience that it is unwise to leave superiors for long years in the same house. Good government requires a change of superiors once in a while. . . .

After Philippine received this letter in early 1832, she informed Rosati of the Mother General's views and then responded to her:

I have received your letter of November 30 in which you tell me your new plan for the convent in St. Louis. My natural tendency toward lowliness will make me find happiness in my position, provided I am not left with nothing to do. And even if you thought that necessary, I believe God would give me the grace to endure it. I am fully convinced that I do not possess the qualifications a superior should have. And for a long time one of my most fervent prayers has been to obtain what I felt should happen and what I hoped would raise the standard of religious observance and schoolwork in this house and draw to it all hearts.

But Rosati was not of the same mind as Mother Barat. He was quite familiar with the houses in both Missouri and Louisiana and their superiors and had heard all the complaints one could hear about Philippine. He told Philippine to remain as superior in the St. Louis house. His letter of February, 1832, to Sophie Barat is a stately defense of Philippine's stewardship. The letter is so rich with details regarding Philippine's character, her situation as superior in St. Louis and the difficulties Europeans had adapting to the American scene, that it merits lengthy quotation:

Madame, Mother Duchesne has informed me, according to your instructions, of your latest letter to her and of the changes you believe it proper and even necessary to make in regard to the government of your institutions in Missouri. After mature reflection on the plan you submitted to me, I have begged Mother Duchesne to suspend its execution until she heard from you again. I want you to think over what I am going to tell you.

In the first place, I believe there is no one among your religious who can gain as much confidence as Mother Duchesne justly receives here. All who know her respect and venerate her because of her virtues, which, joined to age and the experience she has acquired during her long sojourn in this country, make her esteemed by all. There are few persons whom I venerate more than this holy religious. She has the true spirit of her vocation and on many occasions, known only to me, has given most striking proofs of this. In the next place, I see by the complaints that have moved you to decide on the proposed changes that things have been misrepresented to you. I am well aware that no one wished to deceive you, but rather spoke from a lack of insight into the matter. If the boarding school is not larger, this is not the result of lack of space. The house can accommodate twenty-eight and has only eleven boarding pupils. The house is not elegant, as are your European convents, but it is suitable for this country. That is not the reason why parents do not send their children there. You have been told the property has not been properly cultivated; one of your religious newly arrived from France told me the same thing. I replied that after she had been here a while and had made attempts like mine, she would realize that in America, where land is cheap and labor expensive, a religious community cannot obtain profits from its farm produce, for this must be sold at a very low price.

You have been told that she has not cultivated the friendship of the Founder [Mr. Mullanphy] sufficiently, but I can assure you that I do not know anything more Mother Duchesne or anyone else could have done in this respect. Besides, I know the Founder. Once he has done what he planned to do, he will do no more. So I do not think Mother Duchesne should be blamed on this point.

With regard to the religious sent from France, whom Mother Duchesne has not kept here—this action was not prompted by the fact that she did not need them, but rather by her desire to work for the general good of all your convents. This generosity, which I admire and at the same time regret, led her to make sacrifices in order to satisfy the demands of the superiors of the Louisiana houses. These demands were such that had they always been heeded, the houses here would be empty. I speak from firsthand knowledge on this point. More than once she has had to make a change of house or climate to satisfy some of the religious or to prevent complaints. You yourself know that this is not rare in communities, where we feel the effects of human weakness unless we are well advanced on the way of perfection. Religious are also children of Adam, so this is not to be wondered at. On this point in particular Mother Duchesne has suffered very much. Instead of blaming her, we should pity her.

I am speaking very frankly, Madame, because I have at heart the happiness and prosperity of your houses in my diocese. I believe that the contemplated change will in no way contribute to this end. No religious whom you may designate to fill the position now held by Mother Duchesne could really replace her. I greatly fear this excessive desire to enlarge the house, to make it appear more like the French

houses, and to put the houses here on the same footing with
them. You have had an example of that policy at La Fourche.
Very well, here it would be even worse. In this country we
have not the resources nor many wealthy Catholics. At present the Protestants have their own schools and they fear to
send their daughters to a convent lest they be converted to
Catholicism. That is the real reason for the small boarding
school. Is it prudent to go into debt and pay a high rate of
interest to build new additions? As things are now, much
good is being done with the orphans and in the crowded free
school, and there are others who could pay if you received
them as day pupils.

In all the convents good is being done and more is hoped
for in the future. With the growth of population and wealth
will come increased opportunities for good. The Ursulines of
New Orleans and Canada have at times been in conditions
much harder than those of your houses here, but now they
are as well off as their Sisters in Europe, perhaps even better
off. Let us follow, then, the guidance of Divine Providence; it
will not fail to uphold us. That is what those newly come
from Europe do not know and do not want to know. But we
know it after years of experience. Their views must not be
placed before those of experienced persons. I pray you to
pardon me if I speak so frankly. I sincerely desire the prosperity of your convents. . . .

Philippine and Rosati received Mother Barat's responses six
months later, the time it often took for an exchange of letters between
St. Louis and France in the 1830s. Her letter to Rosati is the more
interesting of the two since in it she candidly discusses her own
thoughts on Philippine:

I am very grateful, Bishop, for the frankness with which you
wrote to me of all that concerns our convents in Upper Louisiana, especially the house in St. Louis, about which I have
had much anxiety. Ever since it was opened I have regretted
its failure to prosper, as have the other houses [at St. Michael's and Opelousas]. Many reliable people, as well as several of our Sisters, have told me emphatically that Mother
Duchesne's manner of governing was to a great extent responsible for the failure. I love and revere that dear Mother with
all my heart, Bishop, but I know that even here in France,

where she rendered us such valuable services by her zeal and devotedness, she did not agree entirely with our way of arranging things. As a matter of fact, we never put her in complete charge of a boarding school just for this reason. The representations which have been made to me along these lines did not surprise me. They were in line with my own thoughts and the knowledge I have had for many years of this holy Mother's manner of governing a convent. But, Bishop, I agree with you that she has gained experience through her long years in America and still more, a personal knowledge of the ways of the people, who are so different from ourselves.

Now that you assure me that the abuses which are said to exist there and the slow development of the school are either exaggerations or difficulties inherent in the location of the house, I gladly confirm Mother Duchesne in the position she holds and direct her to make no change for the present. It cost me much to decide to take her from this family which she has established with so much difficulty, but she herself has insistently urged me to do so, and that on the advice of spiritual directors [e.g. Van Quickenborne]. I yielded only to petitions reiterated through many years. I beg Your Lordship to add to the kindness you have already shown in warning me of the disadvantages which would accrue from the change, the favor of confirming Reverend Mother Duchesne in the position she now occupies. I have done so, but a word from you will relieve her of all anxiety and encourage her to continue her self-sacrificing mission with perseverance and confidence.

Mother Barat, even before receiving Rosati's letter, had come to the conclusion that she could no longer govern from France. The confusing and unfortunate failure of La Fourche no doubt helped prompt this decision. In February, 1832, she asked the superiors of the five American houses to recommend one among them as Assistant General for Louisiana and Missouri. This "American" religious would join three other European religious as special assistants to Mother Barat. She would have extensive powers within the Society in the United States and be able to advise the Mother General both by letter and by visits to Europe. In effect, she would replace Philippine as "provincial." In late 1833, word from Europe came that Eugénie Audé had been named Assistant General for the United States. It was good news for Eugénie who had already written to

Sophie Barat about her longing to visit France. She was not well. Her correspondence with Mother Barat suggests that she was suffering both physically and emotionally. Mother Barat tried to calm her anguish of soul and urged her to visit all five United States houses, but only if her strength would allow it. In either case, she was then to return to Europe.[35]

The impoverished conditions of the Missouri houses distressed Philippine. Any ambivalence she had had about her leadership could only have been enhanced by Mother Barat's suggestion that she step down as superior, first in St. Louis, then as leader among the other superiors in the United States. She now worried that Eugénie Audé would judge the Missouri houses harshly and make an unfavorable report to Mother Barat. Fortunately, enrollment in St. Louis had risen slightly by April, 1833, when Eugénie arrived. What was at stake for Philippine in Eugénie Audé's visit to Missouri was the very existence of each of the three houses which she had founded there.

4. PHILIPPINE'S LEADERSHIP

In summing up this chapter on Philippine's leadership, it would be tempting to pit Philippine against the world and show the world to have been wrong. There is certainly material to point to the failings of those who criticized Philippine: the ambitions of Eugénie Audé, the independence of Hélène Dutour, the recalcitrant parents of the St. Louis boarders and the critical, even whining letters sent by religious in Philippine's community to Mother Barat. But this would hardly do justice to the complexity of the situation—nor the complexity of Philippine herself.

Philippine had gifts which recommended her as superior. Her vision inspired the mission to the New World. She was the Society's most eloquent voice on behalf of the poor and marginalized in America. Her tough-spirited temperament could sustain the physical hardships, loneliness and disappointments endemic to missionary life. She never once thought of giving up or going back to France. Unbeknownst to her, Eugénie Audé had written to Mother Barat on several occasions requesting to visit France. Loneliness and the death of loved ones in France surpassed her strength. Eugénie herself acknowledged that Philippine's spiritual stature and wisdom were without equal.

---

[35]See letter of Sophie Barat to Eugénie Audé, November 2, 1833.

But Philippine's weaknesses as superior are also apparent. Again to use Eugénie Audé as a foil, Philippine lacked Eugénie's easy gift for success. Eugénie was a superb administrator and built successful schools on solid foundations. She was quickly loved by religious, parents and clergy alike. Philippine, by contrast, felt ill at ease with many parents. Her inadequate English precluded close relations with many Americans. Her own severity frightened even some of her own religious. Eugénie was arguably a more creative educator than Philippine. While recognizing certain weaknesses, Sophie Barat considered Eugénie to be an outstanding superior. After Eugénie's return to France, Mother Barat wrote in 1836 to Aloysia Hardey, a newly appointed superior in the United States:

Copy in everything the style of government of Mother Audé who succeeded so well in your country.[36]

Eugénie Audé's disagreements with Philippine, even her desire to withdraw her house from Philippine's authority and place it directly under Sophie Barat, derived no doubt from personal convictions regarding the greater good of the Society in the United States. If she lacked some of Philippine's spiritual depth, she nonetheless used well all her other considerable gifts for the sake of establishing excellent educational opportunities for young women on the American frontier. Her impulses regarding new building projects provided a healthy counterbalance to Philippine's excessive fear of construction and debt which derived in part at least from her unhappy experience of building in Florissant.

Philippine's authority was also severely hampered by the fact that all the superiors, indeed many of the religious, continued to depend on Sophie Barat. Mother Barat chose to govern the Society in the United States for as long as she was able. Her own comments indicate that she had reservations about Philippine's capacity to manage boarding schools. Perhaps for that reason she sided with Hélène Dutour and Eugénie Audé, two women she also knew well, when they differed with Philippine.

Philippine's reactions to the numerous circumventions of her authority are also revelatory of her leadership. Although several impor-

---

[36]Quoted in Cunningham, *Eugénie Audé*, pp. 67–68; and see p. 76.

tant decisions were made without her even being consulted, she usually reacted with kindness—or silence. Someone more self-secure in her ability and obligation to lead might have been more forceful. On the other hand, she lived through most of these events with uncommon generosity, concerned more for the welfare of the whole than for herself.

Philippine's commitment to people who had less was the hallmark of her leadership. Sophie Barat recognized this quality as essential to the establishment of the Society in America. Indeed, it was Philippine's concerns for the needs of others which led her to send some of the best nuns to the southern foundations. Already overworked herself in St. Louis, she sacrificed the good of her own particular house, and indirectly impugned her own leadership, because she was concerned with the welfare of other foundations.

Finally, a key element in Philippine's leadership in the United States is the fact that she never wanted to be superior. Her humility, her exaggerated self-effacement, instilled serious self-doubts regarding her capacity to lead. In 1824 she made the following highly revealing remark to Mother Barat:

> I carry in my heart a great fear of spoiling things wherever I shall be, and this because of words I think I heard in the depths of my soul: "You are destined to please Me, not so much by success as by bearing failure." This may have been an illusion or figment of a too lively imagination; still I cannot rid myself of this thought, and so I dread undertaking anything, lest I should hinder its success.

Her personal conviction that God called her to holiness through failure undoubtedly played a powerful role in her life. We are left to speculate as to how such a comment might have affected Sophie Barat's confidence in Philippine's leadership.

When Philippine returned to St. Louis after the superiors' meeting, she was virtually overwhelmed with a sense of her own failure. She was now entering her sixties. One notes a new tiredness in the tone of Philippine's writing after this point. She had received news of the deaths of many loved ones in France. From the moment Sophie Barat had first tried to remove her as superior in St. Louis, she felt that she had shaken her friend's confidence. She perhaps never fully appreciated how much Mother Barat admired her for her staunch defense of the Society's works among the poor. Fears about closures that might take place in Missouri, doubts about herself, not just as superior, but even as a good religious, began to grow in Philippine. Although finally relieved of being provincial over all the United States houses, she was still burdened by the task of being superior in the house in St. Louis.

IX.

Old Age and Life
Among the Potawatomi

The "saint who suffers" is a well-known character in the popular imagination. The most extreme examples astound us with their fortitude: they laugh in the face of death and cheerfully endure inconceivable agonies. The third-century figure, St. Lawrence, is a good example. It is popularly asserted that while he was being burned alive over glowing coals, he calmly turned to his Roman executioner and said, "Let my body be turned; one side is broiled enough." Then there are the less dramatic, but no less painful accounts of saints who suffered years of loneliness, failure, even a sense of being abandoned and unloved by God, but always with smiles on their faces, a kind word to say and an unshakable confidence in God's ultimate goodness. No inner doubts, no deep depressions, no fears regarding God's love for them. At least the popular stereotype would have it this way.

Philippine Duchesne offers us another, more human model of sanctity. The last twenty years of her life are filled not only with exterior struggles—and she had had plenty of these before this period—but also with intense interior trials: loneliness, a penetrating feeling of failure, depression, troubling doubts about God's love for her and anxiety concerning her approaching death. With great feeling, she engaged in the human task of accepting her reality, including her impending death. Philippine's struggle accentuates once again her humanity. Without a doubt, she was a woman who dwelt within the boundaries of our own world.

1. HARD TIMES IN ST. LOUIS

Philippine's sadness was inspired by events already discussed in the last chapter: her failure to establish harmony among the superiors and the contrast between the flourishing southern foundations and the struggling Missouri houses. In addition, Philippine was now in her sixties. She was an old woman by nineteenth-century standards. Old age and its afflictions were an ordeal for her. She said rather matter-of-factly that the children did not like her because she was old. The "advanced sciences" of astronomy, chemistry and philosophy were introduced in the academy and made her feel hopelessly antiquated. Nevertheless, her responsibilities in the convent and school, far from diminishing with her increased age, kept her occupied from four in the morning until eleven o'clock at night. When sickness affected the convent, orphanage or boarding school, it was often Philippine who kept vigil. One religious wrote to Mother Barat in 1831:

> Do ask prayers, dear Mother, for our dear Mother Duchesne. We must beg God to take care of her for us; she certainly does not take care of herself. Just think of it—she has spent eleven successive nights at the bedside of one religious who was very ill, and she does not allow herself any respite from work. I cannot understand how she does it at her age. I think it is miraculous.[1]

One can sense the discouragement in Philippine's heart as she described her life in 1833 to a nun in France:

> Just fancy how cordially we would welcome you here, but accustomed as you are to large convents, you might find it difficult to accept our penitential life, for it calls for great self-renunciation. One has little room in which to move about; there are very few to chant the Office; one must take on many employments and expect them to be upset frequently. A class of five or six children, and frequently less, offers little interest, and success seldom corresponds to the effort one expends in teaching. And after spending oneself on them, one sees little gratitude or piety in them. They go away and there is little to show for all one's solicitude about them. They must

---

[1] Mother Thiéfry to Mother Barat, August 21, 1831.

be coaxed pleasantly to do the will of God, and long afterwards perhaps a soul may be saved eternally. . . .

In keeping with her own ascetical leanings, however, it was the very
difficulty of Philippine's situation which made her cherish it. For example, in 1833, when seven of the thirteen religious in St. Louis were sick
and Philippine had to undertake even more work, she wrote to Josephine:

> I have never been so completely without a moment's peace.
> My heart is never free from suffering—and this is what at-
> taches me most of all to this house, for how could I leave
> these poor, suffering nuns?

There was discord in the St. Louis convent and she knew that more
complaints had been mailed to Mother Barat. The cross, "that good
cross" as she called it, was writ large in her life.

Philippine, as has been touched upon above in chapters two and
four, had never been wholly free of certain religious scruples, a slight
sense of guilt if she did not measure up to the religious Rule or her own
inner standards. She worried if circumstances beyond her control kept
her from mass for many days in a row. She blamed herself for failures
she personally could not have averted. The unrealistic self-
expectations which bound her were clearly standards she had internalized early in life. As her niece, Amélie Jouve, so astutely remarked,
Philippine was "her own heaviest cross."[2]

Philippine's tendency toward scrupulosity became more pronounced as she entered old age. An example revelatory of her character
is the donations she used to make to the needy, especially to missionary
priests. Some religious had complained of this and Philippine had been
duly restricted to giving fifty francs, or ten dollars. It was a rule she
struggled and failed to keep. She was beset by scruples each time her
charity exceeded the prescribed limit of ten dollars. Her anxiety is of a
piece with the guilt she felt about missing mass and her fear of dying
without the last sacraments. Immediately after discussing each of these
in a letter to Sophie Barat in 1834, she confessed:

> I shall have no peace of soul unless I tell you. . . that I have on
> several occasions given more than fifty francs in charity with-

---

[2]Jouve, *Notes concernant la vie de Notre Vénérable Mère Duchesne.*

out asking the advice of my council or your permission, urged as I was by the desire to help a good work. This is just ten dollars here and is considered the least contribution one can make to churches, missions, etc.

In late 1837, she was still giving too much away. By this time, Philippine had realized that her worries were exaggerated, that is, that they were scruples. But they still afflicted her. She wrote to Bishop Rosati:

I am lacking in the zeal that would help me carry my little burden generously, and God allows it to weigh more heavily as I grow older, and draw nearer to judgement. All the scruples I have ever had with regard to obedience and poverty seemed to pile up in my mind one night when I realized that I may soon have to render an account of my stewardship. The things that worry me most are contributions I have made without the permission of our Superior General. When at times I have tried to explain these things to her, either she paid no attention to what I wrote or her answers were so vague I could not decide whether I was acting in agreement with or contrary to her intentions. I said to myself: "Charity is the first, the highest law," yet in the depths of my soul I heard the words: "Obedience is better than sacrifice."

The closing of Philippine's former convent in Grenoble, St. Marie, was a devastating blow to her in this period. It illustrates her growing tendency toward self-blame and guilt. She was over-attached to the monastery, a fact she had realized years earlier. In a retreat in early 1805, only months after becoming a Religious of the Sacred Heart in Grenoble, Philippine had said that this convent was her only attachment in the world. Just a year later, she experienced a sort of religious conversion which she believed had freed her from her attachment:

On the tenth of January [1806], while I was making my meditation in the children's dormitory on the detachment of the three Kings, I was moved by a desire to imitate them. Yielding to grace, I felt freed from my inordinate attachment for this house of Saint Marie, which had cost me so many tears, and I resolved to offer myself for the foreign missions, to teach the pagans of China or any other distant land.[3]

Philippine lived in the Grenoble convent for fifteen years altogether. It had been her first home as a religious and had cost her dearly to reacquire after the Revolution. It was there she had reluctantly resolved to leave the Visitation order and there too that she had met her dear friend, Sophie Barat. Philippine had invested an ample portion of her inherited wealth into its repair, and for years after her departure from France, she was deeply indebted to her cousin Josephine for helping to keep it open. In fact, when Josephine sensed her cousin's fatigue and discouragement on the American frontier in the early 1830s, she had touchingly written to Philippine inviting her back to St. Marie for a rest. Philippine, of course, would never yield to such self-indulgence.

In October, 1833, Sophie Barat broke the news to Philippine about the convent's closing:

> What a heartbreak it is to be forced to give up your cradle, that house so dear to you. We were obliged to do so. The city took it from us.

There is a poignancy in Philippine's polite letter to Mother Barat in December, 1833, which only hints at the loss this signified for her:

> It must have been hard for you to decide to abandon that house. It is still the place to which I am most deeply attached and the greatest sacrifice I could offer at the crib of the Divine Infant. If God strikes the green wood thus, what will He do to the dry, worm-eaten wood we build with here [in America]?

Shortly thereafter she wrote again to Mother Barat:

> I have received the moving details of the downfall of Saint Marie. I would sooner forget my own right hand than that delightful dwelling.[4]

---

[3] *Memoir of Philippine Duchesne.*
[4] Quoted in Cahier, *Vie de la Vénérable Mère Barat*, vol. I, p. 603. Translation mine.

Her letter to her cousin Josephine was particularly candid:

> I wonder why the greatest favor you and your dear husband
> and your splendid brothers all took so much trouble about for
> us now must come to naught. They write me that there is no
> way to save Saint Marie to the Society, that the convent must
> be closed, and that the daughters of Sion can only weep
> because the holy songs of praise are silenced. I never thought
> I might see that beloved place again, but it was a joy for me to
> think of it as a home of God-fearing virtue, zeal, and inno-
> cence. *It is very bitter for me to think that perhaps I am responsible*
> *for the closing of that house, because I did not merit the graces needed*
> *for its support. I have no desire for new endeavors.* It seems to me
> that what we build here is but a house of cards compared
> with the massive pile of that noble monastery, its vast propor-
> tions, its charming situation, its silent church remote from all
> distractions.*

Philippine went on to say that there was nothing left for her but to die,
yet knowing she would still live, she longed at least to have parts of the
holy monastery's altars. The depth of her wound is evident in a letter
written over two years after the monastery's closing. In December,
1835, she rejected one of her cousin Josephine's frequent donations.
She was still too broken to undertake anything new:

> Thank you so much for your generosity in offering me an-
> other gift. Keep it, please. If it reached me before my death, I
> would not use it either to enlarge this house or to improve it.
> The closing of Saint Marie, on which I spent so much money,
> robs me of all initiative, and a three months' illness has weak-
> ened my constitution and made me hope that I shall not be
> much longer in this land of sorrow and tears.

Her grief at St. Marie's closing was also tied to her intense devotion to the French missionary to the poor, St. John Francis Regis. As
discussed in chapter four, she had made a four-point promise to him in
1801 in her efforts to reacquire St. Marie. She was stubbornly faithful
to her part of the bargain. Even after she had moved to Paris in 1815,

---

*Emphasis mine.

she wrote to a religious at Grenoble to ensure that the promise would still be kept:

> I beg you, Mother, have the promises [to honor St. Francis Regis] kept at Saint Marie, and be very exact in saying the prayer to St. Regis, or substitute something else if that promise is not carried out.

And she continued to keep the promise herself. Before sailing for America, Philippine made St. Regis the patron of their new mission. She duly established a shrine to him in St. Charles in 1818 and then transferred it to Florissant the next year when the St. Charles foundation was closed. Philippine's anxiety about keeping all these promises to Regis only intensified in her old age. In 1836, she called it "a trial" for her when the promises could not be kept in Grenoble after the convent's closing. When there were more rumors that year about Florissant's possible closing, and with it Regis' shrine, Philippine wrote to Sophie Barat that she "feared this trial [of not keeping the promises] would go even further." As subsequent pages will show, Philippine eventually attributed an assortment of misfortunes and tragedies to the failure to keep the promises made to St. Regis.

2. FLORISSANT: THE TRANSITION TO OLD AGE

As Assistant General for the United States, Eugénie Audé visited the three Missouri houses before traveling to France to report to Mother Barat. Not surprisingly, Philippine was transferred shortly thereafter from St. Louis to the convent in Florissant. She was to remain as superior within her own house, but Mother Barat contended that the country house of Florissant, an easier foundation than St. Louis, would afford Philippine a much needed rest. Philippine's letters from 1834 to 1840 as superior at Florissant attest to the pain she suffered during her transition into old age.

She was just sixty-five when she arrived in Florissant in October, 1834. Soon after arriving, she made her yearly retreat. New regulations concerning the nuns' method of prayer had been drawn up at the last General Council meeting in France. In a letter to Sophie Barat, Philippine commented on the simplicity of her own prayer, her self-doubts, and the anxieties the new regulations were causing in her:

I have just finished my retreat, which I made by myself shortly after coming here. I wish I could assure you that I shall lead a better life here in solitude and far from the occasions that so often caused me to fail. But it always seems to me that for my own security and for the good of others I should be in a position of lower rank, and I await this second favor from your charity. Besides the experience of my whole past life, these new regulations and directives frighten me. They are so detailed, and my memory is so faulty in regard to new things, much more so than for things of the past. My heart is so dry, I can scarcely think through all these rules and methods, so it will be far worse for me to try to carry them out. There are just three of us together in the evening before night prayers. If I can say three sentences in three minutes on the subject of the morning's meditation, that will be all, and I am sure the others will say nothing. . . . I have never been able to reflect on a subject. I see it as a whole, and what I have once seen I shall see for ten years without change or addition. I never see things in detail or in parts. I see a thing, there is the whole thing; I do not see its divisions. When I hear a sermon or listen to a long instruction, in spite of myself I reduce it all to a few words, and I cannot understand how anyone can develop a topic. In that state of soul all methods and considerations become mere distractions for me, and I am so dry and brief in my words, they only cause aridity and disgust to other people.

I feel that I am a worn-out instrument, a useless walking stick that is fit only to be hidden in a dark corner. God allows everything to deepen this impression in my soul. I have never at any time attracted people's confidence, and the same thing is true here. The religious [at Florissant] quite naturally think they should prefer the superior who preceded me, and not one of them has so far given me a word—I do not say of confidence, but of cordial politeness. Under the eyes of their class mistress two of the pupils wrote me a note asking me not to come to my French class, and they brought it to me with an air of triumph. I just told them to show the note to their mother. I went to the school to replace one of the nuns—the children asked me how soon the other teacher was coming back. A little later they suggested that if I knew how to do multiplication I might show them. Many other disrespectful actions strengthen in me the conviction that I am no longer fit to work with other people.

I came here in great peace of soul as to my assigned post, but the devil did not leave me long in peace. In the letters I received from St. Louis several persons told me the remark was made by some that they *never* wanted to see me again. From that I concluded that they wanted me to be sent further away, and I have not the courage to accept that. Here I have more spiritual help [because of the presence of the Jesuits] than anywhere else in the United States. This is all I ask for the rest of my life. . . . My conscience is not tranquil enough to allow me to live in peace without the possibility of receiving the last sacraments.

Philippine worried most about becoming useless in her old age. She remarked frequently on the sense of isolation produced by her inability to speak or understand fluent English, by then the language of most people in the United States. It frustrated and limited her work with the children in the school. She suffered so deeply in her attempts to speak English that she even assigned speaking English as a penance to a young nun, Gonzague Boilvin, whom she was guiding in the spiritual life.

But Philippine's fears about other matters far exceeded the frustration English caused her. Her paradoxical love of solitude and need for activity comes clearly to the fore during these years. On the one hand, she professed that she loved the solitude of Florissant and longed for a rest from activity. She wrote to Rosati shortly after her transfer to Florissant:

I love the solitude, and I would love it even more had I more of it. I am begging God to grant me this, without much hope of obtaining my request, for our religious are needed everywhere and charity makes it a duty to sacrifice one's personal inclinations. . . .

In fact, she did relish the freedom from "worldly" contacts which the Florissant foundation afforded her, but only as long as her work schedule remained full. She was a personality compelled to remain intensely involved in what, for her, was the struggle of life. Her letters to her cousin Josephine reveal that she feared inactivity almost as much as death itself. She wrote to her in April, 1837:

It seems to me I have outlived myself. I see the time coming when I shall be good for almost nothing. As my health has taken on new vigor, that uselessness will be harder to bear after I have had so much to do. . . .

I dread becoming a doting old lady in second childhood before death catches up with me.

And in March, 1839, she wrote:

I am really healthier than I like. During recent years I have often thought I should die soon. Now I fear I shall live to be a hundred—as there is no prospect of death in the near future. I am troubled at the prospect of the infirmities and useless-ness of old age. However, I am not there yet. The lack of hired servants leaves me plenty to do.

Philippine claimed she preferred "to die at work and, as they say, 'in the fight.' "[5] In a letter to Sophie Barat in 1838, she captured her ambivalent feelings about the rest and inactivity characteristic of old age:

As for myself, I am ready for whatever you may decide. I long for retirement and rest, and I have no hope of finding them in this life. I should not, however, want an inactivity that would expose me to the danger of napping all day long. But everything seems to point to the fact that there is no sweet retreat ahead of me. Wherever I have been, external and distracting work has been my lot and still is, though I am about to begin my seventieth year.

The uselessness Philippine now feared was more than the conse-quence of her energetic spirit. She was beginning the hard human task of confronting her own mortality. She wrote to Josephine in 1838:

As the Society spreads and the older members die [in Eu-rope], we in America must seem like people who lived in ancient history. I am something of an antique myself. I am really ashamed of it, and I have no desire to be considered an Egyptian mummy.

---

[5]June 23, 1833, to Josephine.

She wrote to her sister Euphrosine the same year:

> . . . I have not had a letter from you since the one you wrote after [our sister] Amélie's death. . . . If you want some news about me I shall tell you that going into my seventieth year I feel the infirmities of that age: I cough and totter and fall, and the thought of death is always with me. So many of our family who were younger and stronger than I have died.

She felt that the pain of Amélie's death was like a warning for her to prepare for her own.

References to death become more frequent in Philippine's letters. When she reflected on it theologically, her comments had an unsurprising stoic ring to them, befitting a nineteenth-century religious. For example, in a letter to Josephine in 1839, she wrote:

> Old age and infirmities have changed the outward aspect of our life, but not the Heart of Him whom we took as our model and whom we have followed. He warned us that this would mean carrying His cross, and He promised unending happiness in return for our struggles and sufferings.

But when Philippine reflected on her own particular death, her down-to-earth humanity was conspicuous. She feared her death. There was, as she said to her cousin, so much for her to do "to assure a favorable judgement." She worried that St. Marie's closing was due to her own lack of graces. In her weakest moments, Philippine even imagined God as wrathful and punishing, exacting retribution for worldliness and sin. During the cholera epidemic of 1834, for example, she was afflicted with a sense of personal guilt. She voiced profound misgivings after almost twenty years of selfless service on the American frontier:

> The author of [the fifteenth-century spiritual treatise] the *Imitation* says that those who travel rarely sanctify themselves, and elsewhere, that change of residence deceives many. I had hoped to do out here something for the glory of God and the salvation of His children, and now I find myself with hands as empty—and perhaps not as clean—as when I was in my little cell on our Mountain of Love, Saint Marie.

Like many nineteenth- and even some twentieth-century Christians, Philippine had been exposed to plenty of fire-and-brimstone theology. Impassioned preachers threatened mortals with excruciating tortures for trifling infractions of God's "law." Philippine's memories of this theology often colluded with her own overwhelming sense of worthlessness to fill her heart with fear. To a certain extent, this was a tendency peculiar to Philippine's own personality. But on a more general level, she was simply a woman, like any other, entering into a new stage, the final stage, of life. A rather inadequate theology has encouraged Christians to deny their fear of death. Throughout centuries, preachers and authors of theological treatises have preferred to focus their attention on the joys of the afterlife, a state or place described in surprising detail by countless individuals who have never been there. Given the Christian belief in resurrection, this emphasis on the afterlife is understandable to a certain extent. But even Jesus, the exemplar *par excellence* of human holiness, feared his death. The agony in the garden is not just a stained-glass window in a church: it represents the real human fear that gripped someone who knew he was about to die, did not want to, and did not know what awaited him afterwards. Philippine's realistic fear of diminishment and death, her willingness to speak about it with others, is in this regard a refreshing antidote to an overly-spiritualized theology.

3. THE END OF PHILIPPINE'S SUPERIORSHIP

One of Philippine's joys during these years was that Florissant was "the smallest and lowliest of all the Convents of the Sacred Heart" in the United States.[6] Since at least 1824 she had had to defend it against periodic suggestions that it be closed. Her fight resumed and continued throughout her six years as superior in the 1830s. Sophie Barat was of the opinion that its works were too small. Philippine and the Jesuit pastor of the parish, Father John Theodore De Theux, were of a different mind. De Theux set his argument before Bishop Rosati in 1836. First, closing the convent "would work very serious harm to the village of St. Ferdinand, unfortunately perverse enough already," yet destined to be a place of importance. Second, they would lose "the prayers and good example of these Ladies." Third, they would lose the day school which would eventually strengthen the parish. And finally, he argued:

---

[6]January 1, 1836, to the religious in France.

Who will keep up the church as neatly as they do? And what will their house be used for if they leave? A tavern? I will not insist further. *Fiat voluntas Dei et superiorum* [May the will of God and the superiors be done].

Although Florissant's financial situation briefly improved and it provided an ideal location for the novitiate, the foundation survived as long as it did only by dint of Philippine's determined efforts during her years as superior of the house.

In late 1836, the religious in the United States received news that Eugénie Audé, the Assistant General for the United States, would not be returning to America after all. Her health, they said, was too weak to withstand the hardship of frontier life. But there was more to Eugénie's remaining in France than poor health. On November 28, 1834, Sophie Barat wrote the following intriguing lines to Eugénie in her new house in Marseille:

I am sending you, my daughter, the last letter from St. Louis. It seems that they haven't received our letters in which we indicated the change agreed upon: everyone believes that you are returning. They can wait, but wouldn't it be right to inform them that you are staying in France, at least for a time? *So as not to say everything,* I will respond that you need time to recover your health. It is only too true.[7]

In fact, the voluminous correspondence of Sophie Barat to Eugénie shows clearly that Eugénie was passing through an emotionally and spiritually difficult, even anguished period.[8] Eugénie was convinced, moreover, that the *only* person in the world who could help her out of her tormented state was Sophie Barat.[9] Her incessant and even childish pleas to be near to the Mother General exasperated Sophie. She considered Eugénie's desire to be with her a type of fixed idea.[10] Although deeply concerned for her friend, she could not and would not neglect business elsewhere in the Society just to be with

---

[7]Translation and emphasis mine.

[8]See, for example, letters of Sophie Barat to Eugénie Audé, August 13, 1834; November 11, 1835; September 19 and November 25, 1836; September 5 and December 30, 1837; and February 24, 1838.

[9]See, for example, letter of Sophie Barat to Eugénie Audé, September 19, 1836.

[10]See letters of Sophie Barat to Eugénie Audé, October 10 and 17, 1836.

Eugénie.[11] She urged her repeatedly to open herself to other spiritual advisers.[12] When business delayed the Mother General in Rome, she likewise refused Eugénie's requests to travel there to be with her.[13]

Eugénie's weakened emotional and spiritual state were no doubt related to her poor physical health. It is the ensemble of these and her dependence on, even attachment to Sophie Barat, which explain why she never returned to America. Sophie Barat wanted her to go back, but would not force the hand of a close friend in such a situation of need.[14] It is worth noting that throughout her difficulties, Eugénie still acquitted herself superbly as superior and administrator in Marseille. And after she and Sophie Barat had had an extended stay together in 1839 and 1840, it seems that Eugénie's spiritual difficulties and her dependence on her friend abated. Sophie named her superior of the Trinità dei Monti in Rome where Eugénie died in 1842.

Mother Barat's search for a new Assistant General and for a Mistress of Novices for the United States made it impossible for her to relieve Philippine from her post as superior of the Florissant house. Finally, in 1840, Mother Barat named Russian-born Elizabeth Galitzin as Provincial and Visitatrix for the houses of Missouri and the south. Philippine's liberation was at hand.

She met Galitzin in September, 1840, and was immediately granted her first request, to be relieved from the post of superior, a post she had held against her will for over twenty years. Her second request concerned a desire even older: she wanted to live among the Indians. Philippine was seventy-one years old when she made this request. The discouragement which had undermined her spirit a few years earlier at the closing of St. Marie was still evident in her letters. She wrote to Sophie Barat in September, 1840, just a few days after meeting Galitzin:

> On my side I thank you most sincerely for having at last lifted the burden I have carried so inefficiently, a burden that would have been such a trial in my last hours. I desire death

---

[11]See, for example, letters of Sophie Barat to Eugénie Audé, August 27, September 19, October 10 and 17, November 8 and December 6, 1836; February 20, March 4 and 18, April 30, May 29, June 17, October 14 and December 12, 1837; and February 13, 1838.

[12]See letters of Sophie Barat to Eugénie Audé, October 10, November 8 and December 6, 1836; April 30 and May 29, 1837.

[13]See letters of Sophie Barat to Eugénie Audé, July 22 and August 8, 1837.

[14]See letters of Sophie Barat to Eugénie Audé, July 18 and 28, and December 6 and 14, 1836; and July 20, 1837.

and I fear it. But God, who is so good, will give me the means of expiating my faults, for I realize quite clearly that crosses will follow me, though of quite another kind—if only that of changing from a very busy life to one of almost complete inactivity.

There is no hope of our going to the savages just now. Nothing has been prepared for such a mission. But besides that, I have perceived that whenever I have expressed my desires and my regrets on that subject, I have been judged unfit for the work. And even if there were only my age against me, that would be reason enough for a negative answer.

What is remarkable is that despite Philippine's feelings of inadequacy, fear of death and the depression which weighed on her during her six years as superior of Florissant, her drive to fulfill her original intention in coming to America, to live and work among the Indians, had not diminished in the slightest.

Philippine moved from Florissant to the City House in St. Louis in October, 1840. She was a simple member of the community for the first time, but worries quickly replaced her joy at being released from authority: Mother Galitzin removed the picture of St. Francis Regis from the Florissant chapel and replaced it with another of the Sacred Heart. Philippine became critically ill with a high fever, swollen limbs, labored breathing and an uneven pulse. It was apparently a psychosomatic illness brought on by her anxiety that the promise to Regis was not being fulfilled. She was heard to say as she lay ill, "A vow. . . a promise made in France. . . to God and to Regis." Her reaction seems exaggerated and melodramatic by modern standards. Her own nineteenth-century spirituality emphasized compliance with religious promises and rituals sometimes at the expense of the religious virtues of love and compassion. This tendency naturally engendered profound fear and anxiety in Philippine when she was unable to fulfill her religious duties. But there is a compellingly positive side to Philippine's intense desire to keep her promise to Regis. She knew that she had commended the entire American mission to him. For the good of that mission, she was willing to go to any extreme.

4. LIFE AMONG THE POTAWATOMI

By December, Philippine had recuperated most of her strength. But her life of austerity had changed very little with old age. The poverty, discomfort and solitude of the cubbyhole under the stairway of the convent inspired her to choose it for her sleeping quarters. She undertook the hardest work in the convent and labored long hours. Despite the lack of encouragement she received from Galitzin, Philippine still continued to dream of going to an Indian mission. For years she had been sewing vestments, gathering goods and making donations on behalf of the missionary priests she knew, the Jesuits Charles Van Quickenborne, Peter John Verhaegen and Peter De Smet among them. She had continued to receive invitations from such men to found a community of the Religious of the Sacred Heart among the Indians. Her duties as superior, the need to send religious to other foundations in the United States, and her obedience to ecclesiastical superiors such as Dubourg had always prevented her from accepting these invitations. Now old and infirm, but no longer in authority, she again attempted to make her dream a reality.

In 1840, Bishop Rosati made a trip to Europe and there met with Sophie Barat. They were both eager that the Religious of the Sacred Heart make a foundation among the Indians. Mother Barat told Rosati she could no longer deny her old friend's insistent pleas, regardless of the frail state of Philippine's health. In a letter written from Europe in July, 1840, Rosati rekindled hope in the seventy-year-old Philippine:

The example you have given in leaving Europe to make the first foundation of the Sacred Heart in America is still very powerful in influencing others to follow you. God be praised for this! But I am really surprised to learn that you are now pleading to leave Missouri in order to go among the savages. However, when one loves God, one never says "Enough." If I did not know you well, I might say it is too much for you. But knowing you as I do, I say, "Go! Follow your attraction, or rather the voice of God. He will be with you." I beg Him to bless you.

About this same time, Peter De Smet was trying to convince Galitzin of the importance of such a foundation. De Smet countered Galitzin's reluctance regarding this project and her characteristic sharpness with an absolute statement of his own. He told her that God's very blessing on the Society in America depended on founding an Indian school. In early 1841, De Smet encouraged Philippine to write to Galitzin in New Orleans to try again to sway the superior's will. Philippine wrote an impassioned letter. In it, she recounted her first inspirations to be a missionary, her promise long ago in France to work among the Indians, and her failed attempts to do so ever since her arrival in the United States. In light of her own diminishing health, she also had to persuade Mother Galitzin that she would indeed have the requisite strength to withstand the hardships of a new mission:

> So far we have been disappointed in all our hopes [to work among the Indians]—at least I have, for all my inclinations and desires urge me to work among these tribes. . . . Yesterday, the feast of the Kings, a visit from Father De Smet, who has come back from the Rocky Mountains, roused my ardor once more, and that to such an extent that I experienced a sort of physical resurrection as a result of the hope I feel that I may be among those chosen for a mission that is now offered to us under very favorable auspices.
>
> Beyond the western boundary of Missouri, this Father tells me, there is a very good tribe that comes from Canada, already partly converted to Christianity. They are called the Potawatomi. . . . I showed him the letter you brought me from Bishop Rosati, in which he wrote to me so positively: *Follow your attraction.* At the time I received it, I did not pay much attention to it; for my soul was crushed and all my offers were rejected. Now I think it really is the voice of God. Our Mother General [Barat] has often expressed this desire, and our Lord will so arrange matters that you will lend a hand in this enterprise. . . . God is going to cure me. I shall be just an extra member of the group, helping with the housework and other labors.

Just three weeks later, in late January, 1841, Philippine wrote to Galitzin again. De Smet carried the letter to her personally in New Orleans and showed her five hundred dollars which he had raised to help pay for the foundation. Philippine pressed her argument persuasively regarding the necessity of the Society's works among the poor. Her ideas had matured notably since her works of charity among priests and the poor in Grenoble years earlier. She now spoke with the clarity and conviction developed only with age:

Do hasten your return to St. Louis in order to take care of this important affair. Religious are not lacking for it, and I trust that God will let me be among those who are chosen. I know this work is one of our Mother General's most earnest desires. . . . When I consider how little piety our pupils show after they leave school, I realize how much more glory for God and consolation for ourselves there will be in instructing these fresh souls who are still in their innocence, far from the dangers of the world! What a joy it is to serve God freely, generously, without asking recompense! If we had just four hundred dollars to start with, we could go this coming spring. Our large houses in Louisiana can certainly regard this little gift as a mite in comparison with the huge sums spent on their buildings. It would give God glory if they curtailed some ornamentations in order to furnish the indispensable for our poor Indians.

The radicality of these last lines is true to Philippine's unwavering dedication to those who have less. They must certainly have given Galitzin pause as she considered her new role as superior. The large houses in Louisiana differed considerably from the poorer foundations of Missouri, a disparity which had occasionally been the cause of tension. Philippine, her predecessor as superior, was positively persuaded that the religious should also be living among the oppressed indigenous peoples of America. Although Galitzin initially refused to consider the project, De Smet was relentless. He urged her to take a few days to pray over the matter. Finally, Galitzin acceded to their requests. A month later, she received a letter written by Mother Barat in December, 1840, in which the Mother General also insisted that such a foundation be made. Sophie Barat displayed her clear memory of the vision which first prompted the journey to America twenty-two years earlier:

I am sending you a note from Bishop Rosati on the subject of a foundation which he desires us to make among the savage tribes. This matter should not be neglected. Remember, dear Mother, that our good Mother Duchesne in leaving us for America had only this work in view. It was for the sake of the Indians that she felt inspired to establish the Society in America. I believe it enters into the designs of God that we should profit, if possible, by the opportunity offered us by Bishop Rosati.

The foundation was to be made among the Potawatomi Indians of Sugar Creek. The religious named for the foundation were Lucille Mathevon, who was to be superior, Mary Ann O'Connor, Louise Amyot and Philippine. But Philippine's precarious health imperiled her lifelong desire to live among the Indians. In April, 1841, shortly before the little group was to depart, Lucille Mathevon wrote to Sophie Barat that there was "scarcely a breath of life" left in Philippine. She wrote to Galitzin:

> The doctor thinks she [Philippine] is in continual danger of death, yet she wanted to fast and abstain all during Lent. Since then the swelling has increased, and it extends from her feet up to her chest, so that she is liable to be smothered at any moment. She feels that she is very near to death, yet once our Mother General gives her the permission, she will consider it an order and no one will be able to hold her back.[15]

It is worth noting that Sophie Barat well knew that Philippine was going to Sugar Creek perhaps only to die.[16]

Philippine's chance had finally come, but even she suspected that she was too old and feeble to take it. The cure she had awaited from God to enable her to join the new mission had not come. After an enthusiastic description of what she had heard about Indian life at Sugar Creek, Philippine admitted in a letter to Sophie Barat in May, 1841:

> My writing and my scratching out show you the weakness of both my head and my hand. The miracle of my cure has not taken place. I await the will of God.

Philippine would probably have remained frustrated in this one desire of hers had it not been for the intervention of the Jesuit Father Peter John Verhaegen. For years Philippine had assisted him in his missionary efforts with her prayer, sewing and donations. Verhaegen recognized and admired her passionate dedication to evangelization among the Indians. Since he planned to visit Sugar Creek himself in July, 1841, it occurred to him that the nuns might wish to make the journey to their new mission with him. He took the matter up during a

---

[15]Quoted by Galitzin in a letter to Sophie Barat, September, 1841.
[16]See her letter to Eugénie Audé, May 26, 1841; and also August 23, 1841.

visit to the St. Louis convent. Present during the discussion were Lucille Mathevon, future superior of the Sugar Creek foundation, Eleanor Gray, superior of the City House, and Philippine, now a simple member of the City House community. In the course of their conversation, it suddenly struck Verhaegen that he was speaking of four religious while Mother Mathevon was continually referring to just three. Verhaegen then noticed Philippine's silent tears. The old nun was evidently no longer included in their plans. Verhaegen was the faithful friend in this moment. He knew that going to the Indians had been Philippine's one lifelong desire and he, accordingly, took to the offensive on her behalf. He said to the superior, Mother Gray:

> But *she* must come, too. Even if she can use only one leg, she will come. Why, if we have to carry her all the way on our shoulders, she is coming with us. She may not be able to do much work, but she will assure success to the mission by praying for us. Her very presence will draw down all manner of heavenly favors on the work.[17]

Lucille Mathevon was not entirely persuaded of the prudence of this plan, but she acquiesced to Verhaegen's insistence.

On June 29, 1841, they set off on the four-day river trip up the Missouri River. Philippine was seventy-one years old—and rejuvenated. As Lucille Mathevon described Philippine, "she walked up and down the deck as if she were young again."[18] It was then another four-day journey to Sugar Creek, in present-day Kansas by the Osage River. On the last day of their trip, the gracious Potawatomi Indians posted mounted sentries every two miles to guide the travelers on their way. Since the nuns' house was not yet ready when they arrived, they moved into a twelve-foot-by-fifteen-foot cabin lent to them by a generous Indian. Lucille Mathevon continued in her account to Eleanor Gray:

> We had two chairs, one of them reserved for our dear Mother Duchesne. She made a kind of desk out of the chair and kept her little belongings there—that was the full extent of her

---

[17]Lucille Mathevon, *Notes on the Foundation of the Sugar Creek Mission*, Religious of the Sacred Heart Archives, St. Louis, Missouri.

[18]July, 1841. Lucille Mathevon to Eleanor Gray, written in the form of a journal, Religious of the Sacred Heart Archives, St. Louis, Missouri.

room—and from that chair she wrote to our Mother Foundress with the greatest joy in being able to practice holy poverty in this fashion.

The Indians received the nuns with warmth and friendship. Lucille Mathevon described their first meeting with the Potawatomi at Sugar Creek, many of whom were mestizos, that is, of mixed native American and European descent:

> We were given a reception that far exceeded anything we had expected. A mestizo named Joseph Napoleon Bourassa made a fine speech in the name of the tribe and the seven hundred who were assembled to greet us. He told how glad they were that we had come to instruct their daughters in the true religion. I do not remember all Father Verhaegen said in reply, but he presented Mother Duchesne to the Indians, saying, "Here is a religious who has been asking the dear Lord for thirty years to let her come and teach you, and how happy she is that at last He has heard her prayer."

> Then they all wanted to shake hands, and Mother Duchesne put her arms around all the women and girls; and they all shook hands with us. After that we had a fine dinner at the home of Mr. Joseph Bertrand, a very refined mestizo, whom we regard as a great benefactor. . . .

The white European missionaries considered the Potawatomi tribe especially open to strangers, particularly this group which had had frequent contact with missionaries. Philippine's descriptions of the Christians among them reflects, for her, a veritable ideal. She often compared them to the early Christian communities which the New Testament portrays in such utopian terms. The Potawatomi's life had, in fact, become exceedingly structured through their contact with the Jesuits. From prayer, to work, to schooling, the Christian missionaries made a concerted effort to assimilate these people into the white Christian culture. "Assimilation" for most missionaries meant that the Indians would give up their own cultural heritage in order to adopt that of the white European settlers on the frontier.

In addition, missionaries encouraged a religious lifestyle among the Indians which likened their life in certain respects to religious orders. In September, 1841, Philippine gave the following account of the Indians' life in a letter to her brother Hippolyte:

This is the order of day established for the mission: morning prayers in the church when the bell rings, then holy mass, during which they sing hymns in the Indian language; this is followed by catechism for the children. The principal meal, at ten or eleven o'clock, consists principally of corn and meat. Many of the Indians own cows and horses. In the evening there are prayers again in common in the church. On Saturdays the priest scarcely leaves the confessional, and on August 15 and also today there were more than one hundred communions. In the church the men and women sit on opposite sides, and the boys have a proctor who holds a correction rod in his hand. I assure you there is need for this. The older Indians do not grow weary even during the longest ceremonies. Their good example continually draws other adults and these ask for baptism. Once they receive this sacrament they give up quarreling, drunkenness, stealing, and dancing. Nothing could be more peaceful than this village. One would think the very horses' hooves were cushioned like cats' paws. The animals are tame as human beings.

She wrote similarly to her friend Father De La Croix in February, 1842, contrasting the Catholic Indians of her own mission with "pagan" Indians and adding several other details:

The Catholic Indians live in a village quite separate from the pagans, who honor the evil spirit in order to ward off harm. Among the Catholics there is no drunkenness, no dancing, no gambling. Every Sunday one sees at least a hundred at the Holy Table; at Christmas four hundred received the sacraments. . . . In the church the men and women sit on opposite sides and sing hymns in their own language. They do this also at night and they say the family rosary, each one carrying a pair of beads always. More than two hundred received the scapular of our Lady on a single day. Charity is practiced among them as it was among the early Christians.

The "success" of the Christian missionaries among this little Potawatomi community, which indeed sounds almost like a semimonastic community, can be explained by several factors. First, there were genuinely friendly relations between the missionaries and the Indians. Lucille Mathevon tells of their constant gifts of food to the nuns: "Whatever they have, they bring to the *good old lady*, as they call

Mother Duchesne." Second, the Indian village was a self-contained community in which a concerted effort on the part of missionaries to promote work, religious life and education was relatively easier than among, for example, a population of white settlers. Finally, and related to the last point, the United States government's continual removals of the Potawatomi from one land to another had made the Potawatomi increasingly dependent on aid from the government and missionaries.

The Potawatomi tribe was originally one with the Chippewas and Ottawas. These Algonquian-speaking peoples were residing in the Great Lakes region as early as the seventeenth century. With the arrival of white settlers, they, like so many native American tribes, were killed, driven or bought off their lands. In 1809, for example, the Potawatomi, together with four other tribes, gave three million acres of choice land to the United States government for only 8,200 dollars.[19] In 1830, President Andrew Jackson provided for a policy of "removing" Indians from all the lands where they had hunted and lived whenever those lands were desired by white settlers.[20] Between 1789 and 1837, in fact, the years just preceding Philippine's work among them, the Potawatomi negotiated a total of thirty-nine treaties with the United States government. They lost most of their land in these treaties.[21]

This policy of removal is what brought the Potawatomi to Sugar Creek just a few years before Philippine arrived. The French Sulpician priest, Benjamin Petit, who lived among the Potawatomi of Indiana had commented bitterly in the late 1830s:

The government wants to transport the Indians to the other side of the Mississippi. I live between fear and hope, but I

---

[19]Henry C. Dennis, ed. *The American Indian 1492–1970: A Chronology and Fact Book* (Dobbs Ferry, New York: Oceana Publications, Inc., 1971), p. 23.

[20]Dennis, ed., *The American Indian 1492–1970*, p. 26.

[21]Francis Paul Prucha, *The Great Father: The United States Government and the American Indians*, 2 vols. (Lincoln, Nebraska: University of Nebraska Press, 1984), vol. I, p. 248, and pp. 248–53 on the Potawatomi dispersal. On the history of the Potawatomi tribe from 1500 to 1833, see James A. Clifton, *The Pokagons, 1683–1983: Catholic Potawatomi Indians of the St. Joseph River Valley* (Lanham, New York, London: University Press of America, 1984), pp. 1–41. On the removal of Indian tribes from Kansas after Philippine's death, and on the particular situation of the Prairie Potawatomi who remained in Kansas, see H. Craig Miner and William E. Unrau, *The End of Indian Kansas: A Study of Cultural Revolution, 1854–1871* (Lawrence, Kansas: The Regents Press of Kansas, 1978). See also George E. Fay, ed., *Treaties between the Potawatomi tribe of Indians and the United States of America, 1789–1867*, Occasional publications in anthropology, Ethnology series no. 19 (Greeley, Colorado: University of Northern Colorado, 1971).

entrust my hope and fear to the hands of the Lord. . . . How
little savage at heart they are, these Indians, whom the Americans with their hearts dry as cork and their whole thought
"land and money" fail to appreciate and treat with so much
disdain and injustice.[22]

Just a few years after Philippine's life among them, the Potawatomi
would be moved to yet another location and then yet another. In the
process of being pushed off their native lands, the Potawatomi nation
was splintered into numerous factions.[23] A tribe of hunters, they were
thus obliged to farm and undertake other tasks about which they were
naturally "lazy," according to many white settlers.[24] With hindsight we
can see better than Philippine how such radical social displacement
undermined their lifestyle and made them vulnerable to the white
man's alcohol.

Philippine's periodic references to the drunkenness of some
Potawatomi, to their inherent "laziness," and to the failures experienced by the Jesuits among other tribes are not surprising comments
from a nineteenth-century European missionary. Her concern for their
welfare was genuine, but it assumed the superiority of certain modes of
dress, of work habits and, of course, the Catholic religion.[25] Some
French Catholics had gone so far as to argue explicitly that native
Americans had to be "Frenchified" as a prerequisite to becoming civi-
lized.[26]

Philippine abhorred the fact that so many Indians went hungry
and that others inadequately prepared themselves for the cold of winter. She was also sufficiently astute to recognize that some of these ills,
such as drunkenness, were the fruits of native American contact with
white settlers, and that it was the United States government which had
forced the Potawatomi to Sugar Creek in the first place. She wrote to
her sister Euphrosine in February, 1842:

---

[22]Quoted in Gloria Jahoda, *The Trail of Tears* (New York: Holt, Rinehart and Winston,
1975), pp. 204–205.

[23]For an account of these removals, see R. David Edmunds, *The Potawatomis: Keepers of
the Fire* (Norman, Oklahoma: University of Oklahoma Press, 1978), pp. 240–75.

[24]See Stratton, *Pioneer Women: Voices from the Kansas Frontier*, pp. 107–126, on the clash
between native American culture and nineteenth-century settlers.

[25]On this general topic, see Brian W. Dippie, *The Vanishing American: White Attitudes and
U.S. Indian Policy* (Middletown, Connecticut: Wesleyan University Press, 1982).

[26]Dippie, *The Vanishing American*, p. 9.

Congress forced the Potawatomi to move into this region and will pay them an annual sum of money which, as long as the arrangement lasts, will save them from dire misery. This year we have seen them making good use of part of their money by buying shoes, shirts, and other articles of clothing such as the white people wear. But the blanket is always an important item in their dress. Christianity changes these unfortunate people so noticeably that a pagan among them can always be identified by his fierce and unkempt appearance.

Verhaegen's implicit definition of a "savage" is revealing in this regard. A savage is one whose customs and appearance differ from those of white people. Referring to an Indian chief, he wrote:

He is a savage in the full extent of that term. His face is painted black, with a little red around the eyelids. He prides himself in avoiding entirely the customs of white people.[27]

What Philippine may not fully have appreciated was that the annual sum of money which the government was paying to the Potawatomi, which would "save them from dire misery" as long as the arrangement lasted, was an arrangement forced on them by the removals of the past few decades. It was also an arrangement subject to repeated revisions as the white government and settlers continued to move westward, forcing the unwilling Indians off the new lands "given" to them by the government.

Philippine's age and health kept her from taking a very active part in the mission at Sugar Creek. Except for visiting the sick and lending a little help to the Indian girls with their knitting, there was little else she could do. She had never succeeded in learning English, and the Potawatomi language was "extremely difficult," as she wrote to her brother in September, 1841:

Let me add that some words in this barbaric tongue run to ten, nine, eight syllables, and as yet there is no published dictionary, no grammar, and just one book of prayers. I think I shall never learn such a language.

---

[27]Baunard, *Histoire de Madame Duchesne*, p. 480; translation mine.

Philippine unwittingly betrays the missionaries' limited linguistic abilities when she wrote, seriously, to Sophie Barat in February, 1841, that the Jesuit Father Christian Hoecken concluded that the resemblance he found between some Potawatomi words and Greek and Hebrew pointed to the fact that the Potawatomi were of Jewish descent![28]

The only task at Sugar Creek which Philippine could carry out, in fact, was the one that Verhaegen had foreseen for her: she prayed. In her *Notes on the Foundation of Sugar Creek*, Lucille Mathevon wrote about Philippine:

> She stayed all morning in the church, so Sister Louise would take her a cup of coffee each day, and she drank it at the door of the church. After dinner she went again for three or four hours of prayer. The Indians had the greatest admiration for her, recommended themselves to her prayers and called her Woman-who-prays-always.

Quah-kah-ka-num-ad, Woman-who-prays-always, these people called her. Native Americans, whose traditional religion pervades all aspects of their life, could easily love such a woman. She seemed useless to herself and useless to others from cultures excessively focused on the merit of deeds, but not to them. Their contemplative insight opened them to the fact that the mere presence of someone good, of someone who loves, often has a healing power greater than many mighty deeds. The Potawatomi would draw near to Philippine while she prayed and gently touch her garment. Their gestures were akin to those of people today, many of whom are part or all Indian, from the agrarian regions of Latin America. Still today they can be seen reverently approaching the statues of saints in their village chapels to touch the saint, "to take grace" as they say. It is a gesture of confidence in the goodness of others, that the goodness of any individual somehow heals and makes good all which surrounds and touches them. Philippine is not remembered for any great deeds or accomplishments during her life among the Potawatomi of Sugar Creek. Her legacy is more powerful: Philippine was a presence of goodness and compassion among a suffering people.

Although her sisters recognized this, they also recognized her own

---

[28]See Dippie, *The Vanishing American*, pp. 16–18, on nineteenth-century interest in the question of Indian origins. It is related to the attempt of Europeans settling in America to establish a distinctive national identity for themselves.

physical suffering. Philippine's optimistic reports about her health contrast with those of Lucille Mathevon. For example, Philippine wrote to her sister in February, 1842:

> My health has improved very much in this part of the country. I have gained some strength; my eyesight is better; and I retain the use of all my faculties, though I am in my seventy-third year.

But the very next day, Lucille Mathevon wrote:

> Mother Duchesne is aging more and more. She is often in a very suffering condition. The life here is much too hard for a person her age.

Mother Mathevon had written earlier in a letter to Mother Galitzin in 1841:

> She is here just to suffer, for she has aged much in this short time and is sometimes like a little child. She no longer has the fine mind of other days. She is feeble; her limbs are swollen; her digestion is poor. I fear she will have a stroke. To tell you the truth, we cannot understand how the Father Superior [Verhaegen] could have insisted on bringing her here. But he said that she would pray for the missions and that she must be given the consolation of dying here. All she can do at present is pray, sometimes lying for a little while on her bed, and knit stockings. That is all. It is a great anxiety for us to have to care for her without being able to give her what she needs, for one has to send twenty leagues for things. We are doing all we can for her. She has done so much for the Society, it is only right that we give her all possible care in her old age.

Lucille Mathevon's viewpoint is quite understandable, except perhaps from Philippine's perspective. Philippine drew meaning from her own suffering. In the following letter written to Father De La Croix in February, 1842, Philippine makes explicit the association between her years of suffering and her new life at Sugar Creek:

> Now I come to my own story—the chapter since your departure. If I knew how to profit by suffering, I would be able to

say, like you, that I am perfectly content. But I needed to be
tried, and God has directed my steps along *vias duras* [hard
paths], even while guiding me to the mission for the savages,
so long the goal of my desires. Here I suffer still because I can
do nothing at all. First of all, I was transferred from St. Louis
to St. Ferdinand, where there were continual threats that the
convent would be closed. Then, in answer to prayers and
representations, they placed the novitiate there. I was transferred to St. Louis, passing from a very active life to one of
complete nullity, and I was ill for a long time. Father De
Smet returned from the Flathead mission in the Rockies—a
three months' journey—and his coming gave me new life. He
led me to hope that we would make a foundation there within
two years, and he vigorously urged our Mother Provincial to
send us here to work among these Indians.

Philippine then proceeded to give a full account of the situation of the
Potawatomi mission and Indian missions elsewhere. Her enthusiasm
in such letters is irrepressible. At the same time that she acknowledges
the burden she is to those around her, this seventy-two-year-old
woman was envisioning new missions in the West which she might
help found. She wrote to Sophie Barat in February, 1842:

They tell us that there are many saints buried in the little
[Indian] cemetery. When I walk alone out of doors, I always
go there, and I kneel and beg of God the favor of being buried
beside them. I feel, however, the same longing for the Rocky
Mountain missions and any others like them, that I experienced in France when I first begged to come to America, the
same longing I felt for the Indian missions, once I reached
this country. They say that in the Rockies people live to be a
hundred years old. As my health has improved and I am only
seventy-three [*sic*], I think I shall have at least ten more years
to work.

   I used to think it more perfect to wait for things to take
their course and so decide my fate. But now, Reverend
Mother, will you not authorize me to go farther west if they
want me to do so? Of course, that is still rather doubtful, but
here I am only a burden to others, as I have no real employment, and there is no doubt about it, they would be glad to
have me recalled. I knew from the beginning that I was not
wanted. One of the missionaries got permission to remain as

long as he desired, even though he was wanted at the college.
That makes me hope for a similar favor. . . .

Lucille Mathevon and the other religious who lived with Philippine were faced with a dilemma. They knew Philippine wanted to remain at Sugar Creek, but her declining health made them fear for her life. In the late spring of 1842, Peter Richard Kenrick, the Coadjutor Bishop of St. Louis, came to administer the sacrament of confirmation at Sugar Creek. He considered it unwise for Philippine to remain there. She had obviously been the subject of many letters and conversations. Just a week later, she received a letter from Sophie Barat asking her to sacrifice her dream of living among the Indians. Verhaegen, the man who a year previously had insisted that Philippine be allowed to go to the new mission, had the delicacy to return to Sugar Creek himself to escort his old friend away from the land of her dreams. There was a touching farewell scene with the Potawatomi. One can only imagine the pain in her heart as she boarded the wagon which would take her away. Peter Verhaegen and Philippine reached St. Louis on June 29, 1842, exactly one year after her departure from St. Louis for Sugar Creek. In October, 1842, she wrote to De La Croix, who was then back in France:

> For thirty-eight years my great desire was to work among the savages. I even hoped to go to Father De Smet's mission in the Rockies. Then after one year of uselessness at the Indian mission, I came back here by order of my Superior General, without having accomplished anything and without hope of ever accomplishing anything.

Philippine joined the community of St. Charles, but her thoughts remained in Sugar Creek and with the other Indian missions being established in the West. Her first letters after her departure from Sugar Creek show how she tried not to become self-absorbed with her loss. In August, 1842, she wrote to her friend Mother Gonzague Boilvin:

> From my last letter you learned of my departure from Indian Territory. I cannot forget the savages, even though I am surrounded by everything that can edify me and fill me with gratitude. The religious whom I had never met, as well as those whom I had known for a long time, are full of kind thoughtfulness for me.

In a letter written just before this to Father De La Croix, Philippine expressed her concern that the money she requested for the Sugar Creek mission still reach its destination, even though she was no longer there. Rather than dwell on her own situation, Philippine then described Peter De Smet's missionary work in the West and the situation of the Sacred Heart schools in Missouri. Her acceptance of suffering, a spiritual theme typical of nineteenth-century spirituality and especially strong among women, attains a painful poignancy in this letter:

> As I live a very solitary life [at St. Charles], I can employ all my time in making reparation for the past and in preparing for death. But I cannot put out of my mind the thought of the savages, and my ambition carries me even to the Rockies. I can only adore the designs of God, who has taken from me the thing I had so long desired. . . .

5. ST. CHARLES: LIVING WITH DIMINISHMENT

Philippine was almost seventy-three years old upon her return to St. Charles. She would spend the last ten years of her life in this community. Her letters show a woman deeply affected by a sense of personal failure, her diminishing health and frequent loneliness. Two events which particularly pained her were the closing of Florissant and a misunderstanding she had with her friend Sophie Barat. But perhaps even more than during her years of difficult struggle in Florissant from 1834 to 1840, Philippine stands out as a woman actively committed to her life-long projects and dreams. She voiced her opposition to changes when she thought they were ill-advised. She kept informed regarding the Indian missions and assisted her missionary friends by sewing vestments, writing letters and sending donations. The tone of her letters betrays her state: she was old, infirm and suffering. But what remained in the foreground for Philippine was the world around her and its needs.

It is perhaps not surprising given Philippine's history that by the time she reached the St. Charles community, it had become even poorer than the foundation among the Potawatomi. Indeed, all the convents in Missouri and Louisiana were suffering at this time due to the economic straits of the country. Personal poverty was still Philippine's hallmark. Amélie Jouve, Philippine's niece and fellow religious, wrote to Sophie Barat:

You would be deeply touched, Reverend Mother, by the poverty of St. Charles. It could hardly be greater. Mother Duchesne's room is like a veritable sanctuary of this virtue. Certainly in the whole Society there is no one more poorly housed or clad or shod. . . . And it is quite useless to argue with her in this matter—it is her attraction.

She wrote this shortly after her arrival in the United States in 1847, when she went to see her aunt in St. Charles. It had been almost thirty years since they had seen each other. She has left an account in which she describes Philippine's room alongside the convent chapel. These were the two places in which Philippine spent the greater part of her time, engaged in either prayer or manual labor:

The furniture of her little room consisted of a low cot, a chair, a wooden box in which she kept her treasures—and what treasures they were! Some instruments of penance, some spiritual notebooks, some letters of our Mother General. There were two or three old pictures of pious subjects on the walls and some well worn prayerbooks on a little table.[29]

This room has been preserved and can be visited today.

Although Philippine's educational work was confined to just a few French-speaking children in the free school, she was never idle. She dedicated a great deal of her time to sewing vestments and other garments that could be used by her missionary friends. A few of these Jesuits, Peter Verhaegen and Peter De Smet, remained remarkably dedicated to the old woman. They recognized in her the radical missionary zeal which inspired their own lives. It was a great loss to Philippine when Verhaegen was sent East in 1844. De Smet continued to write her news of his own work in the West. Her own letters to France are replete with information gleaned from his and other reports on the missions among native Americans.

Philippine was gradually failing physically and mentally. Her voice became so faint that she could hardly be heard while doing the refectory readings. Amélie Jouve writes that the other religious kept this fact from her, knowing that her sense of uselessness only depressed her. By 1848, Philippine's eyesight had so weakened that she could hardly read or write on some days. Contending with physical suffering

---

[29]Jouve, *Notes concernant la vie de Notre Vénérable Mère Duchesne.*

and diminishment became a routine part of her life. She wrote to her sister in May, 1845:

> The past winter was very mild. I did not suffer from rheumatism in my limbs this year as I did the winter before, but I did have it in my hands, though I could keep on with ordinary work. Since the twenty-ninth of last August I am in my seventy-sixth year, and I long for, yet fear, the hour of death, for I have amassed so little treasure for heaven, and old age is not the most fervent period of life.

Her reports, however, contrast conspicuously with the accounts of her religious sisters. They were amazed by her stamina.

Philippine experienced two especially painful events in her old age. The first regards her relationship with Sophie Barat and the second the closing of the Florissant foundation. Both events form part of a single narrative. It demonstrates again Philippine's scrupulous attachment to keeping her promises to St. Francis Regis and her unflagging zeal in fighting for principles.

The friendship between Philippine and Sophie Barat, as previously discussed, was especially cherished by Philippine. Her affection for Mother Barat was perhaps second only to that for her cousin Josephine. In the early years of their friendship, Philippine struggled, rather successfully, not to be overly-dependent on Sophie. Her very departure for America attests to the independence she had achieved. Not surprisingly, however, Philippine corresponded frequently with her friend. As superior of all the Sacred Heart houses in the United States and then as superior of the Florissant house, she had ample cause to write Mother Barat. But in addition, Philippine was often rather alone in her life on the frontier. Letters, especially those to and from Sophie Barat, were an important personal support.

The misunderstanding between the two women commenced shortly after Philippine's departure from Sugar Creek for St. Charles. In 1843, just before her own death, Mother Galitzin announced that the St. Charles boarding school would be closed on account of its meager enrollment. Philippine, ever attached to places, all the more so when they were impoverished, hurried to the defense of the establishment. She wrote to her friend Gonzague Boilvin in early 1844:

> You have also learned of the great loss the Society has sustained in the death of Reverend Mother Galitzin. . . . With your sympathetic heart you can easily understand the sorrow

felt in Missouri. Before she left St. Louis, she was ill with fever and so could not visit us at St. Charles. She sent for Mother Hamilton, and on hearing how few children we had and how much sickness there had been in the community, she struck us a severe blow—had the children transferred to St. Louis, along with several of the nuns, and sent others to St. Ferdinand [Florissant]. There are just eight of us left in this big house. Only Mother Hamilton and Sister Couture speak French. In just a few days we found ourselves living in solitude. . . . Our convent was offered to the Visitation religious at Kaskaskia. . . .

I still hold on to some hope that our Mother General will not sanction these measures, which are so heartbreaking, especially for me. I saw the work begin here, and perhaps I shall see it destroyed. I wrote to her with all the urgent entreaties I could employ, begging her to renew the life of this house. . . .

I have written enough to show you the state of my poor heart. Do not fail to get earnest prayers for our resurrection; and when you write to Mother Barat, plead our cause. . . . Pray more earnestly than ever to St. Francis Regis for St. Charles and St. Ferdinand [Florissant]. *I attribute all our troubles and anxieties to the destruction of his shrine.* How I long to erect it again!*

Philippine's passionate commitment to Regis plays a pivotal role in this episode. She learned that Galitzin had in fact offered not only the St. Charles convent, but also the Florissant foundation to the Visitation nuns, although they declined both offers. As Philippine pointed out heatedly in a letter to Mother Boilvin in December, 1844:

Those convents belong to St. Regis, and he saved them, I may say, by a miracle. Comment on these matters is unnecessary.

Philippine went so far as to consider Galitzin's death a sign that the shrine to St. Regis in Florissant, removed by Mother Galitzin in 1840, should never have been dismantled in the first place. Years after the event, in June, 1846, Philippine wrote to Mother Barat:

---

*Emphasis mine.

When I learned that the shrine of Saint Regis had been destroyed, and that the beautiful relics brought from Rome by Bishop Dubourg had been removed from the chapel [of Florissant in 1840], I expected a catastrophe to occur. When Mother Galitzin died [in 1843], I knew it had happened.

In fact, Galitzin's decision to close St. Charles was never approved. Sophie Barat wrote to Regis Hamilton, the superior of St. Charles, informing her so. Yet she sent not a word of reply to Philippine's own entreaties on behalf of St. Charles. Philippine feared that this was a silent, but powerful rebuke. A few years earlier, a directive had gone out to all the religious encouraging them to write to Mother Barat only when necessary. Sophie Barat was then Mother General to about two thousand religious in over sixty foundations in eight countries. Her correspondence was overwhelming. But surely, Philippine had thought, the directive did not apply to a good friend. Besides, her defense of the St. Charles foundation had seemed to her to be urgent business.

If Philippine only suspected a reproval at this point, she was convinced by the Mother General's ensuing absolute silence. Philippine received not a single letter from Sophie Barat for about four years from 1843 until 1847. For her part, Philippine was deeply injured and halted her own communication with her friend.

In June, 1846, Philippine broke the impasse, but only because she felt obliged by duty. Maria Cutts, the new Visitatrix of the Missouri and Louisiana houses after Galitzin, had decided to close the Florissant house. Philippine's formal opening to her friend Sophie Barat alludes in a business-like fashion to the reason for her long silence. It was her way of finally expressing her hurt to her friend:

> My very dear and venerated Mother,
>   It is quite a long time since I wrote to you, but that is because I wished to obey your recommendation not to write except in the case of real necessity. I thought it was such a case when I took the liberty to beg you to re-establish the boarding school here [in St. Charles]. I received no answer, but the Mother who was our superior at that time received one, which proved to me all the more clearly that I ought to be more reserved about writing.

Philippine then represented her reasons in favor of leaving the Florissant foundation open. Although her letter concluded with a formal, superficially apologetic tone, it is once again apparent that this old woman had found her voice. She was strikingly assertive:

> Forgive this long letter. I count on your kindness. If you refuse my petition, I shall submit, but I shall never be reconciled. The wound is too deep. I kneel at your feet awaiting the decision, and I retain always my deep respect for you. . . .
>
>   Your very humble and unworthy servant,
>   Philippine Duchesne

Sophie Barat did not answer this letter either. Those who had tried to cheer Philippine during the preceding years of their silence, who had ascribed the Mother General's lack of communication to the mail's unreliability or Mother Barat's overwhelming workload were left with little to say. The Florissant foundation closed despite Philippine's pleas. She was inconsolable. The injury which this loss signified for her, which she had expounded so eloquently in her letter to Sophie Barat, involved much more than the house of Florissant. She commented on the southern houses in the frank tone that increasingly characterized her mature years:

> If there was less love of external show in our large houses, the small ones would have support. People think they will work wonders by external appearances, but those who are suffering and who see the uselessness of this are able to distinguish in this matter. This passion for external grandeur is accompanied here [in America] by a passion for knowledge. . . . People want to know all the motions of the planets and the stars, when they know nothing about Bible history or the cultivation of a garden.

There was probably a dose of displaced anger here as well. She felt that she had lost a good friend, but on this point, Philippine stoically guarded silence. She suffered another loss when the one person who knew best what she suffered, Regis Hamilton, was transferred to the Society's new foundation in Canada. Philippine's biographer, Louise Callan, suspects that Hamilton wrote to Mother Barat informing her of the pain her silence was causing Philippine.

In September, 1847, Sophie Barat finally wrote to Philippine. The letter was delivered personally by one of Philippine's own nieces, Amélie Jouve, who had come to serve in the Society in America.

Mother Barat had sent her to visit Philippine precisely to assure Philippine of the Mother General's firm affection for her. Amélie Jouve records the scene, referring to herself in the third person:

> That fortunate niece was received by Mother Duchesne as an angel from heaven. After reading the letter sent to her by our Reverend Mother General, who was her dearest friend, she seemed transported with joy. Tears flowed down her cheeks, and she was speechless with emotion. After a little while she exclaimed, "So our Mother General still thinks of me, still loves me? She has been so good as to show me that love by sending you to visit me?" She was radiant with joy.[30]

In a letter written after her arrival in September, 1847, Amélie Jouve recounted her colorful impressions of the seventy-eight-year-old Philippine, likening her to the third-century desert ascetic, Paul:

> I may say with Anthony [another desert dweller] that I have seen Paul in the desert. Yes, I have seen a great saint and one who is drawing near the end of her earthly pilgrimage. I found her very weak and her voice so feeble that it is hard to hear what she says. She received me like an angel come down from heaven. The cross has ever been her portion, and for some time past she has suffered intensely, believing that she had incurred our Mother General's displeasure. An ecstatic happiness lighted up her face when she read our Very Reverend Mother's letter and heard that she had sent me to St. Charles just to see her. We had long talks about the past; the names of our Mothers and Sisters in France recurred over and over again, and the recollections of the early days of the Society.

Jouve also sought to discover what would give her aunt happiness in her old age. Philippine took the opportunity to voice her opinion that Francis Regis' picture should be restored to its proper place of honor, and so it was. The favor granted her a rest which few could fully appreciate.

Correspondence between Sophie and Philippine resumed after Amélie's visit. It too brought solace to the aged missionary, although

---

[30]Jouve, *Notes concernant la vie de Notre Vénérable Mère Duchesne.*

their letters remained sporadic. Each complained that the other did not write enough. Old age was certainly a factor for Philippine, already seventy-eight, and perhaps also for Sophie Barat, ten years her junior. In addition, Mother Barat was kept busy by the myriad responsibilities associated with the congregation's foundations around the world. In the general letters she wrote for common reading by all the superiors and religious throughout the Society, Sophie complains of her lack of time to write to each one personally.

Historians have not agreed on the reasons for Sophie Barat's long silence with her friend Philippine. They variously cite her intense workload, hypothesize about lost letters, simple forgetfulness; it has even been suggested that Philippine's superior, Emilie St. Cyr, had dishonorably purloined the Mother General's letters to Philippine out of jealousy of the old woman. St. Cyr herself vigorously denied the charge, which, in all likelihood, was first made by someone over-anxious to safeguard Sophie Barat's claim to sanctity.[31]

More to the point, the misunderstanding between the two women is revelatory of the tremendous pain it caused Philippine, even after a separation of over twenty-five years. Philippine's life had hardly been easy on the frontier. She experienced little of the comfort of human love in her life, something, indeed, nineteenth-century spirituality did not encourage in religious life. That her cherished friendship with Sophie Barat was finally rescued from misunderstanding was a kind turn of events in her final years.

Philippine's weakened state in this last period allowed her the time she had always desired for prayer. "God is good," she wrote to Sophie Barat in January, 1850,

> . . . always so good. I have the consolation of spending my time in silence close to the chapel. By the grace of God I am still able to be up and around.

But her trials were hardly over. She longed too for human conversation, but was left frequently alone for long periods when the community took its recreations outside. Philippine's niece attributed this to the new superior of St. Charles, Mother St. Cyr:

---

[31]See Baunard, *Histoire de Madame Duchesne*, pp. 513; and Callan's comments in *Philippine Duchesne*, pp. 689–90.

It was not that the religious would not have been happy to spend this time with her, but the superior, young and inexperienced, disapproved of this, fearing that her own authority might suffer by such friendly contacts with this saintly old Mother. God permitted this little trial in order that Mother Duchesne might find her chief support in the cross.[32]

In 1850, Philippine learned of her best friend's, Josephine's, death. She was bitterly disappointed on yet another occasion when she begged two former Jesuit Provincials to write to Mother Barat on behalf of a foundation. In 1851, she wrote to Sophie Barat and minced no words:

> I was completely disappointed in the hopes I set on those two Fathers. Having had occasion to see one of them, I inquired whether he had written to you. He answered "No." That "no" re-echoed in my heart as I thought how, when they first came to Missouri, we had stinted ourselves in order to help them, and all I had asked was a letter that would give you correct information. I know very well that all the Fathers are not so hardhearted. . . .

She never fully recovered from the blow of Florissant's closing and did not lose an opportunity to point out that the Sisters of Loretto, who had taken the foundation over, were prospering. Philippine continued to suffer "the fears and the many intimate afflictions" of old age, as she wrote to Sophie Barat in August, 1851. She told her sister Euphrosine in June, 1852, that old age for her never ceased to be a purgatory.

In the last year of her life, Philippine again enjoyed the comforting presence of her friend Regis Hamilton, returned from Canada. Mother Hamilton slept in the same room with Philippine and gave her every kind attention possible. Philippine experienced periodic mental lapses during this year. A letter she wrote in the summer of 1852 shows how she faced this trial with characteristic frankness and strength:

> The doctor discovered that I had very high fever, but I did not mind that so much as having lost my head for awhile. In order to be able to face my present condition and the prospect of losing my mental balance, I really must hold firmly to the conviction that God does everything for our good.

---

[32]Jouve, *Notes concernant la vie de Notre Vénérable Mère Duchesne.*

Her friend Verhaegen was in St. Charles to give her the last sacraments on August 16, 1852. The next day, she bade good-bye to those she loved who were far away. To Sophie Barat, she wrote:

> According to all appearances this is the last time I shall be able to write to you. Yesterday I received the last sacraments, but God may still keep me waiting for the happiness of seeing Him. The mental wanderings I was suffering from were caused by a high fever that I was going about with all the time. At present I do not know when the end will be, but I come once more to kneel at your feet, beg your pardon, and assure you of my loving veneration.

To her sister Euphrosine, who had reluctantly given several children to religious life, Philippine applied the gospel text usually reserved for religious:

> . . . I am leaving you with sorrow because you are so alone. But God has promised the hundredfold to those who leave father and mother for His sake, and you deserve the hundred-fold, too, for your sacrifices have been far greater than those your children made. You share in the merit of all the good works they accomplish. Courage, then! One is always richer for having made sacrifices for God. Have your pious children pray for me. I carry into eternity with me the memory of them and of you. Adieu, loving and dear Sister.

Her note to Peter De Smet received an almost immediate reply. He wrote to her on August 23:

> I received your good letter of the seventeenth and I cannot tell you what consolation it brought me. Certainly I shall pray to the good God for you. . . . It is I, Madame, and our Indians, who are under great obligation to you for all the prayers you have offered to God for their conversion and welfare and for all your charity in their regard. I do not need to ask you to continue those prayers for us all.

Philippine grew gradually weaker during the next three months. She attended mass every morning, but often needed help from the other nuns to move even between her room and the nearby chapel. On the day of her death, she received a visit from Maria Cutts and Anna

Du Rousier, the Visitatrix representing Mother Barat in America. They were bringing Philippine one last word from her friend Sophie Barat. Mother Du Rousier gave Philippine the Mother General's blessing and then had the wisdom to ask for Philippine's for herself. Just after this, Du Rousier reflected on Philippine's life and its significance for the future:

> Bishop Kenrick declared she was the noblest and most virtuous woman he had ever known. Father De Smet says that while living she was worthy of canonization. Our American houses owe everything to her. She has opened the way to us through many fatigues and privations. . . . I arrived just in time to receive her blessing and to recommend the needs of our missions and she promised me she would treat of them earnestly with our Lord. I count much upon her intercession because I believe she is all-powerful over the Heart of Jesus.[33]

Du Rousier followed in Philippine's missionary footsteps the very next year by founding a convent and school in Santiago, Chile, the first Sacred Heart foundation in South America.

Philippine was true to character even in these last moments. She protested when one of the nuns kindled a fire in her room to cut the chill. When she was offered a little water, she worried lest it break her communion fast. It required Regis Hamilton's firm insistence to reassure Philippine. Verhaegen was present to give her the last sacraments one more time on November 18, 1852. As he said mass in the nearby chapel, she was heard to say, "I give you my heart, my soul, and my life—oh, yes—my life, generously."

Philippine died shortly after noon, November 18, 1852. Her coffin was of plain wood. For one last night, she was left before the tabernacle to be in solitude before her God. Her remains lie now in a simple and austere shrine at the Convent of the Sacred Heart in St. Charles, Missouri. The small chapel there was once part of an elaborate plan to construct a large church in Philippine's honor. The extraordinary expense of building finally prompted her sisters in the Society of the Sacred Heart to interrupt construction and to reconsider the plan. Philippine would never have wanted the attention or understood the expense.

---

[33]Letter to Aloysia Hardey, November, 1852, Religious of the Sacred Heart Archives, St. Louis, Missouri.

This simple, austere chapel is what remains of those unfinished plans. It reminds us of her poverty, her humility and her simple love of God. It reminds us that the work she engaged in on behalf of God's poor also remains unfinished. If Philippine's life could be a letter to each one of us today, it would be a letter laden with passion and it would be about the poor.

SELECTED BIBLIOGRAPHY

Barat, Madeleine-Sophie and Philippine Duchesne. *Correspondance: Texte des manuscrits originaux*. Part I, *Période de Grenoble (1804–1815)*. Ed. Jeanne de Charry. Rome: Tipografia Poliglotta della Pontificia Università Gregoriana, 1988. Part II, to appear.

Baunard, Louis. *Histoire de Madame Duchesne*. Paris: Librairie Poussielgue Frères, 1878.

————. *Life of Mother Duchesne*. Trans. Lady Georgianna Fullerton. Roehampton: n.p., 1879.

Callan, Louise. *Philippine Duchesne: Frontier Missionary of the Sacred Heart 1769–1852*. Westminster, Maryland: The Newman Press, 1957.

————. *The Society of the Sacred Heart in North America*. New York: Longmans, Green and Co., 1937.

de Charry, Jeanne. *Histoire des Constitutions de la Société du Sacré-Coeur*. 2 parts in 5 vols. Rome: Typis Pontificiae Universitatis Gregorianae, 1975–1979; part I, 2nd ed., 1981.

————. *History of the Constitutions of the Society of the Sacred Heart*. Part I, vol. I, *The Formation of the Institute*. Sussex: St. Richard's Press Limited, 1975. Part II, vol. II, *The Definitive Constitutions and Their Approbation by the Holy See*. n.p.: n.p., n.d. Trans. Barbara Hogg.

Erskine, Marjory. *Mother Philippine Duchesne*. New York: Longmans, Green and Co., 1926.

Philippine Duchesne, R.S.C.J.: A Collection. Eds. Catherine Collins, Melanie A. Guste and Anna Thompson. Washington, D.C.: Center for Educational Design, 1988.

Stuart, Janet Erskine. *The Society of the Sacred Heart*. Roehampton, 1914.

Williams, Margaret. *The Society of the Sacred Heart: History of a Spirit 1800–1975*. London: Darton, Longman and Todd, 1978.

GENERAL INDEX

INDEX OF NAMES IN TEXT
AND SELECTED SECONDARY AUTHORS